The Political Economy of Aging
The State, Private Power, and Social Welfare

THE POLITICAL ECONOMY OF AGING

The State, Private Power, and Social Welfare

LAURA KATZ OLSON

New York   Columbia University Press   1982

Library of Congress Cataloging in Publication Data

Olson, Laura Katz, 1945–
The political economy of aging.

Includes bibliographical references and
index.

1. Aged—Government policy—United States
2. Aging—Economic aspects—United States.
3. United States—Social policy—1981–   —
Citizen participation. I. Title.
HQ1064.U5O44   362.6′0973   82-1315
ISBN 0-231-05450-5   AACR2
ISBN 0-231-05451-3 (pbk.)

Columbia University Press
New York and Guildford, Surrey

Clothbound editions of Columbia University Press books are
Smyth-sewn and printed on permanent and durable acid-free paper.

For My Mother,
Dorothy Zager Katz

Contents

Preface

Sarah Cohen, an eighty-three-year-old widow, has lived in her now deteriorating inner-city apartment for over forty years. She has no assets left; her sole source of income, Social Security, barely covers rent, electricity, food, and some winter clothing. Despite her poverty and chronic disabilities, she has managed to survive without public aid. Although her landlord has not repaired the building in years, and often fails to supply adequate heat, Sarah is grateful that the apartment is rent controlled. She has not been told yet that the landlord intends to convert the building into luxury apartments, assisted through city and federal tax benefit programs. She will not be able to find a new dwelling at a rent she can afford. Sarah Cohen will be forced into a nursing home.

PUBLIC OFFICIALS, BANKERS, DEVELOPERS, AND LANDLORDS ARE "REVITALIZING" THE CITY.

Alice Bartell, eighty years old, stares vacantly from her wheelchair parked against the wall of Tannerville nursing home. After two years of twice daily doses of tranquilizers and other drugs, she is not a demanding patient. Although a physician regularly bills the government for his visits to the home, she has not had an examination in over a year. She does not know that the lethargy, dizziness, and tremors she experiences are side effects of large doses of medication she may not actually need, or that her poor eating habits stem from a lack of proper dental care; she needs dentures. She is also unaware that Tannerville, like many nursing homes in the country, has major violations of health and fire safety codes. Alice Bartell entered the home as a private pay resident but the

$16,000 annual cost has depleted her small savings account; she is now supported through Medicaid.

NURSING HOMES ARE A GOOD INVESTMENT.

Donald and Mary Simmons had achieved the American Dream—their own home. Five years ago the couple sent the final mortgage payment on their $50,000 home to the bank. Except for two lengthy periods, Donald had worked steadily for over forty years at a series of low-paid jobs. However, at the age of fifty-nine, he was unemployed and in poor health. Unable to obtain work, and having exhausted his unemployment benefits and savings, he and his wife applied for Social Security as soon as they became eligible. There was an actuarial reduction of over 20 percent on their combined benefits since Donald "chose" early retirement, leaving the couple with $5,300 per year. Donald had been covered under several private retirement plans but never long enough to become vested in any of them.

Since Donald's "retirement," the couple has not been able to afford the rising property taxes or badly needed repairs on their house. They also face mounting heating bills which last year totaled over $600. Donald and Mary Simmons must sell their home.

OIL COMPANIES ACHIEVE RECORD-BREAKING PROFITS.

Robert Jones, seventy years old, has just retired from the presidency of a major company. He will receive over $300,000 annually from his stocks, bonds, savings, private pension plan, and special company bonuses. Since he is over fifty-five, most of the assets from the recent sale of his $180,000 home are tax-exempt. He also is entitled to the double exemption on his federal income taxes, and he does not pay any taxes on the couple's $14,000 annual Social Security benefits. He and his wife are looking forward to spending their retirement years on their newly purchased Florida estate.

ROBERT JONES IS CONCERNED ABOUT THE FINANCIAL HEALTH OF THE SOCIAL SECURITY SYSTEM; HE STRONGLY SUPPORTS COST-CUTTING MEASURES, INCLUDING LOWER BENEFITS FOR EARLY RETIREMENT, AN INCREASE IN THE AGE OF ELIGIBILITY FOR FULL PENSIONS, AND ELIMINATION OF THE MINIMUM BENEFIT.

This book is about growing old under capitalism.

Since the late 1970s, the media, political leaders, social scientists, and others have argued increasingly that American society is spending excessive amounts of its "scarce" public funds on the elderly, contributing both to the overall fiscal crisis and to the critical status of particular programs such as Social Security, Medicare, and Medicaid. At the same time, these sources provide us with compelling evidence on the social ills burdening growing numbers of older people.

My aim in this book is to uncover some of the structural causes of the current crisis in old age policies and programs, and to explore the reasons why a large percentage of the elderly continue to suffer from inadequate retirement income, housing, medical care, and other services, despite vast resources ostensibly committed on their behalf. I also study changes in the political, social, and economic order in the United States, and the deleterious effects of these changes on the elderly population.

My work in public policy over the last several years, and on aging issues in particular, has forced me to conclude that liberal reforms popular among gerontologists, no matter how well intentioned, are ineffectual tools for adequately solving problems faced by the elderly. Unquestionably, such solutions do ease some of their burdens. However, given the constraints of American capitalism, liberal remedies treat only the symptoms rather than fundamental causes of specific problems, generating new ones either for older people, other needy groups, or the economy as a whole. They also tend to enrich service providers, with only limited benefits trickling down to impoverished groups. On the other hand, conservative reforms, such as those proposed and enacted under the Reagan administration, have curtailed the already inadequate relief measures available to the elderly poor, thereby fostering even greater deprivation than had existed previously. The conservative approach also turns solutions over to the same private market forces that have created, and continue to create the social problems of old age.

I contend that the situation of disadvantaged sectors of the older population stems from market and class relationships, along with racist and sexist institutions, that negatively affect workers and families, to varying degrees, throughout their life cycle. Such forces engender even more oppressive conditions during old age. I further argue that American capitalist institutions are not only inherently incapable of meeting the needs of older people, but also that they have fostered many of the problems commonly associated with aging in the United States.

If this book provokes a challenge to basic assumptions underlying aging issues and policies, and encourages greater recognition of factors linking the interests of younger workers with those of older people, it will have served its purpose.

The Political Economy of Aging
The State, Private Power, and Social Welfare

Chapter 1

The Aging Population Today and Tomorrow

Evidently, the American political economy has generated prodigious goods, services, and wealth. Equally clearly, increasing economic inequality, social deprivation, and unemployment coexist with growing affluence, and commodities produced exclusively for profit, despite their abundance, fail wholly to fulfill authentic human needs. The genesis and persistence of a sizable improverished elderly population, and the multifaceted problems associated with its lack of an adequate income, exemplify dramatically major contradictions of capitalist development as well as demonstrate the inability of a market economy to respond adequately to pressing social needs.

American society abounds with serious problems affecting the elderly. Meager retirement incomes, dilapidated but expensive housing, escalating medical costs coupled with insufficient services and facilities, a paucity of social services in general, and high unemployment confront large numbers of older people.

It is my purpose in this book to examine age-based social programs and to explain why they have failed to solve the problems of the elderly despite the receipt of vast and increasing amounts of the nation's monetary resources. Neither the development of public policies for the elderly nor the allocation of immense resources for their needs has substantially improved the relative position of older people, particularly the most disadvantaged. I ask why pressing problems of income, housing, nursing homes, health care, and social services persist and have, in fact, intensified during the last several decades. These problems have proven highly resistent to amelioration through public policy measures. The most serious problem faced by the vast majority of the aged is lack of adequate income. Income levels of all people, including the elderly, are inextricably tied to all other aspects of their well-being.

In my view, the persistence of problems associated with old age is a consequence of policy initiatives that fail to alter existing institutional arrangements and fail as well to redistribute power, income, and wealth in society. I shall argue that the principal barriers to change lie in the nature of capitalism itself. The political institutions that serve the market economy and its dominant interests preserve existing social values and distributions of power, privileges, and resources. Not only is poverty among large segments of the elderly population socially determined, but also their relative material and social deprivation arises from relationships of domination and subordination, power and privilege, dependency and autonomy, fostered by American political and economic structures. Alternative policy solutions for aiding the elderly have been circumscribed by institutional and ideological boundaries that prevent alterations in the basic class relations defining the political economy. I suggest that current age-based legislation tends to perpetuate and reinforce preretirement inequalities of income, wealth, and social benefits among the aged. This legislation also diverts resources and services from the disadvantaged younger population to older people, particularly better-off households. Finally, it benefits primarily entrenched private interests at the expense of both the working class and the low-income elderly population. Age-based classifications obscure class division within society and generate distorted perceptions of what has been and can be accomplished.

I assume that most gerontologists, and other policy analysts studying the aged, while adept at cataloguing and describing the multitude of urgent issues facing the elderly, fail to identify the roots of social ailments and the limits to reform imposed by existing political, social, and economic institutions. As Alford astutely concludes, in his study of health care in the United States:

> The expansion of health insurance and the extension of federal funds to cover health costs for the poor and the elderly can be regarded as real and important, and yet one can still argue that health institutions have not changed and that the barriers to change vitiate those reforms. . . . More generally, reforms such as Medicaid have certain short-term benefits, but do not con-

stitute significant institutional change, since the additional funding they provide simply feeds into increased costs and soon leads to cutbacks of services and payments.[1]

Similarly, other public programs focusing on the elderly population have no substantial impact on the existing maldistribution of benefits in society. Social policies that attempt to address the pressing needs of older people through an accommodation to current political, social, and economic practices will fail ultimately to achieve the desired goals.

AN ISSUE TO BE FACED: CURRENT PUBLIC POLICIES

Although myriad problems have afflicted the elderly for decades, the plight of older people has been, for the most part, invisible until recently. "Crisis" situations affecting the aged and the institutions serving them have erupted intermittently since the 1930s. During the last several decades these have occurred with increased frequency and intensity. Potential insolvency of the Social Security system, vastly insufficient assets to meet state and local pension obligations, corrupt financial administration of some union retirement trusts, periodic bankruptcy of companies and consequently their pension systems, Medicaid/Medicare fraud scandals, and exposures of unscrupulous nursing home operators are among many such crises.

An admixture of declining birth rates, increasing longevity, and a diminishing number of workers relative to the dependent elderly population has broadened the scope as well as highlighted the visibility of economic and social problems associated with old age in the United States. The 65-and-over population has grown dramatically not only in absolute numbers but also as a percentage of the population. In 1900, older Americans totaled 3.1 million people, representing only 4 percent of the population. By 1950, the percentage of elderly had doubled, had grown steadily to 9 percent in 1960, and had reached 11.3 percent by 1981. Currently, over 25 million Americans are sixty-five and over. Projections, varying with a number of factors, particularly fertility rates, indicate that the percentage of older people will soar anywhere from 14 to 22 percent by 2030. That year, perhaps 55 million Americans will be sixty-five and over.[2] At the same time, life expectancy at age sixty-five has increased from 11.9 years to 16.7 years between 1900 and 1981.

The burgeoning of the older population has been coupled with declining economic independence. In the early 1900s, nearly two-thirds of the men aged sixty-five years and over were active in the labor force; most men lived only a few years after they became unable to continue working. The number of dependent elderly, such as the blind, disabled, and widowed, was relatively small. Although the percentage of older females in the labor force has remained relatively constant, at slightly less than 10 percent, since 1950, substantial numbers of older males have withdrawn from the labor market at increasingly earlier ages. While in 1950 46 percent of those sixty-five and over were still in the labor force, this figure steadily decreased to 33 percent, 27 percent, and 19 percent by 1960, 1970, and 1981, respectively.[3] The labor force participation rate of men aged fifty-five to sixty-four dropped from 83 percent in 1970 to 73 percent in 1979 and to 70 percent at the end of 1981. According to a recent study, the major cause of such changes in very early retirement is "chronic unemployment."[4] Most older workers, moreover, have only part-time or low paying jobs.

These trends, fostered through public and private policies, have created a number of serious "crises" for both society in general and the elderly in particular. Increasing numbers of dependent older people have placed substantial strains on the Social Security trust, other retirement programs, and health care delivery systems, all of which are supported, for the most part, directly by the working population. For every ten workers aged twenty to fifty-nine in 1977 there were approximately three nonworkers aged sixty and over.[5] Projections suggest that the ratio of taxpayers to beneficiaries of Social Security will drop from 3.2:1 in 1981 to 2:1 in the 2030s.[6]

Crisis politics has thrust problems related to aging and retirement to the forefront of public policy concerns. During the 1960s and 1970s it prompted political support for a broad variety of legislation and substantial funding commitments. Wide-reaching social policies at the national level attempted to respond to these crises and to ameliorate their impact. Estes has estimated that there are at present approximately eighty separate federal programs that directly or indirectly affect older people.[7] Undoubtedly, both demographic changes and the proliferation of age-based pressure groups expedited recognition of and response to the elderly's plight.

Over the last several decades, Congress substantially strengthened the Social Security Act of 1935, which provided for a public system of retirement income. Amendments expanded coverage to nearly all working people; added survivor and disability benefits; increased payroll tax rates and the wage base on which they are calculated; lowered the age of eligibility; increased real benefit levels; and established automatic cost-of-living adjustments. The Old Age Assistance program, administered by the states, was replaced in 1972 by the Supplementary Security Income Program (SSI), the latter providing a national minimum income level for the indigent elderly.

During the 1960s, Congress instituted a system of health insurance for the aged under Medicare. The enactment of Medicaid made funds for health care services more readily available to the economically disadvantaged population, including the elderly poor, than previously. The Older Americans Act (OAA) of 1965 and subsequent amendments focused on community services and nutritional needs of the 60-and-over population. In 1967 the Age Discrimination in Employment Act prohibited discrimination in hiring, job retention, compensation, and other conditions of employment for those aged forty to sixty-five, and a 1978 amendment extended the protected age to seventy. The Employee Retirement Income Security Act (ERISA) of 1974 attempted to provide greater income security for private sector workers by liberalizing vesting requirements, requiring employers to provide information on retirement trusts and future benefit levels, and establishing the Guaranty Benefit Corporation to insure private systems against bankruptcy. Other legislation, such as the National Housing acts, Food Stamp program, and title XX of the Social Security Act (social services for the poor), provide benefits for older people as well as other needy groups.

As the Federal Council on Aging recently noted: "Without exception, the elderly are treated preferentially at all income levels by the Federal income tax structure."[8] Special provisions for the aged, which will be discussed in the next section, include exclusion of Social Security (and railroad retirement) benefits from taxation, the double exemption, and the retirement income credit. In addition, contributions to, and the accumulated assets of, private sector retirement trusts are exempt from taxation.

The executive branch and Congress also created a number of agencies to respond to the specific needs of the elderly. These include the Administration on Aging, Federal Council on Aging, Senate Special Committee on Aging, and House Select Committee on Aging. The first national conference on aging in 1950, and subsequent White House Conferences in 1961, 1971, and 1981 are additional indications of national attention to older people.

DIMENSIONS OF FEDERAL EXPENDITURES

Age-based programs have entailed the mobilization of significant and rapidly increasing resources for the elderly. As table 1 demonstrates, total federal outlays for income maintenance devoted exclusively to the 65-and-over population in 1980 included approximately $98.3 billion in cash benefits, $41.3 billion in in-kind benefits and $0.9 billion in social services and employment benefits, totaling $140.5 billion. This figure represents about 25 percent of the total national budget accruing to an age group that accounts for 11.3 percent of the population. Estimates for 1981 indicate that these expenses have increased to $162.8 billion, 26 percent of the national budget. This percentage of federal outlays for the elderly has nearly doubled since 1960; in that year older people represented only 13 percent of total national expenditures. An analysis of future changes by James R. Storey shows that "if one simply projects these current programs and assumes that overall Federal spending returns to the 'historic' level of 20 percent of gross national project (it is at 22.5 percent), then the elderly's share of the Federal budget will rise slowly during this century to 32 percent, then leap upward by another 10 percentage points in the next 15 years, and soar to 63 percent by 2025."[9]

Programs supported directly by the working class through payroll taxes account for the bulk of national expenditures for the elderly. Nearly 57 percent of federal outlays for older people in 1980 were allocated to Social Security benefits alone ($79.9 billion), and Medicare represented an additional 21 percent ($30 billion). In fact, increases in Social Security and Medicare outlays over the last fifteen years have accounted for most of the growth in federal fund-

Table 1. Federal Outlays for Income Maintenance, Social Services, and Employment Programs for the Sixty-five and Over Population ($ billion)

Program	1980 estimate	1981 estimate
Cash Benefits		
Social Security (OASDI)	79.9	94.5
Other retired, disabled, and survivors benefits[a]	13.5	15.2
Veterans compensation and pensions	3.1	3.4
Supplementary Income Security (SSI)	1.8	2.0
Subtotal: Cash Benefit Outlays	98.3	115.1
In-Kind Benefits		
Medicare	30.0	33.7
Medicaid	4.8	5.5
Other federal health programs[b]	2.0	2.1
Food stamps	.7	.8
Subsidized public housing	2.1	2.6
Section 202 Elderly Housing Loans	.7	.7
Other	1.0	1.2
Subtotal: In-Kind Benefit Outlays	41.3	46.6
Social Services and Employment		
Administration on Aging (AoA) Programs	.6	.7
Action Older Americans Volunteer programs	.1	.1
Senior Community Service Employment Program and CETA older workers Initiative	.2	.3
Subtotal: Social Services and Employment Outlays	.9	1.1
Total Outlays	140.5	162.8
Total U.S. Budget Outlays	564.0	616.0
Total Outlays for Sixty-five and Over Population as Percent of U.S. Budget	24.9%	26.4%

SOURCE: Office of Management and Budget, in Federal Council on the Aging, *Toward More Effective Implementation of the Older Americans Act*, Staff Report, Washington, D.C., April 1981, p. 43.

[a] Includes the Federal Employee Retirement System, Uniformed Services Retirement System, and the Railroad Retirement System.

[b] Includes health programs administered by the Department of Health and Human Services (DHHS), and Veterans' Administration (VA).

ing for aging programs. It has been estimated that between 1981 and 1984 Social Security costs will increase by at least 11.9 percent per year, and Medicare by 16.2 percent per year.[10] The projected increases in these programs will not be affected by the relatively small cost-saving measures enacted by Congress under the Omnibus Reconciliation Act of 1981. The growth in federal outlays for Social Security and Medicare primarily is due to rapidly rising health care costs, high inflation overall (to which Social Security benefits are indexed), an expanding older population relative to other age groups, and growing unemployment or early retirement among the elderly—increments that the 1981 legislation will not abate.

Retirement benefits for federal employees and their dependents, along with retired railroad workers and military personnel, accounted for $13.5 billion, or 10 percent of outlays for the 65-and-over population in 1980. Federal civilian retirement costs are expected to increase over 10.6 percent annually between 1980 and 1984 alone.[11] Resources available for subsidized public housing, Medicaid, SSI, veterans' pensions, and food stamps, which the national government earmarks for welfare-dependent people, and supports through general revenues, totaled $13.2 billion in 1980, or only 9 percent of federal outlays for older people. Expenditures for Medicare vastly dwarfed those for Medicaid, while SSI represented a fraction of total cash outlays utilized to support income maintenance. National expenditures for the elderly in 1980 also included social services administered by AoA under the Older Americans Act ($0.6 billion), training and employment for older adults ($0.2 billion), programs generated through ACTION ($0.1 billion), other health services ($2 billion), and a wide range of additional benefits less easily calculated, representing another 2 percent of the budget.

The rise in costs for most of these programs, which has been curtailed steadily since the late 1970s, will be lowered even further beginning in the early 1980s. Nearly 70 percent of the approximately $35 billion in total federal spending reductions enacted by Congress for the early 1980s will affect social programs serving the poor, particulaly food stamps, low-income housing, and Medicaid. Although older people will suffer considerably from the severe 1981 cost-cutting measures, the reductions will have a negligible effect on overall spending for this age group. In fact, the evidence suggests that younger welfare recipients, unemployed persons, and the working poor, who will be forced to compete with the elderly over shrinking program resources, may experience the most severe reductions.

Federal outlays shown in table 1 denote only those funds directed at the 65-and-over population. If we were to include beneficiaries between the ages of sixty and sixty-five, or even younger, the level of expenditures would be markedly greater. For example, in 1981 the federal civil service and uniformed services retirement systems paid out over $30 billion to retired workers of all ages. Total outlays of the Social Security Trust Fund in that year amounted to over $100 billion.

Another measure of the allocation of federal resources to the elderly is provided by table 2. Tax expenditure items for selected age-related programs are estimated at $31.7 billion in 1980 and $38.4 billion in 1981. Tax expenditures are:

> revenue losses attributable to provisions of the Federal tax laws which allow a special exclusion, exemption, or deduction from gross income or which provide a special credit, a preferential rate of tax, or a deferral of tax liability. Tax expenditures are one means by which the Federal Government pursues public policy objectives and, in most cases, can be viewed as alternatives to budget outlays, credit assistance or other policy instruments.[12]

Table 2 shows that in 1980, $19.8 billion or 63 percent of the total age-related tax expenditures represented exclusions for employer pension plan contributions and earnings from taxation. This figure rose to $23.6 billion in 1981. Similar exclusions for the self-employed and others with Individual Retirement Accounts (IRAs) amounted to $1.9 billion in 1980, and $2.1 billion in 1981. The projected expansion of Individual Retirement Accounts and Keogh plans, as a result of new tax legislation in 1981, will increase these tax expenditures substantially during the 1980s. Special tax provisions for individuals sixty-five and over without regard to income, such as the double exemption, tax credit, and exclusion of capital gains up to $100,000 ($125,000 beginning in 1982) on the sale of homes, accounted for another $2.6 billion and $3 billion during 1980 and 1981, respectively. The exclusion from taxation of Social

Table 2. Estimates of Selected Age-Related Tax Expenditures ($ billion)

Exclusions by Program	1980	Percent of Total	1981	Percent of Total
Social Security benefits for retirees	$6.9	22	$9.0	23
Railroad retirement benefits for retirees	.3	1	.4	1
Additional personal exemptions for persons 65 and over	2.0	6	2.3	6
Tax credit for the elderly	.1	*	.1	*
Capital gains on sale of homes for persons 65 and over	.5	2	.6	2
Pension plan contributions and earnings				
Employer plans	19.8	63	23.6	62
Self-employed and others	1.9	6	2.1	6
Veterans' pensions	.1	*	.1	*
Disability-related military pensions for current retirees	.1	*	.2	1
Total Tax Expenditure	$31.7	100	$38.4	101†

SOURCE: Adapted from *Special Analysis of the Budget of the U.S. Government, Fiscal Year 1982, Special Analysis G*, (Washington, D.C., GPO, 1981), pp. 226–230.
* Less than 1 percent.
† Total does not add up to 100 percent due to rounding.

Security, railroad retirement, veterans', and disability-related military pension income for retirees totaled $7.4 billion or 23 percent of tax expenditures in 1980 and $9.7 billion or 25 percent in 1981. Tax expenditures for these selected age-related income security measures represented significant revenue losses for the national government.

Middle- and upper-income older people receive greater per capita benefits from preferential tax treatment than do their more disadvantaged cohorts. Major beneficiaries, in fact, have been the 65-and-over population with incomes over $15,000 per year. In 1974, those people receiving an annual income up to $3,000, or 21 percent of the elderly, received $3.56 per capita from the personal exemption, $.51 from the retirement income credit, $239.06 from exclusion of Social Security, and $40.69 for exclusion of dependents—only $283.82 in total national tax preferences for the aged. Those with incomes ranging from $3,000 to $5,000, or 23 percent of the elderly, averaged $47.36 per capita for the personal exemption, $8.97 from the retirement income credit, $229.31 for exclusion of Social security, and $37.39 for exclusion of dependents—an average of

$323.03 per capita in total tax benefits. On the other hand, those with incomes ranging from $20,000 to $50,000, or 8 percent of older households, obtained $307.58 per capita from the personal exemption, $14.58 in retirement income credit, $313.41 for exclusion of Social Security, and $51.02 for exclusion of dependents—an average of $686.59 per capita from the special national tax provisions. Even greater benefits accrued to those with higher incomes.[13]

Moreover, even if Social Security benefits were not tax exempt, most people relying for income exclusively on this source—usually low-income households—would not have been liable for national taxes. Approximately 11 million older people did not receive anything from the other tax exemptions, since most of them had incomes so low after exclusion of their Social Security benefits that they had to file no tax return.[14] In 1978 only about 25 percent of older people had incomes high enough to be liable for federal taxes.[15] Nor will such individuals benefit from the across-the-board cut in individual income tax rates legislated by Congress for fiscal years 1982, 1983, and 1984.

ALTERNATIVE PERSPECTIVES ON THE ROLE OF THE STATE

Several theories of the state provide a variety of perspectives for analyzing age-based public policies and for assessing the potential for ameliorating problems experienced by older people. These theories will be classified as free-market conservative, liberal accommodationist, and radical views of the state. Each focuses on the forces that influence the policy process, the linkages between and among institutional structures and social values, and the impact of these forces on society. Although gerontologists agree that there are numerous age-related social ills, observers differ substantially on the definition of the problems and on their scope, causes, and solutions.

Free-Market Conservative Views

The free-market conservative view of the state, emanating from the American nineteenth-century laissez faire tradition, emphasizes

individualism, economic inequality, competition in market relations, and private solutions for public problems. According to this
approach, individuals in their roles as workers and consumers, and
employers in their perpetual search for profits, rationally seek their
own self-interest in market relations. Through the proper functioning of a free competition for goods, services, and labor, as well as
through unfettered economic growth, the needs of society will be
served, and pressing social problems will be alleviated. For most
people at the lower end of the socioeconomic scale, social mobility
is possible through individual effort as long as the "rules of the
game" are fair, individual liberty is preserved, and opportunities
are accessible to all.

Free-market conservatives assume that the private sector produces and distributes goods and services more effectively and efficiently than the public sector. They urge greater reliance on the
marketplace, along with "sufficient" economic incentives (i.e., government subsidies) for supplying housing, medical care, food, jobs,
and even retirement income. Although inequality of material conditions is inevitable, all groups in society will improve their relative
positions as production increases and the economy expands.

Charles R. Sligh, in *Aging and the Economy*, typifies this position
arguing that, despite the "aging" of American society,

> in recent years the active work force has grown at a faster rate
> than the population as a whole. This means that there will be
> a broader base of support available for retired persons in our
> economy. The economy also has the opportunity to grow, pro-
> vided sufficient investment is made in technological improve-
> ment. When productivity is increased by new methods, again
> the base of support for retired citizens is improved. In short,
> America's retired persons will share the future of the economy
> as a whole. If it is a growing economy it can support its elderly
> in better style. If it does not grow, the prospects of the aged
> in our society are dubious.[16]

Several gerontologists emphasize that, concomitant with the growth
of the American economy, there has been a gradual rise in levels
of living for everyone, including the aged. One observer suggests,
for example, that although improved economic conditions for the
elderly are related to the growth and enhancement of private and

public retirement systems, "basic to all of this has been the continued rise in the gross national product (GNP) of the country, coupled with the participation of the worker in shares of this expansion."[17]

Peter Drucker, Martin Feldstein, and others applaud the fact that the private sector has produced, in their view, viable income maintenance schemes through its pension trusts. They advocate efforts to encourage their growth and expansion. Drucker insists:

> one might without much exaggeration say that it [the private pension system] is the *only* economic and social program of the last thirty years that has truly produced results and delivered what it promised. . . . Pension funds . . . offer one example of the efficacy of using the existing private non-governmental institutions of our "society of organizations" for the formulation and achievement of social goals and the satisfaction of social needs.[18]

Persistent major social problems in society, according to free-market conservatives, are "pathological abnormalities" of the political process in general and of certain sectors of society specifically. Expansion of misguided governmental programs imposes artificial restrictions on economic activities, stifles individual initiatives, and gives birth to a labyrinth of self-perpetuating and inefficient bureaucratic structures concerned primarily with internal needs and requirements. The growth of the welfare state has not alleviated major problems but, on the contrary, has aggravated or caused them.

Milton Friedman argues that the packaging of Social Security "has made the public willing to accept a capricious system of benefits and to support a mammoth bureaucracy that could never have arisen separately. The ultimate effect has been to foster the growth of government and, above all, central government."[19] Free-market conservatives thus have begun to focus on reducing what they consider to be excessive benefit levels, including overcompensation for inflation during the retirement span, and other cost-cutting measures. Others point out that Social Security contains several disincentive effects, such as those that discourage personal savings, reduce incentives to work, and limit employment opportunities by increasing labor costs.[20] Feldstein attacks Social Security for contributing to capital shortages in the country. Due to its reliance on a pay-as-you-go system, Feldstein argues, it adversely affects the American economy and its productive capacity.[21] Further, free-market conservatives view Social Security as a coercive system that limits individual freedom while simultaneously encouraging inefficiencies by artificial channeling of retirement income decisions.

Similarly, Alford observes that free-market reformers blame bureaucratic interference for ineffective and inefficient American health care systems. In their view, restored market competition among health facilities, physicians, and other health providers and expanded private insurance options would improve dramatically the quantity and quality of health services.[22] Free-market conservatives also argue that the primary barriers to improved housing for the elderly are insufficient economic incentives to spur residential construction and rehabilitation and overly restrictive governmental regulations, such as rent controls and housing maintenance codes. They also advocate increased privatization of subsidized low-cost housing efforts.

That certain categories of people fail to solve their pressing needs, the free-market conservatives attribute predominantly to attitudes, values, and modes of behavior that render some individuals incapable of taking, or unwilling to take, advantage of opportunities available through existing institutions for their own support and advancement. That is, the poor, themselves, are responsible for their own condition.[23]

Though many market reformers view the elderly as a special case of poverty (i.e., "worthy" poor), their underlying assumption tends to be that older people are, in fact, responsible for their own material deprivation. Workers willing to sacrifice some present consumption needs and to save and invest for the future are rewarded with higher benefits during their old age than those who expect and depend on state support. The state should encourage individuals to provide for their own retirement needs through measures such as an extention of the Keogh Plan, expansion of Individual Retirement Accounts (IRAs), initiation of "retirement bonds," and enhancement of retirement counseling opportunities.

According to Wilensky and Lebeaux, this perspective (which they label "residualism") holds that older people should satisfy their own social service needs through the two "natural" channels of support: the family and the private market. Public aid should be provided only to those older people who, due to particular adverse circumstances, cannot avail themselves of these "preferred" institutions. In order to discourage excessive or unnecessary utilization of social services, according to this view, public facilities and programs must inevitably carry a stigma of dole or charity.[24] Cottrell further explains that residualism implies private and voluntary agency support for those in need of special services: "public agencies should come into the picture only when such resources are exhausted. . . . It is argued that public aid should go only to the "vulnerable aged" and that others must "accept their lot" as a reward or punishment for their success or failure to achieve a decent old age through their previous compliance with the legitimate demands of American society."[25] Some analysts even suggest that the elderly are to blame, in part, for their poor housing situation since they are unwilling to leave familiar neighborhoods, family, and friends.

A significant number of gerontologists, although not adhering entirely to the free-market perspective, tend to imply individual responsibility for alleviating problems of old age. In fact, major theories in social gerontology, including disengagement theory, activity theory, developmental theory, and even social environmentalist and age stratification theories, represent attempts to explain existing conditions in terms of individual adjustment.[26]

For free-market conservatives, then, the state should play a more limited role in society than it plays at present. Its major functions are to maintain conditions for economic growth; provide economic incentives to the private sector; insure that market forces are competitive and open; protect private property; and preserve order. For groups suffering "cultural deprivation," governmental initiatives should provide opportunities for individuals to adapt to the needs and requirements of the prevailing system so that they can compete more effectively in the market process. Public policy alternatives for the aged range from removing barriers to employment opportunities, stimulating the economy so as to create more jobs, and encouraging personal savings, to generating more competitive health care facilities, mobilizing private sector resources for housing and social services, and buttressing the private pension system.

Liberal Accommodationist Views

The liberal accommodationist view of the state, the perspective most prominent among social gerontologists, emphasizes societal

rather than individual deficiencies as major causes of social problems. Although maintaining a strong commitment to existing political, social, and economic arrangements, accommodationists focus
on the intrinsic shortcomings of community and environmental
forces, particularly those of the market system, that hamper opportunities and fail to provide adequately for the disadvantaged elderly
or that relegate them to poverty. The thrust of their argument is
that current public programs must be revised substantially in order
to remedy some of the deficiencies of the market economy.

Most accommodationists insist that all older Americans possess
inviolable rights to employment opportunities, adequate retirement
income, decent housing, and good health care. The poverty that
affects large numbers of the elderly is not only morally wrong but
also avoidable through appropriate governmental action and expanded funding commitments. According to this view, the pressing
needs of the older population can be satisfied within society's current structural arrangements through improved public policies.

The fact that accommodationists perceive the problems of old
age, in the main, as socially induced justifies their call for comprehensive and special public remedies. Though other sectors of society may encounter myriad difficulties as a consequence of rapid
industrialization, automation, and other technological or structural
changes—inflation, recession, and the like—the aged are particularly vulnerable to vicissitudes in the economy. In addition, since
many have been forced into dependency, they tend to lack sufficient resources for dealing with these problems effectively.

Liberal accommodationists point out that technological advances
in drugs, sanitation facilities, and health care have contributed to
increased life expectancies and greater numbers of older people in
the population, while at the same time dislocations caused by technological unemployment have made it particularly difficult for the
elderly to retain or obtain jobs. Encumbered by obsolete skills,
negative stereotypes about their efficiency as employees, and mandatory retirement policies, substantial numbers of elderly are forced
either to work in low-paying, part-time positions or to subsist on
meager pension incomes. Moreover, according to liberal accommodationists, although extended family ties tend to remain strong,
urbanization and industrialization have affected the willingness or
ability of families to care for aged parents on a regular basis. Even
those older people who have been able to save for their old age

find their assets ravaged by inflation and other forces beyond their control. For those fortunate enough to live beyond seventy-five, stretching meager savings becomes even more problematic. Thus this perspective, which is categorized as the "institutional view" of social welfare by Lowy, Wilensky, Lebeaux, and others, "recognizes the complexity and vicissitudes of modern life, [and] the inability of individuals to provide fully for themselves or to meet all their needs in family and work settings."[27]

Accommodationists imply that the economic position of the elderly would be improved substantially by dispelling "myths" about their productive capacity, overcoming ageist employment practices, and providing opportunities for retraining and second career education. Consequently, gerontologists must provide evidence to convince employers that older people are not ineffectual employees and to persuade public officials that employed older people require educational opportunities in order to stay current. Unemployed middle-aged and older workers who have been displaced from the labor market because of forced retirement or technological innovations should be provided with second career training. According to Sheppard, "legislation to protect workers ... against age discrimination may be a major weapon in the war against poverty."[28]

Liberal accommodationists often note that age-related problems are inextricably linked with sexism and racism. Some social analysts validly point out that the aged are not a homogeneous aggregate but rather consist of distinct subgroups, such as women and minorities, who are more likely to be destitute during their old age than are white males. To aid these subgroups, state action is required to combat these "isms," to ease personal burdens through an admixture of larger cash subsidies, expanded income in-kind programs, and improved service delivery systems, and to overcome other artificial barriers to societal benefits.

Accommodationists also point to inherent imperfections in the market system that have engendered, among other things, gaps in available social services, particularly for the multiproblem elderly poor, an inadequate private pension system, dilapidated housing, and deteriorating neighborhoods. More generally, other private sector practices make self-provision for all income and service needs impossible for the vast majority of elderly. To overcome market deficiencies in housing, community services, transportation, medical care, and the like, accommodationists advocate such reforms as enhanced public planning, greater coordination of fragmented services and facilities, and stronger political controls over private sector initiatives.

Although Zeckhauser and Viscusi argue that "a compulsory social insurance program such as social security can be justified as a response to imperfections in the market for capital and in the type of insurance represented by annuities,"[29] accommodationists also tend to support the continuation of private retirement systems, albeit with substantial revisions and controls. While some accommodationists are satisfied that the Employee Retirement Income Security Act (ERISA) will eventually mitigate the most blatant problems and abuses of these private trusts, others argue that these reforms are insufficient. They propose further strengthening the system by providing for immediate vesting, portability, automatic cost-of-living increases, and improved survivor's benefits.

Liberal accommodationists tend to applaud the gains achieved through such public measures as Social Security, Medicare, Medicaid, the Older Americans Act, and subsidized housing. They insist that, without these programs, economic and social deprivation among older people would be even more widespread than it is. However, they argue that these programs must be revamped and better funded in order to enhance their effectiveness and to surmount particular programmatic features that adversely affect the position of the elderly poor. As Butler notes: "serious questions have been raised since the beginning of social security about the adequacy of the concept behind the system as well as the level of benefits."[30] Thus Social Security is attacked for its low wage base, work penalties, and other inequities and gaps. In addition to various reforms of the Social Security system itself, liberal accommodationists frequently urge increased benefits for those relying on Social Security as the sole means of support. They assume, however, that the calculation of benefits on the basis of past work histories must be retained. Furthermore, since free-market conservatives increasingly have been able to limit the scope of public discourse to ways of maintaining the Social Security system's economic viability, all within their definition of the problem, many liberal accommodationists also have begun to accept cost reductions as both necessary and inevitable.

Both liberal accommodationists and free-market conservatives often cite Medicaid and Medicare as examples of programs where the solutions themselves have created acute problems, although the two groups differ considerably in their proposals for reform. Alford points out that free-market reformers blame "bureaucratic interference and cumbersomeness for the defects of the system and [call] for the restoration of market competition and pluralism in health care institutions." On the other hand, liberal accommodationists blame "market competition for the defects of the system and [call] for increased administrative regulation and government financing and control of health care."[31] The latter group's reform proposals include greater coverage for such items as hearing aids, dental work, office visits, and other medical expenses, controls over physician and hospital costs, and partial funding for Medicare from general revenues.

Liberal accommodationists point out that shortages in available middle- and low-income housing, coupled with urban redevelopment programs which force the elderly from deteriorated but affordable homes, are major causes of the elderly's housing problems. Greater financial commitments to subsidized housing programs, expanded efforts to rehabilitate existing dwellings, improved enforcement of housing code violations, rent controls, lowered property tax liabilities, and more public funding to offset growing utility costs, are among the solutions offered.

Welfare programs, such as food stamps, SSI, public housing, Medicaid, and title XX of the Social Security Act (social services), pose a dilemma for accommodationists. They perceive these measures as antithetical to the values of pride and independence held by large numbers of older people. On the one hand, since liberal accommodationists assume that resources for social programs are limited, they argue that, without rigid eligibility standards, the government would not provide sufficient aid to the most disadvantaged elderly. On the other hand, many needy older people do not qualify for the programs when eligibility ceilings are very low. Moreover, a large number of destitute older Americans are reluctant to take advantage of these "stigmatized" programs. For the aged who do participate, benefit levels are insufficient to meet their needs. Consequently, reform proposals range from liberalizing the needs test, enlarging benefits currently available, and increasing efforts to enroll eligible clients, to providing universal eligibility for the 65-and-over population.

Finally liberal reformers tend to assume a pluralist view of power.

That is, society is characterized by disparate groups seeking access to the state, with public policies derived from bargaining and compromise among these interests. From this perspective, although the emergence and establishment of old age organizations have been critical factors in the successful efforts to secure benefits on behalf of the elderly, the persistence of the latter's relative material deprivation denotes insufficient political power. If age consciousness grows, and age-based organizations continue to proliferate and expand, the elderly will become an increasingly effective political force. Older people will be able to contend successfully for available social benefits. Several gerontologists suggest that the issue of resource allocation is becoming increasingly age based, and warn that some age conflict is inevitable, particularly given the increasing number of dependent elderly relative to the working population.

Liberal accommodationists imply that, although public policy should aim at bringing all the elderly to a decent standard of living and at providing them sufficient and effective services, achievement of these objectives will be limited by the requirements of other sectors of society. Moreover, liberal reformers attempt to secure a "fair share" of available resources for older people without altering substantially existing institutional structures and practices or the general distribution of income and wealth in society. That accommodationist policies can provide the elderly with an adequate standard of living and sufficient public services, without affecting negatively other needy groups, is highly questionable. Many reform proposals would merely shift resources from one sector of society (the working poor) to another (the aged). As Wachtel astutely observes, the liberal reformer's "commitment to 'alleviating' poverty without systemic changes is as deep as any conservative's."[32]

Radical Views

Whereas the free-market perspective sees improvement in the condition of the aged as the result of new encouragement of private delivery systems and on a change in the attitudes and values of "deficient" individuals, and accommodationists would compensate for the shortcomings of "deficient" institutions and reform particular public programs, a radical theory of the state, which I will adopt in this book, views the origins and persistence of age-related problems as inherent in the normal functioning of American capitalism. Capitalist imperatives for unfettered capital accumulation and maximization of profits are inextricably linked with a ceaseless drive for growth; increasing concentration of private market activities; increasing socialization of production costs with profits appropriated privately; rising structural unemployment; cyclical economic crises; significant and growing inequalities in income, wealth, and power; and production for profit at the expense of satisfying human needs. Radicals note that, under capitalism, the government is committed not only to the values of private ownership and private profits but also to the necessity of economic and social inequality. These factors profoundly affect the distribution of benefits and deprivations among the population, including older people.

To understand fully both the roots of the problems affecting the aged and the limits to free-market conservative and liberal accommodationist reforms, it is necessary to analyze older Americans' past and present relationships to the means of production, the social stratification among workers which continues unabated during old age, the role of the state in enhancing and maintaining existing institutional arrangements, and basic class relationships within society. The "crises" associated with aging are crises only because, as Katznelson and Kesselman observe, "they are manifestations of contradictions rooted in the social structure; and, from the vantage point of those on top, they potentially threaten existing patterns of dominance."[33]

In chapter 2 I discuss the growth and expansion of monopoly capitalism, the rise of the positive state, and the impact of these changes on the nature of class relationships in general and on the elderly in particular. I argue that public and private policies serve to advance the interests of those who own and control the means of production, while fostering the pressing social and economic problems experienced by a large sector of older people. The capitalist class, representing a small minority of the population, holds vast economic and political power with which to strengthen the political, social, and economic relationships that serve its needs. Since, under capitalism, there is a tendency for the private sector to require growing public financial support, and the primary role of the state has been to buttress capital accumulation and private profits, the capitalist class has sought and benefited from the state's growing involvement in the economy.

The increasing proletarianization of once independent workers, including farmers, has forced the vast majority of the population to become dependent solely on selling its labor power for subsistence. Simultaneously, the private sector's ceaseless drive for economic growth and profits, supported by state policies, and the increasing pace of the technological changes, mechanization, and cyclical economic crises generated as a result, have contributed to the creation of a large pool of workers, especially at older ages, who are discarded from the productive order without sufficient resources to meet their needs.

Widespread, pressing social problems have ensued from the growth and support of private economic interests. These, in turn, have produced calls for state action by diverse sectors of the working class, the unemployed, the aged, and other adversely affected groups. The state has responded with policies and programs to legitimate the capitalist order and to achieve stability and social harmony—the latter goals receiving increasingly less emphasis since the mid-1970s. Moreover, the state has shaped public programs meeting these demands in ways that do not threaten prevailing institutional arrangements, private profits, or other benefits accruing to the dominant class. The boundaries of public policy are determined primarily by the ideas, values, and biases emanating from private economic interests. The latter successfully promote, protect, and enhance their benefits and advantages.

Aging programs and policy enactments mirror the dual, and often contradictory, state functions of private accumulation and legitimization. Their effect has been to reinforce existing inequalities within society. Income maintenance programs for the elderly make no alterations in the distribution of resources between the classes. In fact, the net effect of Social Security, the private retirement systems, SSI, and public pension programs has been to increase income and wealth inequalities between capitalists and workers, between older and younger generations, among sectors of the labor force, and among the elderly themselves.

Chapter 3 will show that Social Security is basically a conservative instrument of social control. It rests largely on the principle of social insurance which, according to Binstock, "does not affect the class structure, the sum total of opportunity, or anything else;

on the contrary, it tends to maintain existing patterns."[34] Relief arrangements, such as the Supplementary Security Income (SSI) program for the elderly poor, regulate and control workers even more effectively than payroll-supported programs. SSI, which guarantees an income minimum that does not meet even the officially defined poverty level, is vastly inadequate, restrictive, and punitive. This legislation serves, as Piven and Cloward argue, "to instill in the laboring masses a fear of the fate that awaits them should they relax into beggary and pauperism. To demean and punish those who do not work is to exalt by constrast even the meanest labor at the meanest wages."[35]

In chapter 3 I also note that the modern capitalist system in the United States is distinguished by the vast concentration of wealth and power in a few corporate and financial monopolies, alongside of which operate a large number of competitive firms.[36] This dual private economy, coupled with a significant public sector, finds its counterparts in the division and organization of the working class, and consequently of the aged population.

Monopoly sector workers, who are for the most part unionized, have been able to secure relatively decent wages and coverage by private pension systems. Similarly, public sector employees have obtained comparable—and sometimes more than comparable—retirement benefits through federal civil service, military, state, and local retirement systems. Competitive sector employment, on the other hand, is characterized by low wages, job insecurity, a large number of poorly paid part-time positions, and a paucity of private retirement systems and other benefits. This sector includes the vast majority of female and minority group employees as well as technologically displaced older workers.

This tripartite division of labor, each group with its own distinguishing characteristics, has produced three general classes of retirees and dependent spouses. Moreover, rewards accrue primarily to those retirees in the monopoly and state sectors having long and continuous employment histories.

Inequalities within the labor market, which are perpetuated into the retirement years, also have important implications for the status of minority and female older Americans. The prevalence of poverty among particular groups of older people, and the complex social problems associated with their lack of an adequate income, are clearly related to such characteristics as sex and race. But, as Wachtel cogently argues, these innate traits are not causes of social and economic problems. Nonrandom distribution of need among female and minority elderly, rather, is evidence that certain groups are affected most adversely by capitalist practices, particularly markets for labor.[37]

Chapter 4 will argue that private, state, and local pension systems, buttressed through state policies, play a crucial (and growing) role in private capital accumulation. These retirement trusts have become a major source of capital in the American economy. At the end of 1980, they held $653 billion and over 20 percent of common stocks of companies listed on the New York and American exchanges. Managed and controlled by large institutional investors, particularly commercial banks, pension trusts have contributed, among other things, to the concentration of capital, the growing power of financial institutions, and the support of corporate practices that tend to be antithetical to working class interests and socially desirable goals. At the same time they have failed to meet the retirement income needs of workers.

The major public policies aimed at improving medical care, housing conditions, and social services for the elderly—problems that have been generated through capitalist development itself—reinforce existing social, economic, and power relationships and institutional practices that benefit disproportionately the relatively affluent income groups. They enrich considerably private providers of goods and services, such as doctors, hospitals, nursing home operators, landlords, and developers, and foster the exploitation of social needs for private gain. They fail conspicuously to meet the pressing and growing needs of the elderly poor. Moreover, since health, housing, and service needs of certain sectors of older people stem from such factors as inadequate resources, poor nutrition, deficient medical care, and unhealthy working and living environments during workers' younger years, efforts directed exclusively at the aged fail to address the root causes of their problems.

In chapter 5 I point out that Medicare, Medicaid, and other health-related measures purporting to serve the elderly have been superimposed on a privately controlled medical market that has been designed, established, and controlled by special provider groups, such as hospitals, doctors, drug companies, and nursing homes, to serve their own interests. Age-based health programs have buttressed and exacerbated ineffective, inequitable, and overly costly medical care practices in the United States. I also contend that the equation of health care with medical services and the growth of technological medicine, both promoted by corporate and provider interests, have diverted attention from industrial, environmental, social, and economic causes of disease. Addressing a 1975 American Medical Association Convention, Dr. Theodore Cooper, previously assistant HEW Secretary for Health, commented: "It is one of the great and sobering truths of our profession that modern health care probably has less impact on the health of the population than economic status, education, housing, nutrition and sanitation, and the impact of changing technologies on working conditions and the environment."[38] Despite the enormous economic resources devoted to Medicare and, to a lesser extent, Medicaid, health-related problems of the aged have not improved markedly.

Chapter 6 provides evidence about the housing problems of older people. Physically inadequate units, absence of essential facilities and services, high and rising costs relative to income, and deteriorating and high-crime neighborhoods typify these problems. They stem predominantly from (a) the disproportionate representation of the elderly in low and poverty level income classes and (b) housing policies that focus on subsidizing and benefiting financial institutions, developers, the construction industry, and other private interests. The profit-oriented activities of such groups are unrelated to the quality and affordability of shelter among the general population, particularly such disadvantaged groups as the elderly poor.

Chapter 7 assesses the Older Americans Act (OAA) and related service programs. I suggest that the thrust of the service intervention strategy is to compensate for the assumed personal deficiencies of beneficiaries or, alternatively, specified community defects.[39] Thus services focus on correcting the supposed ignorance of the aged or their personal problems. Special transportation services and information and referral programs aim at ameliorating community deficiencies that prevent adequate utilization of public and private services, but affect neither the quality nor the quantity of existing services and facilities. By segregating service programs according to age, the government implies that certain needs are the inevitable and accepted consequences of growing old. Thus the thrust of OAA is on multiproblems of advanced age. The activities of powerful private interests and the public-policies they influence, which have created the pressing problems affecting the elderly and which continue to oppress them, remain untouched. Without addressing the basic cause of the aged's urgent needs, and the larger structural issues those needs reveal, OAA and similar programs serve to maintain existing allocations of power and benefits in society.

Chapter 8 provides some concluding observations on the role of age-based social policies. I also note some of the inherent limitations of free-market and liberal accommodationist reforms under prevailing institutional arrangements. I contend that progressive changes—those that move society in the direction of democratic socialism—are necessary for solving general social problems as well as those experienced by older people.

Chapter 2

A Brief History of the Economic Problems of Aging

This chapter seeks to explore the historical relationships among capital, labor, and the national state, and their impacts on the older population. I argue that deep transformations in the American economy and civil society, fostered by industrial leaders to meet their own needs and supported by growing national state activities on behalf of capital, have had pernicious effects on the elderly. The rise of monopoly capitalism was accompanied by a steady proletarianization and de-skilling of the work force. These changes, along with other corporate and governmental practices intended to enhance private accumulation and profits as well as to control and motivate workers, generated increasing unemployment, forced retirement, economic dependency, and poverty among older people. I further contend that the belated political response to economic aging, through the Social Security Act of 1935, was primarily an attempt by the national state to preserve established economic and political arrangements, including the class system; to curtail growing support among the masses for fundamental systemic changes; and to force the working class to save for their own old age.

THE EMERGING INDUSTRIAL ORDER

Until the nineteenth-century industrial revolution, wage labor was rare in the United States. A rural and predominantly agricultural society, its social, political, and economic relationships were connected with land holdings; the vast majority of the nonslave population worked as independent farmers. Artisans, merchants, small producers, traders, lawyers, and other professionals were also self-employed and often cultivated small plots of land to supplement their income.

The family was a relatively independent, integrated production unit, with older male parents generally having power even over their grown children. Before the advent of factories and mechanized farming, economic superannuation was unknown. Few people attained old age,[1] but those who did experienced economic insecurity, along with the rest of the household, primarily through crop failures, pestilence, and other natural disasters, rather than as a result of forced retirement and loss of wages. On the farm, or in trade and business, only physical incapacity determined whether an individual would withdraw from full-time productive labor. Greenough and King note: "Although the physical labor of older family members decreased, the aged still played an important supervisory role in the family structure, participating in the productive enterprise of the farm or artisanship and sharing in the working and supportive processes."[2] Since family ties tended to be strong and binding, most older people who were no longer able to work were cared for and supported by their children and relatives. In fact, grown children, particularly those who were to inherit the farm or family business, often remained economically dependent on their parents, the latter generally retaining ownership and control over the land or trade nearly until death.[3]

On the other hand, older people who were too infirm to labor and who lacked independent or family means of support, although their number was small, suffered severe economic deprivation and social sanctions. According to Fischer: "To be old and poor and outcast in early America was certainly not to be venerated, but rather to be despised. . . . old age seems actually to have intensified the contempt visited upon a poor man."[4]

During the 1800s American social and economic structures were radically transformed. The emergence of the merchant-capitalist, and soon after, factory production, was fostered by and influenced the growth of cities, improvements in transportation facilities, settlement of the frontier, and consequently enlarged markets for manufactured products. The merchant-capitalist, who had relatively easy access to credit, soon dominated the economy while, by the 1860s, the work force had become increasingly proletarianized.[5]

The labor required for the developing factory system was drawn primarily from the influx of immigrants during the 1840s and to a lesser extent from surplus agricultural workers in surrounding communities. Moreover, as a result of competition from machine production, craftsmen and other self-employed people were steadily forced into wage labor.[6]

However, production took place mostly in small local workshops and factories organized by single entrepreneurs or small family groups. Since these early enterprises relied on traditional craft methods, middle-aged and older men, who possessed specialized knowledge and skills, were not denied employment. Voluntary or mandatory retirement at a prescribed age was, for the most part, nonexistent. Moreover, over half of the laboring masses, particularly in the West and South, continued their independent agricultural pursuits. Older people, in fact, were disproportionately represented among the farming population.[7] As a result, the proportion of elderly men who continued to perform labor remained relatively constant during this period.

After the Civil War the pace of urbanization, expansion of the factory system, mechanization, railroad construction, and growth and concentration of industry and finance, as well as the proletarianization and deskilling of the work force all intensified rapidly. In 1850 about 70 percent of manufactured goods were produced in the handicraft workshop; by 1890 80 percent were produced in factories.[8] The proportion of the population dependent on a wage for subsistence reached nearly two-thirds of the adult work force by 1890 and steadily increased during the 1900s. Small manufacturers, craftsmen, and other independent producers, unable to compete effectively, were driven out of business and transformed into wage laborers. Growing concentration of land, mechanized agriculture, and high interest rates forced a large percentage of independent farmers off the land and into the cities and factories. The percentage of the labor force engaged in farming decreased from 59 percent in 1865 to 26 percent by 1914.[9] At the same time, vastly increased productivity and falling prices within the agricultural sector depressed considerably the incomes of those remaining on the land. Blacks, who had worked primarily as farm tenants or sharecroppers after the Civil War, joined the urban proletariat at the turn of the century, although not in great numbers until the 1940s and 1950s.

Mass immigration from eastern and southern Europe, encouraged through public policy and private efforts, was most instrumental in expanding wage labor. Between 1861 and 1900 over 28 million people immigrated to the United States. Settling in the growing cities where industrial activity was concentrated, these new arrivals provided a major portion of the workers required by large-scale industry.[10]

Although smaller firms were increasingly engulfed by larger companies, intense competition that characterized the latter half of the nineteenth century precluded monopoly control over the economy or within particular industries. Not only did corporations face competition from existing concerns, but also new enterprises swiftly might make old ones obsolete. As a result of relatively free trade, competitive labor and market conditions, and rapid technological innovation, production grew enormously while at the same time prices dropped precipitously. Unable to control and stabilize labor, output, markets, or prices within an industry, the emerging industrial corporations experienced severe pressures on profits. As Kolko notes: "Expansion and competition, and with them instability and economic crisis, had become the essential hallmarks of the main branches of the American economic structure during the first half of modern American history."[11] The paramount problem for industrialists of the late nineteenth century was how to control both internal and external relationships associated with the production process.

In confronting their external challenges, corporate leaders instituted voluntary output and price agreements through newly organized business trade associations, industry pools, and similar entities. In addition, mergers, trusts, and holding companies proliferated. However, these innovations failed to curtail competition or to reduce pressures on profits sufficiently for meeting corporate needs. Informal agreements were often broken as small firms sought to increase their share of growing markets. Even corporate giants were unable to prevent the emergence of new enterprises. By the beginning of the twentieth century, chaos and economic instability continued to threaten major industrial interests. Big business turned increasingly to the national state for stable market conditions to ensure profitability.

Moreover, to cut costs, large corporations intermittently reduced their workers' already low wages, resulting in severe economic hardship and growing militancy among the laboring masses. Ray-bach reports that "in 1884 the average [wage] cut was 15 percent; in 1885 the cuts were even deeper."[12] Arbitrary and harsh practices intended to increase worker discipline, such as mass dismissals, also furthered unionization, labor violence, and costly strikes. Consequently, industrial leaders sought the power of the national state to contain labor strife through the use of repressive sanctions.

THE RISE OF MONOPOLY CAPITALISM

In the United States the major role of the national government until the late nineteenth century had been to set the framework for and encourage the expansion of industrial capitalism. Although prevailing views among political and economic leaders supported the notion of a "minimal" state, government intervention in the economy was substantial. As Wolfe argues, the early accumulative state paved the way for the rise of industrial capitalism: "A collective effort was necessary to unleash the phenomenal power of modern industrial production, and it was government that provided, to one degree or another, the core of that effort. Modern capitalism could not have existed without the state."[13] The federal government established legal codes and maintained order for the protection and advancement of private production and property, allowed massive exploitation of public lands and other natural resources, and adopted tariff policies which prevented foreign competition.

After the Civil War, as laissez faire capitalism triumphed, direct and indirect governmental intervention on behalf of industry continued, albeit in altered form. Faced with an economy characterized by intense and vigorous market competition, the national state sought to discipline the work force, preserve order, and protect existing property relationships. For example, the government sent federal troops to break up strikes and obstruct workers' efforts to obtain better wages and improved working conditions. In fact, the evidence suggests that the state lived up to its laissez faire, minimalist ideals only when confronted with the needs of the working class, their dependents, and the aged.

By the end of the nineteenth century, the state began to take a more active role in the economy and civil society. Unable to control what they perceived as intense competition and falling profits through private efforts alone, large-scale industrialists successfully procured protective measures from the government. Industry's own activities had depressed wages and increased the frequency of industrial accidents, unemployment, oppressive working conditions, and unethical business practices, and served both to intensify working class militancy and elicit public support for labor. Consequently, under the guise of reform, the state implemented various "regulatory" mechanisms and other measures. With the dual goals of social control and market stability, the progressive era substantially benefited capital and quieted public discontent while failing to ameliorate the growing problems of active and retired workers, widows, and other needy groups.

According to Kolko, the integration of economic and political institutions "on behalf of the greater interests of capitalism" met with only limited success during the progressive era. It was the more extensive cooperation between big business and government during World War I, including massive government subsidies and loans, that institutionalized political capitalism, producing high profits, aiding the growth of monopolies and oligopolies, and generally solving the problems for large-scale business that had existed under laissez faire capitalism.[14] In sum, as Katznelson and Kesselman argue, "if it had not been for government intervention, the new breed of industrial giants might have continued to decline."[15]

After the war the government lifted most controls on corporations and a new wave of mergers and consolidations ensued. By 1930, 50 percent of all banking capital was held by one percent of the nation's banks, four companies produced 64 percent of America's iron and steel, and three corporations manufactured 90 percent of all automobiles:

> Between 1919 and 1930 nearly six thousand independent manufacturing and mining companies disappeared as a result of mergers. . . . In 1910 the two hundred largest corporations in the country did thirty-three percent of the business; by 1930 the two hundred largest . . . controlled half the corporate wealth, a third of the business, and one-fifth of the total wealth in the U.S.[16]

At the same time a growing, if peripheral, competitive sector coexisted alongside the industrial giants, creating a dual private economy in the nation. Though the number of people employed in manufacturing increased by 50 percent from 1900 to 1940, this number represented only about one-fourth of the total labor force. In addition, other monopoly sector enterprises, particularly banking, finance, and insurance, accounted for an increasing share of the total. On the other hand, the largest rise in employment occurred in the burgeoning competitive service industries, including the wholesale trade, retail shops, and domestic service.[17]

THE GROWTH OF DEPENDENCY AND POVERTY IN OLD AGE

Welfare Capitalism: Forced Retirement and Private Pension Systems

To provide for their own long-term stability, the giant corporations also restructured internal processes and instituted measures aimed at curtailing and destroying growing unionization. Within larger firms, where increased profits depended on labor stability, and technological innovations for improving worker productivity, the nature and organization of work processes were radically transformed. First, during the 1920s, vastly increased mechanization, narrower divisions of labor, and the acceleration of the productive process itself all increased efficiency, allowing rapid replacement of skilled by unskilled or semiskilled labor, reducing the numbers of workers necessary overall, and enabling employers to gain control over the work process. By the 1920s, as Brecher and Costello note, "little skill was required in most industries either using or building materials, such as steel, shoes, clothing, meat-packing, baking, cannery, hardware and tobacco."[18] Second, employers adopted new and subtle means for controlling and motivating employees. Hierarchical arrangements, divisions into job grades and categories, and bureaucratic controls were instituted to motivate employee production and to create internal labor markets. Just as important, according to Edwards, Reich, and Gordon: "the new needs of monopoly capitalism for control were threatened by the tremendous upsurge in labor conflict, already apparent as early as the 1870s, and reaching new levels of militancy around the turn of the century."[19] Welfare capitalism therefore provided another means for advancing labor stability, improving efficiency, and weakening the growing union movement.

For older workers these monopoly sector practices had pernicious effects. As assembly lines moved faster and efficiency was stressed, employers viewed the aged not only as "unable to maintain the pace"[20] but also as a retarding influence on the production rate of younger employees. Consequently, as Achenbaum contends, "new bureaucratic principles were applied in a deliberate effort to eliminate those who, from a 'rational' point of view, appeared to be inefficient human machines."[21] For the first time, mandatory retirement at a fixed age, usually between sixty-five and seventy, was adopted by large enterprises. Between 1874 and 1918, according to Achenbaum, "the idea of requiring people to retire or offering them the option to do so because they had attained a particular age was gaining acceptance in the private sector."[22]

As a central component of welfare capitalism major corporations established noncontributory, employer-controlled pension systems during the late 1800s and early 1900s. Organized labor strongly opposed these retirement programs, viewing them as antithetical to worker interests and preferring higher wages instead. In fact, the evidence suggests that among the large industries wages were lower in those corporations that had the better pension systems.[23] As Lubove and others have argued: "the industrial pension was, first and foremost, a technique of labor control. This helps to explain the indifference to funding and especially to vesting employees with legal rights."[24] Employers assumed that not only would retirement programs provide opportunities for removing less productive workers, but they would also improve morale and efficiency among younger employees by imbuing the latter with a sense of economic security. Drawing from an article written in 1906 entitled *Insurance from the Employer's Standpoint*, Lubove noted a growing viewpoint among corporate leaders:

> An "intelligent employer" had to recognize that fear of the consequences of disability or old age demoralized the average worker. Lack of security acted as an "incubus to his efforts and progress." Permanent industrial peace depended upon the employer's understanding that it was "just as important to furnish security for the job as it is to furnish security for the investment."[25]

Employers also saw pensions as an important instrument for attracting an ambitious and proficient work force who would be bound to the firm. Wage competition and high labor turnover had deleterious effects on corporate attempts to stabilize the labor market. Pension promises would weaken labor mobility and aid in the creation of internal markets, particularly since eligibility required long tenure with the firm (generally between twenty and thirty years).

Finally, employers considered their pension systems a means of discouraging workers from forming unions for the regulation of hours, wages, and working conditions, as well as of reducing strikes. Their major goal was the inculcation of loyalty to the employer rather than to the trade union. Louis Brandeis, for example, condemned these early retirement schemes as a "form of 'strike insurance,' to rob the worker of any industrial liberty."[26] Since the administration of the funds was in the hands of employers, any workers attempting to unionize could be threatened with a denial of their pensions. Those retired workers receiving benefits were sometimes even recalled during strikes. If they refused to cooperate their pensions were forfeited.[27]

Following the first formal private pension plans (American Express Company, 1875; Baltimore and Ohio Railroad Company, 1880), other corporations instituted retirement systems. There were only twelve such plans in 1900, primarily in the railroad industry. By the 1920s, according to Greenough and King, "most of the major railroads, utility companies, banks, mining companies, and petroleum companies had set up formal pension plans, and parallel pension plans was recorded for manufacturers of machinery, agricultural implements, chemicals, paints and varnishes, food products, rubber, paper and printing products and electrical apparatus."[28] By the end of 1929 about 397 retirement systems were operating in the country.[29]

Despite the establishment of private pension plans in many industries, most of the aged forced to retire at a prescribed age were ineligible for, or unable to obtain, pension income. Eligibility criteria were restrictive, requiring long, continuous tenure with a firm. In addition, pensions were rarely sufficient to maintain an adequate standard of living. They were controlled exclusively by employers, who viewed them as gratuities subject to the company's discretion. Clauses in all plans stated clearly that retirement benefits were voluntary gifts rather than contractual obligations; employers did not have to provide an annuity, continue the system, or guarantee that renumeration would be permanent. The uncertain nature of pensions was compounded by the fact that most plans were financed from a corporation's current income. Even the resources of funded plans—those that accumulated reserves—were vastly insufficient to meet their "obligations." During business depressions, pensioners' benefits were either drastically reduced or suspended altogether, and retiring workers were denied initial payments.[30] If a firm went bankrupt, all pension obligations ceased since employees, as affirmed by the courts, had no claim on a company's assets.[31]

Consequently, few older people employed in industries with retirement systems actually received a pension. Epstein has pointed out that the Pennsylvania Railroad, which employed 300,000 workers, provided pensions for only 9,129 people between 1900 and 1919. Similarly, the Philadelphia and Reading Railroad had only 976 pensioners between 1902 and 1920, while the Baltimore and Ohio Railroad Company retired under 3,000 workers with old age benefits during the same period.[32] In fact, less than 1 percent of the nonagricultural labor force qualified for a pension by the 1920s. In sum, the combination of forced retirement with few, inadequate pension systems made poverty and dependency in old age two of the most serious social problems fostered by industrial capitalism.

Structural Unemployment

For workers dependent on a wage for subsistence, unemployment often meant poverty and dependency even before they reached age sixty-five. The speed, strain, and harshness of industrial conditions adversely affected all workers, and, since expertise and experience lost their value in large, mass production enterprises, employers downgraded or discharged without compensation employees unable to maintain their efficiency. Writing in 1922, Epstein observed that industrial workers were often eliminated from productive industry as early as their fiftieth year.[33] As noted by Achenbaum, employees "over fifty-five who were worn out or displaced by machines found reemployment opportunities limited. . . . If employment prospects were poor for those in their fifties, they were even worse for people in their sixties."[34] Many larger industries set their hiring age at below forty.[35] Welfare capitalism further served to reduce employment opportunities for middle-aged and older workers because, since the cost of many pension plans was determined by the average age of a company's work force, a youthful work force saved employers money.

Achenbaum has estimated that the number of elderly men working decreased less than 5 percent from 1840 to 1890.[36] However, as a result of new monopoly sector practices, mechanization, and unemployment, the rate of older men participating in the labor force dropped from 63.1 percent in 1900 to 55.6 percent in 1920 and steadily declined thereafter.[37] Although production increased dramatically and real wages expanded somewhat during the prosperous 1920s, while total unemployment in the nation hovered between 2 and 4 percent, nearly half of all male wage-earners sixty-five and over were without work.

The Changing Situation of Older Farmers

Despite rapidly declining numbers of people working on farms, as late as 1900 the majority of all older people continued agricultural pursuits.[38] However, the problems of farm workers also intensified considerably after the turn of the century. Although many elderly farmers owned their own land and thus were not dependent on a wage for subsistence, they were plagued by rapidly falling farm prices resulting from increasing mechanization and overproduction fostered by big landowners. Moreover, since the children of agricultural workers were likely to be living in urban areas, usually earning very low wages, care and support of elderly farmers who could no longer work, or of widows unable to manage the farm alone, became increasingly difficult.

Deep changes in the American economy had profound and negative effects on the conditions of all workers. However, the economic problems of the elderly were particularly acute. Given the large percentage of the elderly engaged in agriculture, the older population was highly likely to be affected by the growing poverty experienced by all small-scale farmers. Their poor prospects for alternative employment also placed them at a greater disadvantage than younger adults. Mechanization, bureaucratic controls, and mandatory retirement policies instituted by giant corporations, coupled with illusory private pension systems, forced retirement, unemployment, and low wages all contributed to the worsening economic situation of elderly industrial workers. Consequently, by the 1920s the majority of people sixty-five and over were partially or entirely dependent on others for support.[39]

POLITICAL RESPONSES TO ECONOMIC PROBLEMS OF AGING

The steady expansion of activities by the national state and its intervention in the economy did not lead to substantially revised approaches to the needs of the elderly despite the latter's growing destitution and poverty. Until the upsurge of mass protest, radical political movements, and serious threats to the established order during the 1930s, the federal government assumed no responsibility for the plight of superannuated workers. National political leaders viewed problems related to economic aging primarily as an individual responsibility and pauperism as a local obligation. They assumed that family support and savings would be the primary form of subsistence for "retired" wage-earners and their dependents.

However, in his study of wage levels between 1890 and 1900, John Ryan concluded that most employees earned substantially less than they needed to support a family at subsistence level.[40] Workers who could barely meet current needs clearly could not accrue sufficient resources for their old age. Moreover, industrial accidents and sickness could deplete any savings or assets a worker had managed to accumulate. A study of the elderly in Pennsylvania during 1919, for example, revealed that most of the aged had disposed of property, possessions, and savings in order to meet emergencies.[41]

Lacking savings or other forms of support, unemployed and retired workers, as well as their wives and widows, tended to be dependent on children and relatives who themselves were usually struggling to maintain an adequate standard of living. However, studies of old age during the early 1900s show that, in most cases, children sacrificed in order to provide for their elderly parents.

Until the 1920s there were no publicly supported state or local old age assistance programs. According to Lubove, the latter were eschewed by government officials who assumed that these types of economic assistance "allocated goods or services on the basis of need rather than participation in the labor force. In providing a form of guaranteed income they undermined incentive and work discipline," and encouraged dependency instead of self-support.[42]

Older paupers without relatives, or those whose families were unwilling or unable to assist them, were relegated to county almshouses and private charitable institutions. To a lesser extent they might be provided with "outdoor relief" in the form of food and clothing by local poor boards and charitable institutions. The American Poor Law System, derived from Elizabethan England, was predicated on the assumption that older people (as well as other needy groups) were responsible for their own condition. Since their framers hoped that the poor laws would stimulate hard work and savings among the laboring masses and deter their future dependency on government, it is no surprise that public relief was a degrading and humiliating experience.

By the 1920s there were over 2,400 almshouses in the nation.[43] Conditions in these public poorhouses tended to be miserable; the elderly were not infrequently housed with the insane, alcoholics, and petty criminals. Dread and fear of the consequences of dependency, then, served to discipline the working class. Moreover, to avoid the indignities of the almshouse and other repressive relief measures, and to avoid burdening their children, a substantial percentage of the elderly population suffered severe economic deprivation quietly, without drawing attention to their problems.

As the number of older people rose and dependency grew, the scope of the "aging problem" widened and old age emerged as a social problem.[44] The underlying concern of state and local governments, however, appears to have been the increasing burdens on public resources. The primary political response to the plight of the elderly was at the state level in the form of family responsibility laws. By 1914 two-thirds of the states had enacted measures that made children legally responsible for incapacitated and indigent relatives; between World War 1 and 1929, legislation in eleven states stipulated that failure to provide for destitute parents was a criminal offense.[45]

During the 1920s a number of states also passed laws allowing counties to provide aid for the elderly, but these laws were operative only in six states by 1929. Most local programs were not functioning since counties, which were free to choose whether or not to participate, rarely received state funding. Moreover, these old age assistance acts were an attempt "to improve the poor relief programs, rather than an effort to institute a plan of general pensions."[46] Older people whose relatives could support them were not eligible. Encumbered by repressive needs tests to prove indigency, and supported by very low levels of funding, these programs further ensured that work discipline would be maintained. Strict residency requirements also prevented minorities and other newly urbanized groups from receiving any aid. Since the vast majority of states did not have any old age assistance laws, and counties within those that did generally refused to participate in their programs, the major form of public relief during the 1920s continued to be the poorhouse and "outdoor relief" systems.

There were some attempts to establish a publicly funded national system of old age pensions. A socialist legislator in 1909 introduced the "Old Age Home Guard of U.S." bill, but it died in committee. Similar proposals also attracted public attention. But old age assistance at the federal level was opposed vigorously by both big business and the emerging unions, and these proposals were all unsuccessful.

In order to attract members, trade unions had established their own pension plans. By 1928 nearly 40 percent of unionized workers belonged to national labor organizations offering some kind of old age and disability benefits. These limited systems were funded through assessments on participating employees. Labor leaders viewed compulsory government insurance as a means of increasing governmental control over workers, weakening the fledgling labor movement, and reducing the appeal of unions. Instead, labor advocated government financial assistance for existing trade union plans. According to Samuel Gompers, while private employer-controlled pensions "implied an industrial feudalism," publicly funded insurance symbolized "a labor movement subordinate to the state." He further observed that if the worker was paid enough he "could provide for all his needs."[47] Industrial employers, who also strongly opposed national old age insurance, argued that such a government program would constrict the role of their private pension systems and undermine worker discipline. They contended that employer-controlled pensions served to maintain incentives and deterrents "which sustained the work culture."[48]

THE ROLE OF PUBLIC RETIREMENT SYSTEMS

Public retirement systems established prior to the 1890s covered only those occupations serving to maintain public order and stability as well as to support expansionist international policies required by the growing industrial order. In order to attract more competent employees and to remove the superannuated and disabled who were viewed as inefficient, localities began instituting retirement plans for their police and fire workers in the 1850s.[49] By 1910 most such workers were covered and—besides teachers for whom pension systems were established in the 1890s—these were the only classes of workers enrolled in local plans prior to the 1900s.

Similarly, the federal government established pension programs only for military personnel who, as early as the eighteenth century, had received increasingly expensive annuities for their involvement in the Revolutionary War. In 1861, Congress enacted the first of a series of pension legislation for military personnel engaged in the Civil War. Although eligibility for these pensions originally was based on war-related disabilities, Congress eventually provided some benefits for all survivors of the Civil War and their dependents under universal service pension acts.[50] Outlays for these pension benefits which, according to Fischer and others, "had become primarily a system of old age assistance," represented a substantial and growing portion of the federal budget. Fischer observes: "At the same time that compulsory old age pensions were condemned as un-American, the U.S. maintained the largest public pension system in the world."[51] Between 1866 and 1917 the military pension system cost the national government $5.3 billion. By 1902 it was disbursing $138.5 million annually in pension benefits, reaching $161 million a year by 1917.[52] The total national budget in 1902 was approximately $562 million.

Moreover, according to Rubinow, most of the military annuities accrued only to "the native American white population who, financially, were least in need."[53] Similarly, in his comprehensive study of federal military pensions in the United States, Glasson argues that these generous pension laws, particularly the universal service pension legislation, placed burdensome taxes on the poor while paying out "gratuities to persons who were better off than a large proportion of the taxpayers."[54]

By the early 1900s, officials at all levels of government had "found the absence of pensions as a frustrating obstacle to efficiency."[55] For example, a 1908 study of elderly employees in Boston, by the Massachusetts Commission on Old Age Pensions, concluded that "the percentage of inefficient employees over 65 is strikingly large in many departments."[56] Similarly, by 1917 many federal officials were arguing that the efficiency of workers was declining. According to Epstein, "In one federal department it was estimated that 250 people could do the work at present performed by 1,000 superannuated employees."[57] Further, prewar figures showed that turnover of workers was inordinately high in the public sector; 20 percent of federal employees left within the first year, and another 10 percent by the second year.[58]

In 1911 Massachusetts enacted the first statewide retirement plan and shortly after pension systems were established in other parts of the country. During the 1920s, state and local governments expanded their pension systems to include greater coverage for public sector workers. Over 12 percent of the largest state and local plans operating in the 1970s were established prior to 1930.[59] Moreover, in 1920 the national government enacted the Federal Civil Service Retirement System for its nonmilitary employees.

Public retirement programs, viewed as a means of raising the standards of government performance, were based on goals of efficiency and scientific management characteristic of the progressive era. Public sector employers expected that such programs would enable them to recruit and retain better workers; increase the morale and economic security of their employees; and retire inefficient older people at a set age. Just as important, since the federal and most state and local retirement plans were contributory, these pension systems would force government employees to save for their own old age, thus reducing public obligations for their support. However, pensions were extremely low and, similar to the private systems, required long tenure for eligibility.

THE SOCIAL SECURITY ACT OF 1935

The prosperous 1920s obscured the growing contradictions of monopoly capitalism that would usher in more than a decade of economic and social collapse before public policies and a world war superficially and temporarily rejuvenated the system. With vastly growing industrial concentration, inequalities in wealth and income among the population, and greater technological efficiency in the productive processes, the period was characterized by shrinking consumer demand in the face of rising productive output, eventually culminating in the Great Depression of the 1930s. This severe economic crisis prompted an even greater role by the national state both in supporting private accumulation and promoting legitimization of the capitalist system, particularly through social controls and other political expedients.

Retrenched production, persistently high unemployement, and a massive decline in purchasing power during the Great Depression adversely affected all sectors of society, although, as Holzman noted, "the precipitous and widespread decline in employment was more severely felt by the old people than by any other group except the Negro." As the depression grew more severe, unemployment among the 65-and-over population rose dramatically, reaching well over 50 percent by 1935, and rendering approximately 3.5 million older people jobless.[60]

Traditional income support mechanisms proved vastly inadequate to meet the needs of the elderly. Rampant unemployment and poverty among the general population left most families incapable of providing support for aging relatives. In an effort to sustain profits, corporations decreased private retirement benefits, temporarily suspended pension plans, or abolished their retirement systems entirely. In 1935, less than 15 percent of wage and salary workers were covered by private plans; only 165,000 older people, representing fewer than 2.5 percent of private sector employees, were receiving any income from them. Moreover, the average benefit was so low that even private pension recipients were living in poverty. At the same time, nearly all trade union welfare plans collapsed. Shrinking state and local tax revenues also left many public pension systems insolvent, while others, liable to dissolution at any time, decreased or discontinued pension payments.

As the number of indigent older people grew, twenty-eight states revised or passed new old age assistance programs, most of which mandated county participation. In thirteen states the county was fully responsible for funding; in six, the state assumed the entire financial burden; and in eight, the state and county governments shared the costs.[61] However, in most localities children remained legally responsible for the support of their aged parents, program qualifying criteria were strict, and the amount of aid was minimal. Where county programs were optional (seven states), they covered only 28 percent of the aged. Soaring relief costs and declining tax revenues as the depression worsened increased the inability of state and local governments to meet their growing financial burdens. Many state legislators failed to appropriate sufficient funds for their share of the old age programs. Furthermore, twenty states—generally those with a predominantly agricultural economy or located in the South—had enacted no laws for aiding the indigent elderly.[62] The number of older people receiving aid through publicly supported old age assistance programs actually declined during the 1930s; by the end of the 1934 only 180,000 of the elderly received assistance.[63]

The evidence suggests, however, that Congress did not necessarily intend the enactment of national old age insurance as part of the Social Security legislation to alleviate the pressing economic problems of the older population. As noted earlier, deprivation and dependency among the elderly had grown dramatically even before the depression took effect, without causing the national government to enact relief measures. Not until 1934 was a special committee appointed by the President to study issues of economic insecurity, and the particular problems of the elderly were low priority items on its agenda. National old age insurance emerged as an integral part of the New Deal's attempt to preserve existing institutional arrangements, including the class system; to deflect demands for radical change; and to prevent future dependency on public resources.

The underlying concern of the Social Security Act was to control the turbulent masses who, in response to widespread unemployment, mortgage foreclosures, depletion of savings, and destitution, were raiding local relief agencies, mobilizing rent riots, participating in Communist-led marches, and organizing violent protests. By the mid-1930s, despite earlier efforts by the national government to buttress the industrial sector, over 20 percent of the population was still unemployed, and nearly 22 million people were dependent on public aid or private charities. As growing numbers of people began to question the legitimacy of existing institutional structures, a clear threat to monopoly capitalism and the political system materialized.[64] The sheer size of the surplus labor population and its explosive potential threatened the survival of established political and economic relationships. To promote stability and restore confidence in the system, the Social Security Act aimed at mitigating economic insecurity among selected sectors of the working class.

Consequently, old age insurance provisions not only excluded a high proportion of those in need, such as agricultural workers, domestics, state and local employees, the self-employed, and irregularly employed labor, but also omitted all older people at that time, as well as those who would shortly reach sixty-five.[65] Pensions were scheduled to begin in 1942 (later revised to 1940) and full annuities were not to be available for many years thereafter. Initial pensions were also completely insufficient for a decent standard of living. In 1940, older workers averaged $22.60 per month; spouses received $12.13, and widows $20.28. Five years later, benefit levels were only $24.19, $12.82, and $20.19, respectively. Even more significant, eligibility for even these sorely inadequate benefits depended upon a worker's adherence to strict retirement from income-producing labor, a provision which government leaders assumed would enhance job opportunities for younger adults by discouraging older workers from continuing or seeking employment.

In fact, right up to the introduction of the Social Security Act the principal interest of those committees and individuals concerned with its development was to provide a system of unemployment insurance.[66] The last minute inclusion of old age insurance was a direct response to the increasing popularity of more radical alternatives, such as those offered by the Townsend movement and the Lundeen bill.

Emerging in 1933, the Townsend movement advocated a flat pension of $200 a month for every older American, with the provision that it be spent immediately. As opposed to contributory insurance, the Townsend Plan implied that old age benefits were a matter of right, regardless of previous labor force participation. As such it was viewed by national political and economic leaders as threatening to worker discipline, the work ethic, the class structure, individual responsibility, and other values of capitalist society. At its peak the Townsend movement claimed a membership of over 2.2 million people, including 1.5 million elderly Americans, nearly 10 percent of the 65-and-over population.[67] As several observers noted, the Townsend Plan—along with Senator Huey Long's

"Share the Wealth Movement"—"posed the threat of . . . funda-mental change and in this way exercised strong pressure for action," while stimultaneously weakening opposition to the more conser-vative social security legislation.[68] Significantly, passage of the So-cial Security Act and its 1939 amendments reduced substantially the intensity of support for the Townsend movement.

An even more radical scheme, the Lundeen bill, was introduced in Congress during 1934 and again in 1935.[69] With the collapse of union pension and welfare funds, and mass destitution among the population, national union leaders had reversed their opposition to federal old age insurance. They focused their energies on active support for the Social Security Act. However, the Lundeen bill appears to have elicited substantial support among local affiliates of national unions as well as other sectors of the working class. In contrast to the Social Security Act, the Lundeen legislation pro-posed unemployment compensation for everyone over eighteen who was jobless, including the aged, with benefits continuing until the worker found suitable employment; annuities equivalent to prevailing local wages; funding from taxes on inheritances, gifts, and personal annual incomes over $5,000; and administrative con-trol of the program by representatives of workers' and farmers' or-ganizations. Under existing institutional arrangements it would have been difficult to pay for the sweeping coverage and benefit amounts offered in the bill. But this problem was a critical point for some of the Lundeen bill's proponents, who viewed the measure as a preliminary step toward nationalization of industry and even-tually socialism. According to Douglas, they argued that, if it passed, "the people of the country would then demand a reorganization of industry and would insist that men had to be put to work under a program of production for use rather than profit."[70] Support for the bill was so strong during hearings held by the House Committee on Labor that, by a close vote, the committee recommended that it be enacted. Only pressure from the executive branch prevented the bill from coming before the full House. However, when it was offered as an amendment to the Social Security Act the following year, the bill obtained fifty votes. Paul Douglas noted in 1936: "The radical and sweeping nature of its proposals enabled the Admin-istration's forces to say to the indifferent and to the conservatives that unless the latter accepted the moderate program put forward by the Administration they might be forced to accept the radical and far-reaching provisions of the Lundeen bill."[71]

Prospects for reduced relief costs were an additional factor that spurred the enactment of old age insurance both for workers, and in 1939, for their dependents and widows. In order to lighten the potential burden of mass dependency on the state, particularly in view of projected rises in the number of older people who, if left to their own devices, would be unwilling or unable to save, the Social Security Act provided for compulsory participation of covered workers. In other words, employees would be forced to save for their old age. By taxing the working class directly the national state would be relieved of responsibility for supporting potentially large numbers of indigent elderly in future years.

The 1935 act had failed to protect dependents and widows from the threat of dependency and not only would have left a large number of people as wards of the state but also would have impeded the act's primary goal of inculcating a sense of economic security among participating workers. Direct pressure from labor and other groups, as well as the indirect influence of the Townsend movement, were instrumental in persuading national leaders to add coverage for wives and surviving spouses in the 1939 amendments. As Robert and Rosemary Stevens argue: "with the optimisim that accompanies new 'solutions' to major problems, there was an expectation that social security and unemployment insurance would ultimately monopolize income security and that public assistance would 'wither away.'"[72]

Most important—as will be argued more extensively in chapter 3—the Social Security Act was designed to preserve and reinforce the capitalist system of production and distribution, existing income and wealth inequalities, and worker discipline. In contrast to the Social Security systems developed in nearly all other industrialized countries, the United States' system was structured so as to avoid direct government support for older people. Both the ability of large-scale capital to pass on the employer's share of the payroll tax to consumers and workers, and provisions in the act that allowed employer contributions to be deducted from profits for income tax purposes, effectively absolved monopoly enterprises of most responsibility for their retired employees.

Individualization of benefit rights, based on participation in the work force, simultaneously reinforced worker discipline and income inequalities. Only covered workers with five years of regular labor force participation prior to 1940 were eligible for the initial pensions. Low benefit levels would maintain individual initiative, thrift, and responsibility by necessitating additional savings for an adequate income during old age. By not taxing "unearned income," such as interest on savings, rents, and dividends, and by imposing a regressive tax structure with annuity amounts tied to wages, the system further reinforced existing income inequalities in society. The system's overriding principle—"social equity" based on "earned" benefits—precluded benefit levels that met a criterion of "social adequacy." The Social Security Act of 1935 ensured the majority of covered workers a retirement income vastly below that necessary for a decent standard of living.

THE OLD AGE ASSISTANCE PROGRAM

The Social Security Act also provided aid to the welfare-dependent older population. However, the Old Age Assistance measure and its subsequent revisions did little more than contribute federal funds to existing state programs and spur the enactment of new or revised state laws. Low benefit levels and rigid eligibility standards were not significantly altered. Many states retained laws demanding that relatives assume primary responsibility for the indigent elderly, and kept the right to place liens on a welfare recipient's property in exchange for support. Although the original legislative proposal had stated that "old-age assistance grants must be sufficient, with other income, to provide a reasonable subsistence compatible with decency and health," this clause was eliminated in the final version of the Social Security Act.[73] Political leaders argued that adequate and easily obtainable benefits would encourage lower income groups to depend on the state for support and undermine their initiative to work and save. Moreover, many states and localities strongly opposed national standards requiring them to assist blacks in the South or Mexicans and Indians in the Southwest and West. Consequently, state programs varied widely in the criteria by which they determined need and levels of support. Many states, hard-pressed to match federal contributions, provided vastly insufficient assistance. By 1952 average monthly payments ranged from \$21.85 in Alabama to \$80.43 in Colorado. Some states even used rising federal matching grants to lower state expenditures for the programs rather than to increase benefit amounts.[74] In sum, "the federal-state program of old-age assistance ... was, at best, a temporary makeshift which improved somewhat a patchwork of needs-tested relief."[75]

THE NEW DEAL UNFOLDS: 1940 TO THE PRESENT

Expansion of the Social Security System

Despite the persistence of poverty among large sectors of the aged population between 1941 and 1949, Congress enacted few changes in coverage, benefits, and the like of the Social Security system. By the 1950s, however, growing dependency of indigent older people on public assistance began to strain the inadequate federal-state old age assistance program which, in 1950, provided at least some aid to 2.8 million aged Americans, representing 23 percent of all older people.[76] As noted by Sanders, "The sweeping changes in eligibility requirements as well as the substantial increases in benefits and expanded coverage [of the Social Security Act), were approved by Congress in the hope of eliminating the need for further expansion in public assistance."[77]

Pressure by organized labor and large-scale industrial leaders was instrumental in prompting a series of amendments to the Social Security Act in the 1950s and 1960s. The former groups, concerned over decreasing job opportunities as well as low Social Security benefit levels, lobbied vigorously for expansion and liberalization of the system. Corporate leaders, on the other hand, anticipated that an enhanced Social Security scheme would abate pressures by unions for higher pensions and other liberalizing features in the growing private retirement systems. For example, Walter Reuther, head of the United Auto Workers, argued that attempts by workers to improve noncontributory private pension plans provided incentives for employers to fight for larger Social Security benefits.[78]

Responding to these pressures, Congress expanded coverage, eased eligibility requirements, added disability insurance, and increased pension benefits, although the latter remained insufficient to ensure an adequate income for older people. For example, in 1959, 38 percent of the elderly were living in poverty.[79] Farmers, the self-employed, domestics, military personnel, and professionals were included under mandatory coverage, while employees of state and local governments and nonprofit organizations were allowed to enroll in the program. Divorced spouses became eligible for benefits and female workers and dependents were permitted to receive their initial annuities at age sixty-two. However, most of these changes were accompanied by higher wage base levels and taxes, further increasing the regressive nature of the Social Security system and ensuring that the working class would support the growing sector of unemployed and "retired" aged. With the enactment of Medicare in 1965 (see chapter 5), an additional tax was placed on the wages of the working class. From 1935 to 1972 the wage base of the old age insurance program increased from $3,000 to $9,000 while tax rates on employees grew from 1 percent to 5.2 percent. Moreover, the expanding number of workers contributing to the system also allowed Congress to pass periodic benefit increases.

Recurring high rates of unemployment in the country, which reached particularly high levels from 1957 until the early 1960s, influenced Congress to lower the age of eligibility for pensions to sixty-two. Saville argues that the reduction of the retirement age for men "was founded under the simple assumption that earlier retirement would reduce unemployment in the short run."[80] Finally, in the 1970s Congress enacted substantial across-the-board pension increases and beginning in 1975 benefit levels were indexed automatically to rises in the Consumer Price Index. Again, these revisions were accompanied by larger wage bases and tax rates. The current status of the Social Security system, including more recent revisions in 1977, will be discussed in the next chapter. Importantly, Social Security has become the most costly social program administered by the national government.

The Growth of Private Retirement Systems

During World War II, the national government raised corporate taxes and instituted wage and price controls. These factors, coupled with a scarcity of labor, were influential in promoting a renewal of interest by corporations in private retirement systems. First, as suggested earlier, corporate officers viewed pension plans as a viable means of attracting and retaining proficient workers, goals that became particularly important as a result of severe labor shortages in the 1940s. Second, the 1942 Revenue Act—which clarified earlier provisions relating to the tax-exempt status of both employer contributions to and interest on the assets of pension trusts—made the establishment of retirement systems attractive as a means of lowering corporate taxes. Third, confronted with strong demands by labor for increased wages, the War Labor Board ruled in 1944 that the provision or expansion of fringe benefits, including pensions, would be allowed in lieu of an upward adjustment in earnings. Thus, according to a Conference Board report, "employers . . . were able to offer substantially improved employee benefits in lieu of salary increases with very little impact on their net profits."[81] However, labor organizations, which favored higher wages, reaffirmed their earlier opposition to these company-initiated plans.

By the late 1940s, organized labor began to reevaluate its negative attitude toward private pension systems. In order to decrease industrial turmoil and class conflict during the depression, the Wagner Act of 1935 granted labor unions the right to organize and bargain "with respect to wages, hours and other terms and conditions of employment." In 1948 a confrontation arose between the Inland Steel Company and the steelworkers' union as to whether the compulsory retirement feature of the company-controlled pension plan was a negotiable issue. In allowing pension plans as legitimate subjects for collective bargaining, the National Labor Relations Board (NLRB) argued that provisions of retirement plans can be considered among "conditions of employment." As Greenough and King note, the Inland Steel case, by forcing employers to negotiate on pension issues, "marked a turning point in the unions' attitude toward pension plans. Thereafter, many private plans ceased to be a matter of voluntary, unilateral action by an employer."[82] Unions now would have at least some influence, through negotiation, over their private pension plans.

Labor achieved further support for collectively bargained plans in 1949, although at the expense of wage increases. A special commission appointed by President Truman for the purpose of averting a steel strike refused to grant demands for higher wages, arguing that the latter would interfere with business growth. However, in forcing steel to bargain on pension issues, the commission noted that retirement systems would not adversely affect profits.

Other factors were also instrumental in persuading labor organizations to value private plans. The failure of trade union welfare systems and their ineffectiveness in attracting union members convinced labor leaders that union pension plans were not viable alternatives to private plans. Moreover, the granting of pensions in lieu of wage increases during the war established a presumption among workers that they were entitled to such retirement income as a matter of right. Labor adopted the argument that employers were obligated to provide for the "repair and retirement" of workers as they do the "repair and retirement" of equipment and machinery.[83] Most important, the inadequacy of Social Security benefits spurred demands by organized labor for supplementary retirement income. Several union leaders, particularly those in the CIO, viewed private pensions as a means of closing the gap between Social Security annuity levels, which in 1949 averaged only $39 per month for a retired worker and his wife, and the national government's "decent standard of living budget," then set at $148 per month. Although most unions still considered higher wages, better working conditions, and various other issues to be greater priorities than pensions, retirement systems emerged as a serious concern during collective bargaining.

Several key pension issues, however, were resolved in favor of industrial employers. For example, the first demands for a negotiated multi-employer plan were initiated by John L. Lewis, president of the United Mine Workers, in 1946. After a lengthy strike, and seizure of the mines by the national government, an agreement was reached which established, among other things, a pooled welfare and retirement fund. However, partly in reaction to Lewis' attempt to have the unions control the pension system, Congress added section 302 to the 1947 Taft-Hartley law. The provision prohibited unions from obtaining exclusive power over any multi-employer trusts. Moreover, nearly all single-employer schemes contained provisions providing for company control over these retirement funds. Congress also failed to protect employee pension rights. In particular, it did not require actuarially sound systems, and even vested workers were not protected against business failure or bankruptcy of the trust. This problem was demonstrated dramatically after a Studebaker plant in Indiana was shut down permanently during the 1960s and the firm's employees were forced to forfeit their future pension entitlements. Moreover, at least 2,000 retired workers were left without their annuities.

In fact, with the exception of the Internal Revenue Codes and the Taft-Hartley provisions relating to pooled schemes, the federal government exercised extremely limited control of private pension systems until the enactment of the Employee Retirement Income Security Act (ERISA) in 1974. The major benefits of the Internal Revenue Codes, such as tax exemptions for qualified plans, tended to accrue to industry. Moreover, a proposal to incorporate immediate and full vesting rights for workers into the 1942 Internal Revenue Act was contested successfully by employers. Restrictive vesting rules often required as long as twenty or even thirty years of continuous service for workers to become eligible for benefits, a length of employment reached by few. The primary, although inadequate, protection for employees included provisions mandating the use of trust assets exclusively in the interest of workers and their beneficiaries, and prohibiting plans from discriminating in favor of officers, stockholders, or highly paid personnel.

After the inital, and often acrimonious encounters between labor and capital, the number of collectively bargained single-employer and multiemployer private pension plans grew rapidly. While in 1950, 11.2 million workers were covered under private plans, the number rose to 18.7 million and 26.3 million in 1960 and 1970, respectively. By 1981, nearly 50 percent of the labor force participated in a private scheme.

It will be argued in chapters 3 and 4, however, that the private retirement systems inadequately serve the interests of most retired workers and their dependents, although they continue to afford substantial benefits to monopoly capital. The enactment of ERISA, which was partly in response to the Studebaker debacle, provided greater involvement by the national government in the area of private plans. It mandated limited improvements in vesting, eligibility requirements, funding, and actuarial standards. However, the legislation failed to address fundamental issues pertaining to income protection in old age and the critical and growing role of retirement trust assets in the American economy.

Capital and State Policies

The Social Security Act conspicuously failed either to ameliorate immediate problems faced by the aged or to address the underlying causes of insecurity and poverty among workers, superannuated employees, and their dependents or widows. Thus the legislation, or for that matter other New Deal measures, did not resolve the host of structural problems inherent within monopoly capitalism.

Underconsumption, a direct consequence of vast income inequalities, was not redressed by the Social Security Act. Without redistribution of income and wealth, consumer purchasing power continued to be inadequate for encouraging industrial expansion and employment opportunities. In fact, according to Katznelson and Kesselman, "the top 100 corporations increased their control of all corporate assets during the new deal, and the highest income group increased its share of the country's personal wealth."[84]

On the other hand, the continued growth of structural unemployment was not abated through New Deal initiatives. Thus the number of jobless decreased only somewhat among younger adults and actually increased among the aged. By 1940, 14.6 percent of workers and 42.2 percent of those sixty-five and over, representing 13 percent of all unemployed people actively seeking jobs, still were unemployed. Moreover, as suggested earlier, the latter were ineligible for Social Security pensions. As late as 1948, only 10 percent of those people sixty-five and over were receiving such benefits and these individuals were not necessarily the most needy.[85]

It was through the substantial increases in defense spending immediately prior to, and rapidly expanded during World War II that the problems of insufficient demand and oversupply of labor were temporarily resolved. As production expanded dramatically, unemployment temporarily ceased to be a major issue.[86] However, though employment opportunities increased for older people during the war, and some corporations even suspended compulsory retirement for a short period, participation by the aged in the labor force continued to decline steadily.[87]

Intense collaboration between big business and the state during the war completed the consolidation of political and economic power that had its genesis during the early twentieth century, and prompted an ever-expanding state role in the private accumulation process. The state emerged as a necessary consumer of defense-industry and related products, supplier of capital, and direct and indirect subsidizer of private interests and profits, activities which became permanent features of the political economy.[88] Moreover, as Kolko observes, "the bulk of the war's economic gains still fell predominantly to big business and reinforced its relative control over the economy."[89] A tidal wave of mergers, which was buttressed through state policies, continued unabated throughout subsequent decades, and into the 1980s, producing an ever-increasing concentration of economic power. The postwar decades also witnessed the rise and expansion of multinational corporations, as well as a growing export of capital and jobs.

The steady growth of federal expenditures for costly social programs during the postwar years escalated during the 1960s. It also contributed to the burgeoning national budget, rising deficit spending, and inflation. In order to maintain social order, absorb some of the costs of capitalist development and private accumulation, and even at times to fashion winning electoral coalitions, national political leaders have been forced to respond to the increasing needs and demands of workers, unemployed people, consumers, minorities, women, the elderly, and other social groups. During the decades of sustained economic growth government intervention was possible, to a limited extent, on behalf of these diverse group interests, including older people. While most of the social programs were structured and implemented in such a way as to protect inter- and intraclass inequalities in income, privilege, and power, massive government spending allowed some tangible benefits to "trickle down" to the welfare-dependent populations. However, federally funded programs during the 1950s and 1960s did not serve to promote fundamental structural reform.

Consequently, by the early 1970s, the contradictions of advanced capitalism unleashed, among other things, souring levels of structural unemployment and inflation, declining productivity in the monopoly sector, an increasing fiscal crisis, and economic chaos in general. These problems have become increasingly difficult to solve within existing institutional arrangements, given persistently low levels of economic growth, the decline of American hegemony in the world system, spiraling costs for commodities basic to expansion (e.g., oil and other energy sources), and the decline of the dollar in the international market. In attempting to reverse the disaccumulation process and buttress the faltering American economy, the state has embarked on a period of steady retrenchment in social programs for less affluent groups.

Chapter 3

Income Maintenance and the Pension Games: Winners and Losers Under Capitalism

The most pressing problem for the vast majority of the elderly population is its lack of sufficient economic resources. All other aspects of well-being are closely linked to income level. The 1976 Harris survey, *Myth and Reality of Aging in America*, showed that older people at the bottom of the income scale suffer disproportionately from poor health, fear of crime, loneliness, inadequate medical services, deficient housing, and lack of employment opportunities.[1]

In this chapter I argue that the economic situation of the elderly reflects the contradiction between governmental policies that support private accumulation of capital and profits and government's attempts to provide for people considered no longer productive. I further contend that both the economic inequality found among the aged, and the significant percentage of them living in situations of economic deprivation, are functions of market, property, and power relationships set prior to old age. The elderly are highly dependent on public and private programs for their support. The goals of these income-maintenance systems, and the concepts underlying income adequacy itself, have been defined by social analysts within the context of capitalist market relationships. Vast extremes of wealth and income in society, coupled with class, racial, and sexual stratifications, are perpetuated and legitimized through the educational system and reinforced through work roles and market relations. Income support programs for the elderly not only maintain but also strengthen these divisions during retirement years. The net effect of public and private pension systems also has been to increase economic inequalities among younger adults.

The chapter is divided into two major sections. In the first part I focus on the two gauges used by social analysts in the United States to assess income adequacy and the effectiveness of public and private income policies: (a) the percentage of elderly households with an income level above official poverty lines; (b) the extent to which preretirement standards of living are maintained through the mix of public and private resources. Both strategies share debatable assumptions about potential societal sources of retirement income, the actual needs of the elderly, and income standards that allow the national government to define "economic deprivation" so narrowly as to make most of the aged appear free of such problems, and to limit markedly the scope of income goals.

The second part analyzes the Social Security system, the Supplementary Security Income (SSI) program, private and public pension systems, and other income-maintenance measures. Old age support in the United States can be viewed as a four-tier system. The major objective of the first tier, Social Security, is to provide a partial replacement of wages for those employees covered by the program who have substantially withdrawn from the labor market. Social Security, however, was never intended to serve as the sole means of support for the aged, or to replace entirely preretirement earnings. Consequently, the second tier is considered essential for supplementing income needs. This level consists of public and private employee retirement systems, as well as Individual Retirement Accounts (IRAs). For federal employees and the 30 percent of state and local workers not covered under Social Security, public employee retirement systems are expected to furnish both first and second tier of retirement income support. Political officials assume that savings and other assets, such as property, stocks, and bonds, will provide the third tier. Finally, for those older Americans lacking sufficient resources from the other sources, SSI provides a minimum income guarantee.

MEASUREMENTS OF INCOME ADEQUACY

Defining the Poverty Population

The most extensively used gauge of income adequacy has been the poverty index developed in 1964 by Mollie Orshansky of the

Social Security Administration (SSA). She based her initial calculations on a 1955 Household Food Consumption Survey, which showed that the average American family spent one-third of its income on food, and a 1961 Department of Agriculture economy food budget, viewed only as a temporary, emergency diet when it was created.[2] Although local welfare departments had been utilizing a "low-income" food plan designed to meet essential nutritional requirements, SSA opted for the economy plan which was 20 percent lower in cost. The Orshansky index, designated in 1969 by the Office of Management and Budget (OMB) as the offficial system of poverty thresholds, multiplied the cost of the economy food budget by three. Until 1969 the index was revised to account for yearly changes in the cost of the economy food budget. Since that time the proverty thresholds have been updated annually to reflect changes in the Consumer Price Index (CPI).

As Rodgers notes, "Quite clearly, SSA did not decide to use the economy budget as a base because it was deemed adequate for poor people's needs. It was chosen because it kept the poverty standard low."[3] Higher standards, such as might have been based on the low-income food plan, would have shown a larger percentage of the population to have inadequate incomes, exposing more fully the failure of the American capitalist system to meet even essential human needs.

Official poverty standards vary according to the age and sex of household heads and family size, with a 15 percent reduction in the various standards for people living on farms. Thresholds for single- and two-family older households are also nearly 10 percent lower than those for younger people similarly situated, since officials assume that the aged require less income. Accordingly, in 1979 the federal government officially classified 3.6 million older people, representing 15.1 percent of the 65-and-over population, as poor.

In 1979, poverty levels for older families with heads sixty-five and over, and elderly unrelated individuals, were $4,364 and $3,472, respectively. (The corresponding figures for 1981 are $5,475 and $4,340.) The monthly food budget for an older couple who actually had to live within this statistically defined income, and who allotted one-third of it to food, would consist of $60.61 per person (or $1.99 daily), with $242.44 remaining for housing, health care, heating, electricity, household items, transportation, recreation, and other needs for the family. A single elderly person who similarly allotted one-third of his or her monthly budget to food would spend $96.44 (or $3.17 daily), leaving $192.89 for all other items. Clearly, these are unrealistic figures: it would be impossible for older households to subsist on such meager budgets.

Not only is the allowance for food vastly insufficient where the government uses the economy food budget as the basis for its calculations, but also spiraling costs for other necessities (such as heating and health services) have outpaced increases in the CPI, to which the poverty threshold is tied. Between 1972 and 1976, for example, while the CPI rose by 37.6 percent, the cost of food grew by 45.6 percent, fuel oil by 42.2 percent, and medical care by 41.2 percent.[4]

As early as the 1960s, the one-to-three relationship between food requirements and income needs was challenged by a number of knowledgeable observers. Michael Harrington noted, for example, that former director of the Bureau of the Census, Herman Miller, argued that the cost of the economy food budget should be multiplied by a factor of four to obtain more realistic income standards.[5] In fact, an April 1976 study by the Department of Health, Education, and Welfare (HEW) concluded that raising the multiplier to five and substituting the higher low cost food budget as a base would be "within the range of reasonable judgement."[6] The one to five ratio has also been supported by other studies, including the Department of Labor Expenditure Surveys in 1970.[7] If we estimate a low-income food plan[8] for couples and unrelated individuals age sixty-five and over and calculate food costs as one-fifth of income needs, then a minimum poverty level for older couples would rise to $8,728, and for older individuals to $6,944. Approximately half of older families and three-fourths of older individuals living alone had incomes below these revised poverty levels in 1979.

Measurements of abject poverty through the official poverty indices fail to reveal fully the number of older people who face serious economic hardship and who cannot afford to provide for needs deemed essential by ordinary societal standards. Accordingly, HEW created the near-poor threshold, which is calculated at 125 percent of the poverty standards. In 1979 these thresholds were $5,455 for older couples and $4,340 for older people living alone. Of the 65-and-over population, 25 percent or 5.9 million people, had incomes at or below this alternative standard.[9]

In 1971 the White House Conference on Aging concluded that the intermediate budget developed by the Bureau of Labor Statistics for elderly couples would provide an improved minimum standard for gauging income adequacy. Conference delegates suggested that 75 percent of this figure would be an appropriate benchmark for older single people.[10] The Bureau of Labor Statistics set an intermediate budget for older couples at $8,562 in 1979. Approximately 36 percent of older couples (2.2 million households) failed to have incomes that reached this very modest standard of living. Seventy-five percent of this budget (the conference's recommended index for older single people) would have amounted to $6,422, a moderate threshold level greater than the actual income of over two-thirds of the single elderly in 1979.

Despite White House Conference recommendations to adjust indices of income standards for changes in both the CPI and rising national income levels, the Department of Labor has indexed its moderate couples budget exclusively to the CPI. Since all the income standards discussed above also are not adjusted to overall growth in the economy, it is assumed by government officials that the elderly poor will not, and should not, share in society's rising standard of living.

Opposition to the assumptions underlying official measurements of poverty and the conclusions drawn from them have been argued persuasively in a number of publications, including such seminal works as Michael Harrington's *The Other America*, in the 1960s, and Robert Butler's *Why Survive? Being Old in America*, in the 1970s.[11] Yet official poverty indices continue to be used unequivocally by social gerontologists and government officials as evidence that older people have achieved significant gains over the last several decades. Studies often point out that the percentage of older families regarded as "poor" has declined steadily: 30 percent in 1959, 23 percent in 1965, 9 percent in 1978. For older unrelated individuals the proportion has also been reduced: 66 percent in 1959, 57 percent in 1965, 30 percent by 1978. However, the percentage of elderly living at or below the poverty line remained stagnant from 1974 to 1978, and has increased slightly since 1978.[12] Despite the obvious limitations of BLS poverty and near-poverty thresholds for measuring the real income needs of older people, their official acceptance has allowed the government and many social analysts literally to define away the extent of severe deprivation among the elderly, to argue that economic conditions for older people are improving, and to applaud the effectiveness of public and private programs, particularly Social Security, in meeting national income goals.

In order further to obliterate poverty statistically, the Congressional Budget Office (CBO) has provided an alternative definition of income that includes not only transfer income but also in-kind benefits such as Medicare, Medicaid, food stamps, and housing subsidies. When these factors were taken into account, the Budget Office concluded, only 4 percent of older people could be considered poor in 1976.[13] However, as Harrington points out in his 1977 article, "Hiding the Other America," in-kind goods and services are valued "at their dollar cost to the federal government. Thus part of the increased 'income' [of the poor] is that cost of unnecessary, and even harmful medical care at inflated prices in medicare mills; and the money which various real estate speculators rip off from housing subsidy programs." In equating outlays for these programs with income accruing to the elderly poor, the government assumes that older people are primary beneficiaries of such programs, that all "needy" people have access to or take advantage of their services, and that benefits received by the elderly under these various programs are related to costs. These assumptions are of doubtful validity. For example, many older Americans—for a variety of reasons—are reluctant to participate in needs-tested programs such as food stamps. Ironically, as Harrington further notes, "on the CBO assumptions people can enormously increase their income—and even enter the middle class—by suffering a catastrophic illness at government expense."[14]

The Untapped Pool of Income and Wealth

The unwillingness to revise upward official estimates of poverty stems partly from major suppositions about potential sources of economic support that can be mobilized on behalf of older people under capitalism. Social gerontologists, for example, often argue that the basic issue "has to do with the willingness of other segments of the population to allocate funds to those who are no longer seen as "productive." We can categorize those segments of the population to whom money resources are allocated as the young who are being trained to take their place in the economy; those who are currently employed and producing goods or services; and those who are older, retired and considered "unproductive." Any society must divide up its monetary pie among these sectors of the population."[15] Given these assumptions and current means for financing income-maintenance programs, a growing beneficiary-to-worker ratio has burdened, and will continue to burden substantially, younger wage earners, thus limiting total public resources available for the aged, particularly the elderly poor.

However, such an analysis is based on two implicit presuppositions that require further examination: 1) the poverty and low standards of living affecting a large percentage of America's elderly result from society's inability to produce enough income and wealth to go around; 2) wage earners should continue to shoulder the burden of support for a growing "dependent" older population. Evidence suggests, however, that both the maldistribution of income and wealth among the population, and current transfer programs that fail to tap vast economic resources held by more affluent groups, severely restrict the quantity of potential resources available for meeting the income needs of deprived older people.

Since 1947 the poorest 20 percent of the population has received only 5 percent while the richest 20 percent has obtained 41 percent of aggregate pretax family income in the United States. In fact, the wealthiest 5 percent of the population alone obtains approximately 15 percent of the total.[16] These figures, which do not include stocks, bonds, land, and other forms of wealth held primarily by the highest income groups, severely underestimate the extent of economic inequality in the United States. Moreover, "in recent years, after-tax income has been even more heavily skewed in favor of top-income earners,"[17] a situation that is likely to be exacerbated by the newly-enacted Economic Recovery Tax Act of 1981.

The control and ownership of wealth is even more highly concentrated than income. According to a 1978 analysis, the wealthiest 1 percent and 5 percent of the population hold about 33 and 53 percent, respectively, of all assets in the nation. On the other hand, the bottom 60 percent of the population owns only 8 percent of the total.[18] Moreover, assets held by the lowest income groups are, for the most part, personal property producing no revenues. Capitalism provides no mechanism for sharing total economic resources which accrue disproportionately to the owners of capital. If capitalist society continues to define responsibility for old age support as a working class burden, and does not allow transfer programs to alter significantly the current concentration of societal income and wealth in the hands of the few, then the pool of resources available for the elderly will continue to be limited indeed.

Income Replacement

A second measure of income adequacy for the elderly currently used in the United States concentrates on the extent to which a preretirement standard of living is maintained during old age. Social analysts using this approach presume that older people require less income during their retirement years, since they pay lower, or no taxes, receive special tax subsidies and have reduced travel and other work-related expenses, diminished family responsibilities, and a lesser need to save. Consequently, gerontologists estimate, between 60 and 80 percent of a retiree's previous gross earnings, calculated on the basis of his earning's during his last five years of full-time employment, would allow his family to sustain its pre-retirement level of living. Schulz and his colleagues, for example, argue that between 60 and 65 percent of the retiree's previous gross earnings would suffice.[19]

Low-wage earners and their families have less margin for reduction in their income when the worker retires since a significant portion of their total income provides for such necessities as housing, food, and energy. Consequently, analysts tend to agree that these workers require a greater replacement rate than do high-income earners in order to maintain pre-retirement standards of living. In 1980, the President's Commission on Pension Policy, after surveying available data, concluded that the replacement rate for workers retiring in 1980 with final wages of $6,500 should be from 75 to 85 percent. The suggested replacement rates for persons earning $20,000 and $55,000 were 60 to 65 percent, and 45 to 55 percent, respectively.[20]

Instead of focusing on the real needs of the elderly and the underlying causes of their economic deprivation, which are rooted in the labor market itself, social analysts emphasize replacement of wages, which merely perpetuates income inequalities among workers on into the retirement years. In addition, even full replacement of wages would not automatically keep the elderly's standard of living in line with rising national levels or even maintain purchasing power throughout the retirement span. Growing income gaps between the generations, as well as between the younger and older elderly populations, are inevitable unless retirement income is tied both to growth in the economy and to inflation.

Moreover, by reducing the already inadequate wages of low-income working adults, a disproportionate number of whom are women and minorities, a policy of partial replacement of earnings relegates many to poverty. Sixty percent, or even 80 percent, of very low earnings inevitably results in heightened deprivation during old age. On the other hand, sizable wage replacement rates for the highest income earners (who tend to have large amounts of income-producing wealth as well) not only provide these retirees with a standard of living considerably higher than that reached by the average active worker but may also entail a transfer of income from low-income current employees to affluent older people.

The wage replacement approach serves, in part, to reinforce labor discipline. Methods that relate income adequacy to past earning histories place severe hardships on employees with long periods of unemployment. When the five years prior to retirement are used as the base on which retirement income is calculated, the temporarily unemployed middle-aged worker is particularly disadvantaged. At the end of 1977, 73.8 percent of workers aged forty-five to fifty-four, and only 57 percent of those aged fifty-five to sixty-four, were employed. A recent report by the Senate Committee on Aging notes: "middle-aged and older workers face formidable employment barriers. They run a substantially greater risk of being without a job for a long period of time after becoming unemployed. The average duration of unemployment for middle-aged and older workers is more than 19 weeks, or nearly 5 months."[21] Even if an average of lifetime earnings, or some variation, is taken into account, long periods without earnings depress preretirement income bases considerably. This method has obviously negative impact upon older women who have sporadic employment histories due to child-care and homemaking responsibilities.

Whether older people need fewer resources than younger adults is, in itself, highly questionable. Most likely this assumption is rooted in what Kolko calls "the functional ethos of our economy" which "dictates that the comparatively unproductive old-age population should consume in accordance with their output rather than their requirements."[22] In fact, some observers argue that as people age their costs may actually increase. For example, average annual out-of-pocket health-related expenses of older people tend to be higher than those of other age groups. Although many studies show relatively low average expenditures by older people for food, housing, clothing, and recreation, they tend to overlook the fact that people with limited resources are simply forced to purchase less and forego goods and services viewed as essential by the rest of the population.

In any event, neither current income standards nor income maintenance programs are in practice effective barriers to the impoverishment of a large percentage of the nation's elderly. Despite vastly insufficient gauges of income adequacy, pension systems and other income support programs in the United States fail to protect all older people from living at or below officially defined poverty levels or to provide many of them with even 65 percent of preretirement earnings.

SOCIAL SECURITY

Social Security is the central component of old age economic assistance in the United States. In 1981, 93 percent of all Americans sixty-five and over were covered by or drawing annuities from the system. Despite myriad amendments throughout the last several decades, and substantial revisions in benefits and other provisions, the basic philosophy underlying the program has remained intact since its inception in 1935. Its tax and benefit structures simultaneously discriminate between and within classes. The funding mechanisms are not only class biased against labor but also tend, along with the method of calculating benefits, "to redistribute income from competitive sector to monopoly sector workers and reproduce and deepen the divisions within the work force."[23] The legislation, which entails forced savings, serves to control labor by ensuring that workers forego current consumption needs in order to provide for their own old age. In addition, it regulates workers throughout their life cycle by rewarding long and continuous labor force participation and providing for the orderly removal of older people from the work place. The latter function aids capital by forcing out economically redundant and highly paid older workers, thus lowering the cost of labor for employers, while at the same time inculcating a false sense of economic security among the employed. As O'Connor observes, this sense of security raises morale and reinforces discipline.

> This contributes to harmonious management-labor relations which are indispensable to capital accumulation and growth of production. Thus the fundamental intent and effect of social security is to expand productivity, production and profits. Seen in this way, social insurance is not primarily for workers, but a kind of insurance for capitalists and corporations.[24]

Social Security purports both to replace a portion of preretirement wages (the "insurance concept") as well as to maintain a minimum income level (the "adequacy concept.") The objective of the insurance concept is to replace a worker's wages up to a maximum percentage. Its emphasis on "earned" (or wage-related) annuities assures that preretirement economic stratification of the population will not be disturbed. In complying with the adequacy concept, the system provides a greater replacement of preretirement wages for low-income earners than for high-income earners, and a minimum benefit, regardless of the wage base. Nevertheless, a person who earned an inadequate income prior to retirement and benefits from a replacement level even less than his lifetime average earnings will, of course, be even poorer than before.

Replacement ratios have fluctuated from 25 to 33 percent of preretirement wages for those with maximum creditable earnings, from 41 to 44 percent for average wage earners, and from 47 to 60 percent for low-income workers.[25] However, in response to the growing fiscal crisis of the Social Security system, and in order to maintain the self-supporting nature of the program, Congress modified substantially both the taxation and benefit levels in 1977. The revision of benefits focused on stabilizing wage replacement levels which had been expected to climb steadily. Under the new provisions, the countable average monthly earnings for persons who retire, die, or become disabled after 1978 will be indexed automatically to the general growth in wages, rather than to both wages and prices, as the 1972 amendments had directed. A specified PIA formula is then applied to the worker's updated wage record.[26] Once benefits are received they are indexed exclusively to the CPI. By 1985 the gross wage replacement rates will stabilize at approximately 53 percent for low-income, 42 percent for average-income, and 28 percent for high-income earners. For workers with a dependent spouse, the replacement rate is 50 percent greater in all of the categories.[27]

These replacement rates are misleading, however, since they are related to average monthly indexed earnings (AMIE) over a worker's lifetime and apply only to retirees and dependent spouses who receive their initial pensions at age sixty-five. The Social Security system ensures that the highest benefits accrue to those employees within each income group who have had long and continuous attachments to the labor force. The PIA is computed from an average of updated wages earned from 1950 (or age twenty-one, if later) until the worker reaches sixty-two, becomes disabled, or dies. Only the five lowest earning years are excluded from the average. Consequently, a substantial length of time without earnings, whether due to long periods of unemployment, illness, or family responsibilities (such as child care), will depress the AMIE considerably. Because of both intermittent work histories and very low earnings, the PIA for a significant percentage of retirees is at the lower end of the scale. In 1979, 46 percent of retired workers had a PIA under $280 per month or $3,360 for the year. Twenty percent of the beneficiaries had a monthly PIA under $180 or $2,160 on an annual basis. Nineteen percent of all female retired workers had a monthly PIA under $134.00 ($1,607 annually), as compared to only 5 percent of male retired workers. The average PIA was $299.30 or $3,592 for the year.[28]

Moreover, pensions are substantially reduced, and remain at the lower levels for life, when recipients obtain their initial benefits prior to age sixty-five. A worker's benefits are actuarially reduced by up to 20 percent, and his dependent's supplement by up to 25 percent, depending upon the age at which a worker or spouse apply for the initial pension. Widows, widowers, and surviving divorced spouses face possible reductions of up to 28.5 percent. Even the already insufficient minimum benefit is subject to actuarial reduction when acquired prior to age sixty-five.

A 1968 survey of newly entitled beneficiaries by the Social Security Administration revealed that 50 percent of men and 68 percent of women received their initial Social Security annuities prior to reaching age sixty-five. Approximately 20 percent of the men had not worked for twelve months before entitlement and 40 percent had earnings so low that they qualified for some benefits at the earliest age of eligibility.[29] In 1976, 8 percent of couples, 38 percent of unmarried women, and 26 percent of unmarried men had no earnings from age fifty-five to sixty-one. Twenty percent, 54 percent, and 39 percent, respectively, had no earnings between ages sixty-two and sixty-four.[30] A significant portion of these older people were forced to apply for benefits at actuarially reduced levels. By 1980, about 60 percent of all retired workers, representing 55 percent of the men and 69 percent of the women, received Social Security benefits prior to attaining age sixty-five, and increasingly at the earliest eligibility age of sixty-two.[31]

High-income workers tend to receive maximum full annuities since they are less likely, than are their lower-paid cohorts, to apply for initial benefits before age sixty-five, or to face unemployment or poor health during their working years. They also are more likely to be eligible for the 1 percent annual increase in the PIA (3 percent per year beginning in 1982), up to a maximum of 15 percent, for each year that retirement is delayed after age sixty-five. The maximum initial PIA applicable for a high-income earner, which was $752.90 in June 1981, potentially could rise to $865.83 if the worker delays retirement until after age seventy. In combination with the spouses benefit, such a worker would receive $1,242 monthly, or $14,904 on an annual basis. Average life expectancy of high-income workers is also longer than that of lower-paid workers, and therefore they can expect to receive compensation over a greater retirement span.[32]

In addition, one-earner couples must subsist on a single benefit if the insured worker becomes eligible for Social Security before his wife. This is a particular hardship for low-income households, given their vastly inadequate single worker's income. According to a 1980 report by the House Select Committee on Aging, "an individual who has worked forty years full-time at the minimum wage would be entitled to a monthly benefit of $330 in 1982—$17 per month under the poverty line." Yet Social Security has replaced 47 percent of his or her pre-retirement wages.[33]

Working women and minorities are represented disproportionately at the lower end of the Social Security benefit scale. Concentrated in low-paying jobs, they are also likely to have experienced long periods of unemployment which further depress their lifetime average earnings. The average monthly benefit actually received by retired female workers in 1979 was $256.50, compared with $326.80 for men. (The average for white males, black males, white females, and black females was $332.00, $271.40, $260.90, and $210.10, respectively.) Moreover, 32 percent of male and 61 percent of female retirees received monthly worker benefits of $279.90 or less, a figure under the official poverty index for single older people in that year. Approximately one-fourth of retired workers receiving a spouse benefit accrued average monthly annuities that similarly were below the poverty level for older couples.[34]

Widows dependent on their husband's Social Security benefits, whose spouses have died prior to reaching retirement age, often receive inadequate benefits, since the PIA is wage-indexed only to the year of the spouse's death. Widowed homemakers under age sixty often find themselves caught in the so-called "widow's gap," since they are too young to receive Social Security (if they do not have dependent children) but are often unable to obtain employment. They are usually forced to apply for Social Security at sixty, when the benefit based on the worker's PIA is reduced by 28.5 percent, or at sixty-two, when it is reduced by 17.1 percent. The average monthly benefit for older widows at the end of 1979 was $269.80, or $3,238 for the year—a figure below the official poverty threshold.[35] In 1979, 19 percent of all women between the ages of fifty-five and sixty-four, and 41 percent between the ages of sixty-five and seventy-four, were widowed, compared to only 3 percent and 9 percent, respectively, of men.[36]

Divorced homemakers are entitled to only 50 percent of their ex-spouse's single worker's pension upon becoming sixty-two (and only after ten years of marriage). Their ex-husbands, however, receive full single worker's benefits. Moreover, despite the fact that an ex-husband may not be providing any support for his former wife, she receives no benefits until he decides to retire. When the retired worker dies the surviving divorced spouse is then entitled to full compensation. In 1979, approximately 7 percent of all women between the ages of fifty-five and sixty-four, 4 percent between the ages of sixty-five and seventy-four, and 2 percent who were seventy-five or over were divorced or separated.[37] The average monthly benefit payable to divorced wives at the end of 1979 was $153.50.[38]

Consequently, a substantial number of low-income households and divorced, separated, or widowed women receive Social Security benefits that leave them in abject poverty. Eight percent of older couples, 21 percent of older unmarried men, and 21 percent of older unmarried women receiving Social Security benefits in 1978 had no other source of retirement income. Moreover, the median Social Security benefit of $4,820, and $3,130, received by older couples and older unmarried men, respectively, was not sufficient to bring their households over the official near-poor threshold. The median pension of older unmarried women in 1978 was $2,830. This benefit amount was even lower than the official poverty level in that year.[39] Further, 3 million Social Security recipients, who are disproportionately single elderly women, receive the minimum benefit. The initial amount payable to a single person is frozen at $122 per month, $1,464 for the year. This is about one-third of the poverty index for single older households in 1981.[40]

Parsons and Munro have found that compensation levels for couples under Social Security have followed a pattern similar to those of payments under welfare programs such as Aid to Families with Dependent Children (AFDC), particularly since 1950. They conclude, "apparently the worker and nonworking spouse with no assets or pension other than Social Security receive on average the same income as couples on welfare."[41] It would appear that "nonproductive" labor, regardless of age, is subject to similar sanctions in a capitalist economy.

Since Social Security is financed through a uniform payroll tax rather than through a tax on total income and wealth, the tax structure is not only regressive but also limits the sources of societal resources that can be redistributed in order to provide adequate benefits. Both workers and employers pay a percentage of earnings up to a maximum covered amount. The taxable wage base, which was raised to $9,000 in 1972, has steadily increased to $22,900 in 1979, $25,900 in 1980, and $29,700 in 1981. Thereafter it will be automatically adjusted to rise with overall wages in the economy. Employees with earnings at or below the maximum covered amount pay a higher percentage of their total wages than those with earnings above the current taxable amount. Thus an employee earning $22,900 in 1979 paid the same Social Security tax as a corporate executive earning $200,000. The $1,404 maximum payment into Social Security in that year represented 6.13 percent of the former's wage income and only .007 of the latter's. Although Social Security contributions will be deducted from the total wages paid most workers by 1982, the wealthiest earners will continue to find large portions of their income excluded from Social Security taxation.[42]

Significant income-producing assets—such as dividends, rents, and capital gains, which are highly concentrated among the top 5 percent of households in the United States—are also untapped, thus excluding a formidable pool of wealth for funding benefits. The ownership class obtains most of its income from "unearned" rather than earned sources.[43] This factor serves further to reduce the percentage of total resources paid into the Social Security system by the highest income classes. The corporate executive earning $200,000 annually in wages, who receives an additional $500,00 from his income-producing assets not taxed under Social Security, will actually contribute only .002 percent of his total income into the Social Security trust.

In its support of private accumulation, the state also loses a significant funding source by failing to tax corporate wealth and profits directly. Though the employer is forced to match each worker's contributions, it is generally agreed among economists that the former's share is shifted either directly to his employees or to both employees and consumers in the form of higher prices.[44] As Milton Friedman admits, "the tax, whether nominally paid by the worker or the employer, is borne by the worker. His employer simply transmits the amount."[45] According to a recent study, under one set of premises (the "most progressive" view) the entire employer tax is transferred to the workers; under alternative assumptions (the "least progressive" view), one-half of the employer payroll tax is shifted to employees and the other half to consumers.[46] Either case affects lower income people more adversely than higher paid, while leaving corporate wealth untouched. Under monopoly capitalism, substantial constraints militate against touching corporate wealth and profits. Since the first priority of capital is to sustain profits, any attempt by the state to draw upon the vast resources held by giant corporations would lead to threats of greater unemployment, higher prices and inflation, depressed real wages, and even lower business investment in plants and equipment.

The large across-the-board increases in real Social Security benefits in the 1970s, and automatic increases tied to the CPI since 1975, have heightened inequities both in the funding and benefit structures. Though these changes have aided the elderly overall, they have coincided with commensurate upward adjustments in the tax rate, broadening the regressive features of the system. The government also has further institutionalized the maldistribution of pension income by allowing, at best, each older income group to maintain its relative purchasing power while placing responsibility for the costs on the backs of labor, particularly the working poor. The worker and employer tax rate, each increased from 5.2 percent in 1972 to 5.85 percent in 1973, will climb steadily to 6.7 percent in 1982 and reach 7.15 percent in 1987. Pechman noted that in 1977 the federal payroll tax for Social Security was "the highest tax paid by about two-thirds of the nation's income recipients, and $2.5 billion [was] paid by persons officially classified as living in poverty."[47] Accounting for an estimated 31 percent of total tax receipts in 1981, Social Security, coupled with other payroll-supported social programs, tended to vitiate progressive features of the national tax structure.

Across-the-board pension increases also have widened the dollar income gap among beneficiary groups. For example, assuming a constant 6 percent growth in the CPI (and thus in Social Security benefit levels) for five years, the income gap in actual dollars between a low-earning couple whose initial benefit was $3,000, and a high-earning couple whose initial benefit was $7,000, would steadily rise from $4,000 to approximately $5,353 by the fifth year. This gap would even be larger using more realistic higher CPI growth rates over the last several years. In addition, since benefit levels fail to keep pace with overall growth in the economy, the economic situation of the oldest retirees steadily falls relative to both younger beneficiaries (whose initial PIA is indexed to the growth in wage levels) and to active workers. This particularly affects women, since they are concentrated disproportionately in the oldest age categories.

Pension increases in the past have been facilitated by a growing population, an expansion of occupations covered by, and thus contributing to, the trust, and the rising percentage of women entering the paid labor force. In fact, older people who have retired prior to the system's maturity receive, as a group, far greater benefits than they paid into the system. With declining birth rates, a probable leveling off in the percentage of new female workers, and nearly universal coverage of occupations, the possibility of expanding the base of employees supporting the program is more limited than in the past. Rising numbers of older people, and workers who are retiring at increasingly earlier ages, have further worsened the financial viability of the system. The Social Security Administration has estimated that by the year 2000 there will be about fifty people receiving benefits for every one hundred workers. Restricting potential revenues to current sources will increasingly burden labor, particularly the working poor, and limit even further the ability of society to provide for the pressing needs of older people.

Social security's "retirement test," which is based solely on wages, is also class-biased. Pension benefits are reduced for workers age sixty-five to seventy-two (lowered to age seventy beginning in 1983) at the rate of $1.00 for each $2 earned in wages above $5,500 during 1981. The exempt amount will increase to $6,000 by 1982, and will be automatically adjusted upward thereafter.[48] However, unearned income does not have any upper limit, thus allowing affluent older people to receive both their high Social Security annuities and substantial resources from income-producing assets, as well. The earnings test also serves to create a pool of part-time, low-wage labor. In order to supplement vastly inadequate Social Security benefits without earning incomes over the eligibility ceiling, the elderly poor often are forced to secure jobs at even lower wages than they had obtained prior to "retirement." A job, even at minimal wages, is the primary means for an older household to overcome poverty.

Although the retirement test negatively affects older people by forcing some individuals into low-wage or part-time employment, and discriminates against earners whose income is derived from work, rather than investments, its liberalization or elimination would not remedy the inequities. According to a study by Esposito, Mallon, and Podoff, the recent changes in the earnings test legislated by the 1977 amendments will aid primarily persons at the top and middle of the earnings distribution who will receive 48 percent, and 45 percent, respectively, of the total additional benefits. They argue that "successive increases in the annual exempt amount concentrates additional benefits among groups with higher and higher earnings," while increasing it "within the $6,000-$10,000 range primarily helps individuals in the middle of the earnings distribution. Neither change has an appreciable effect on individuals at the lower end." The authors further contend that "lowering the age at which the earnings test no longer applies will be advantageous to the 5 percent of the aged population at the top of the earnings distribution."[49]

Despite an interest in reducing Social Security expenditures, the Reagan Administration has proposed phasing out the earnings test, and eliminating it entirely by 1986 for all workers aged sixty-five and over. It has been estimated that the cost of these changes would be $0.6 billion in 1983, $1.2 billion in 1984, $1.8 billion in 1985, and $2.9 billion in 1986. Yet, as the authors cited above note, less than 2 percent of the aged population, representing those at the highest income level, would receive 60 percent of the additional benefits from such a revision of the Social Security Act.[50]

Social analysts recently have raised a number of "equity" issues pertaining to the program's treatment of women. For example, the Social Security system duplicates coverage for female workers who are also entitled to benefits as dependents. At retirement age a previously employed female receives either 50 percent of her husband's pension or her own, whichever is greater. However, since the spouse benefit tends to be larger, many female workers who have paid into the system throughout their working lives may receive no return from their own contributions. At the same time, a low-income worker married to a high-earning spouse may receive a larger annuity than a single female employee with the same AMIE. In addition, one-earner couples tend to receive higher benefits than two-earner households with an equivalent total AMIE. A one-earner couple retiring in 1985 with average monthly indexed earnings of $1,258 would be eligible for $990 per month. On the other hand, if each partner had average monthly indexed earnings of $629, the Social Security benefits for the household would amount to only $845, or 85 percent of that received by the one-earner couple. Similarly, the survivor of a two-earner couple obtains a lower benefit than the survivor of a one-earner household with the same total average monthly indexed earnings.[51] Some analysts have also pointed out that since blacks have lower average life expectancies, and are more apt to receive actuarially reduced pensions, they often accrue substantially lower total benefits than do whites with similar earning histories.

The inequities outlined above, however real, are usually viewed by social analysts as violations of the social insurance philosophy of the system rather than as questions of social adequacy. Thus, gerontologists, government officials, and other interested groups have offered proposals which redress some of the imbalances between contributions and benefits without seriously improving the system's ability to meet the economic needs of impoverished older households. Moreover, they attempt to resolve equity problems without altering substantially the existing wage-based benefit or revenue structures. As persuasively argued by Tish Sommers, these types of approaches inevitably pit one group of disadvantaged older people against another, as well as the elderly poor against low-income younger workers.[52] Basic class issues, racial and sexual stratifications within the labor market that the program perpetuates during old age, and the general inability of Social Security to meet the real income needs of the aged within the context of capitalist market relations are the fundamental questions that should be addressed.

THE WELFARE PROGRAMS

Supplementary Security Income

Enactment of the Supplementary Security Income (SSI) program in 1972, which guarantees a national income floor for the elderly poor, blind, and disabled, replaced federal grants to the states for the Old-Age Assistance (OAA) programs, Aid to the Blind (AB), and Aid to the Disabled. Financed from general revenues and administered by the Social Security Administration, the act provides for uniform eligibility requirements and benefits levels across the country. People sixty-five and over qualify for the needs-tested program if their countable income is under the annual federal guarantee. In 1981, monthly wages of up to $65 and $20 in income from other sources were disregarded when determining eligibility. SSI payments were reduced by $1 for each $2 earned above $65 per month in wages. In addition, total assets (except for a house, an automobile worth less than $4,500, household goods worth less than $2,000, and a life insurance policy worth less than $1,500) had to be under $1,500 for individuals and $2,250 for couples. Older people having meager savings over the upper limits must exhaust their assets until they meet the eligibility requirements, a regulation forcing them into abject poverty.

The states are allowed to supplement the national pension; by 1980 thirty-seven states had taken this option. However, these additional benefits vary widely, ranging from a monthly average of $10.52 in Mississippi to $193.00 in California for single older people.[53] Some states have maintained their restrictive relative responsibility provisions, as well as liens on homes, as bases for eligibility in the state programs.[54]

SSI alone, or even in combination with Social Security, may not provide an income that meets even the officially defined poverty levels. In 1981, the national government guaranteed a single person only $3,176 and a couple $4,764 annually under SSI, amounts well below the poverty lines of $4,390 and $5,540, respectively, in that year. Although benefits are tied to increases in the CPI, this relationship merely ensures that current below-poverty purchasing power will be sustained. The program also provides for a reduction of benefits to $25 per month when the beneficiary is institutionalized for as little as one month in any public (and in most private) hospitals or nursing homes. Since older people, particularly women, tend to live alone, and often are unable to continue rental or mortgage payments during these periods, they can lose their place of residence and be forced into permanent institutionalization.[55]

In 1981, 2.2 million older people, or nearly 9 percent of the 65-and-over population, were receiving SSI. Nearly 10 percent of Social Security recipients receive benefits that are low enough to qualify them for SSI supplements. Aged women, who are most likely to receive the lowest Social Security amounts while lacking other sources of retirement income, comprise 72 percent of older SSI beneficiaries.[56]

SSI serves to compel labor and reinforce work norms by assuring that poor people who are outside of the paid labor force for substantial periods during their younger years will continue to live at a degrading level during old age. Its intent is to maintain the prior income gap between younger low wage earners and younger public assistance recipients. The longer a low wage earner participates in the labor force, the larger the differential will be between his or her retirement income and that of SSI recipients.

The Veterans' Administration Program

The Veterans' and Survivors' Pension Plan, which provides benefits to veterans or their surviving dependents, is also a restrictive, needs-tested program. In 1977, 538,000 older veterans and 1.7 million surviving spouses received pensions under the system. However, both the monthly $185 in annuities for individuals and $199 for veterans with one dependent were under the poverty threshold. Significantly, 15 percent of recipients had no other income, and over 100,000 beneficiaries were also eligible for some SSI payments. In 1978 benefit levels and asset eligibility criteria were liberalized somewhat and pension adjustments were tied to increases in Social Security benefits. At the same time many of the income exclusions, which allow up to $3,000 annually in earnings, were eliminated, thereby reducing the number of recipients who would receive the new higher compensation levels. Moreover, since benefits have risen, usually over SSI guarantees, many beneficiaries will become ineligible for Medicaid or state-run programs for the medically needy.[57]

PRIVATE AND PUBLIC RETIREMENT SYSTEMS

Under advanced capitalism a dual private market has emerged, dominated by giant corporations (the monopoly sector) with extensive yet peripheral smaller-scale firms alongside (the competitive sector). The monopoly sector includes such industries as finance, insurance, steel, aluminum, rubber, automobiles, communications, and oil. Services and retail outlets (e.g., restaurants, grocery stores, gas stations, and apparel), as well as mining, construction, and textiles, are examples of competitive sector firms. Concomitantly, considerable and growing economic activities are organized by the state (the public sector). This tripartite division of the economy is reflected in a corresponding differentiation of markets for labor, employment conditions, and the presence (or lack) of retirement systems. Each sector comprises about one-third of the labor force. A person's economic situation in old age is dependent not only on Social Security benefits but also on the availability of secondary pensions, savings, and job opportunities. I argue in the next several pages that these diverse labor markets further intensify stratifications among workers and retirees by offering (or withholding) substantially different opportunities for old age income supplements.

Where workers are covered under public and private retirement systems, benefit amounts are closely related to length of employment at the same job and wage levels. The public and private pension programs sharpen inequalities among these retirees and attempt to discipline labor even more markedly than Social Security. How they do so will be demonstrated below in discussions of the monopoly, competitive, and public sectors.

Despite the difficulty of separating, for purposes of analysis, sometimes overlapping areas of economic activity into three concrete sectors, and other related problems, this type of approach can aid substantially in understanding economic stratifications among older people and the role of pensions in a capitalist system.[58]

The Monopoly Sector

Large, capital intensive oligopolistic and monopolistic corporations have relatively high productivity per worker. They are capable of reducing unit costs through technological advancement, mechanization, and market economies of scale, and can regularize production and stabilize their product and labor markets. These factors, coupled with their longstanding taboos against competitive price cutting, tend to permit giant industries to accrue higher profit rates than competitive firms.

As noted by O'Connor, the monopoly sector labor force consists predominantly of "(1) blue-collar production, maintenance, and similar workers and (2) a so-called middle class of white-collar, technical, administrative workers (the great majority white adult males)."[59] These workers have usually organized themselves into powerful labor unions which, through years of struggle, have been able to wrest major concessions from employers. With current earnings as a primary concern, unions have demanded and often have obtained wage increments for their members that rise in a rough ratio to growth in production. In some cases, they have also received annual upward adjustments in earnings commensurate with increases in the CPI, as well.

Union bargaining efforts also have encouraged the development and growth of private pension systems. The control exercised by large corporations over markets and prices, and their ability to sustain relatively high profit *rates*, have rendered possible their ability to accede to wage and pension-related union demands. Corporations can also pass off the costs of worker retirement benefits either to consumers, in the form of higher prices, or to the workers themselves.

Nearly all large-scale enterprises have established capital-producing retirement systems. As argued in the previous chapter, tax incentives that disproportionately benefit monopoly industries and their highly paid executives, as well as the need to stabilize their labor markets, are additional factors encouraging the provision of pension systems in this sector. Ball notes that "private plans can offer various provisions that the employer sees as advantageous in attracting and holding workers to his firm, and can also make it easier to retire them when he believes it is desireable to do so."[60] Over half of the workers covered by these private plans are subject to compulsory retirement provisions.

Relatively high wage and pension gains have often been attained by unions at the expense of employment security for those employees at the less prestigious job levels. Moreover, as O'Connor argues, "low-seniority workers and many in unskilled and semi-skilled jobs are frequently little better off than their counterparts in competitive industries."[61] I will show in the section on private retirement systems that though these latter workers (of whom women and minorities comprise a disproportionate number) may be covered under monopoly sector pension systems, they benefit little, if at all, from them.

The Competitive Sector

Competitive sector firms tend to be relatively small scale and labor intensive, with low productivity per worker. Business and labor conditions are characterized by periodic overcrowding and instability, and sometimes irregular or seasonal product and labor markets. According to O'Connor, "workers who want and are unable to find full-time, year-round well-paid work in the monopolistic or state sectors will accept employment in the competitive sector on almost any terms."[62] Because of fewer employment opportunities in the monopoly sector for minorities, due particularly to racism, black workers are heavily concentrated in this sector. Sexism and sex-role stereotyping have also led to a preponderance of females in competitive sector jobs. In addition, the mandatory retirement policies of large corporations, coupled with inadequate pension incomes, have forced many older workers to seek second-ary, sometimes part-time, employment in the competitive labor market.

An abundance of potential workers, the relative ease with which new firms enter the field, and prices and salaries determined, for the most part, by competitive forces, are all factors that tend to depress both profit rates and wages, relative to those characteristic in the monopoly sector. Workers in this sector are less likely to be organized than monopoly sector workers; where unions exist, they are usually weaker than those in the monopoly sector. As O'Connor suggests, "the social characteristics of the work force, the multitude of firms in a particular industry, and the small-scale, localized na-ture of production obstruct the organization of strong unions. Fur-ther, highly competitive product markets, rapid business turnover, and small profit margins make it costly for employers to recognize unions."[63]

Accordingly, in addition to suffering the burdens of inadequate wages, high rates of unemployment, and an inability to save for their old age, workers in this sector usually find themselves covered by no private retirement systems. High business mortality rates discourage companies from initiating pension plans which involve long-range financial commitments; for the same reason, they have little incentive to initiate plans geared at retaining employees. Ex-tremely low wages and competitive product markets make it dif-ficult to pass pension costs on to either workers or consumers. Weak unions—or none—exert little pressure on employers over pensions, generally giving priority to wage increases when using whatever bargaining power they may have obtained. While pension-related tax incentives aid giant corporations substantially, they provide fewer economic gains for the smaller, competitive sector firms. Moreover, because of economies of scale, the latter tend to have higher pension administrative costs, which sometimes reach 10 percent of total expenses, as compared to 1 percent for the larger systems. This factor also discourages the initiation or retention of retirement trusts in the competitive sector.

However, some industries within this sector, particularly those with numerous unionized firms, have attempted to stabilize their labor markets by agreeing to contribute to multiemployer pension funds. These plans are concentrated in mining, construction, motor transportation, printing, wholesale trade, and service industries.

Pension benefits provided through competitive sector retirement systems tend to be smaller (whether measured in absolute amounts or by preretirement wage replacement levels) and more uncertain than those furnished through monopoly-sector programs.

In sum, employees in the competitive sector generally have low wages during their active years. In old age these workers are forced to rely either exclusively on Social Security pensions, often at the lowest benefit levels, or, in limited cases, on Social Security in combination with a meager secondary private pension. Competitive sector households tend to have the most severely depressed retirement incomes.

The Private Retirement Systems

By 1979 about 30 million full-time wage and salary workers, representing slightly less than half of the private work force, were covered by approximately half a million private retirement systems. In that year 40 percent of female and 55 percent of male full-time, private sector employees worked in jobs covered by such plans.[64] Only 10 percent of employees earning less than $5,000 participated in a private pension system as compared to 31 percent of workers earning from $5,000 to $9,999 and 54 percent of those earning from $10,000 to $14,999. Over three-fourths of all private-sector employees with earnings of $20,000 or over were covered by these plans.[65] Fifty percent of eligible workers participated in employer-initiated plans, 25 percent in a single-employer collectively bargained systems, and another 25 percent in multiemployer (or union) plans.[66] However, covered workers are highly concentrated in the largest pension systems within these groupings.

In addition to limited coverage, particularly in the competitive sector, most workers who participate in private retirement systems do not gain substantially from them, for four main reasons. First, "covering" workers and providing them with retirement benefits are not necessarily the same thing. Participating workers and their surviving spouses are entitled to a pension only after satisfying specific, often stringent eligibility requirements. By 1979, only 23 percent of all persons sixty-five and over actually received annuities from the private systems. These beneficiaries represented 31 percent of white older couples, 14 percent of white elderly unmarried women, and 25 percent of white elderly unmarried men in the United States. Only 15 percent of aged black couples, 4 percent of single, aged black women and 13 percent of single, aged black men received private pension income.[67]

A primary reason for the relatively low number of pensioners is restrictive vesting regulations—the number of years a worker must be continuously employed with a firm before becoming eligible for a pension—set by private companies. These have been liberalized only to a limited extent by the Employee Retirement Income Security Act (ERISA) of 1974. Prior to its enactment, 45 percent of covered workers were vested after ten years of continuous service, 39 percent after fifteen years, 12 percent after twenty years, and 3 percent after more than twenty years.[68] ERISA did not provide for full and immediate vesting but rather offered three options to private employers: (a) 100 percent vesting after ten years; (b) five to fifteen year graded vesting (at least 25 percent of the pension vested after five years of covered service, 5 percent more for each of the next five years, and 10 percent each year after until full vesting is reached); or (c) the "rule of forty-five" (an employee with five years of employment under a plan must be 50 percent vested when age and service total forty-five years, and receive 10 percent vesting for each subsequent year until fully vested). Most employers who had to amend their plans to conform with the legislative requirements chose the first option.

Consequently, private pension systems continue to reward only those workers who are willing and able to tie themselves to a single employer (or industry, in the case of multiemployer systems). Greenough and King note that in 1973 only about 30 percent of male and 18 percent of female workers had been continuously employed at the same job for eleven years or more.[69] On average, full-time male workers change jobs every 9.2 years, full-time female workers every 6.8 years. Among all employees the average is 4.6 and 2.8 years, respectively.[70] As a result, most private pension systems fail to provide benefits to a significant number of covered workers. In 1979, only 48 perecent of all full-time employees participating in a private retirement system, and 66 percent of those aged 45 or over, had vested pension rights.[71]

Second, even employees eligible for a private pension may find benefit levels vastly inadequate to their supplementary retirement income needs. Meaningful private pensions usually accrue only to those retirees at the upper end of the income scale or with a record of long and continuous employment with the sponsoring companies. In 1978 the annual median pensions received by single women, single men, and couples sixty-five and over were only $1,400, $2,340, and $2,540, respectively.[72] The mean benefit during 1979 was $2,919 for individuals, and $3,689 for couples.[73] An analysis of the distribution of private system benefits in 1972, based on the Social Security Administration's retirement history study, showed that 44 percent of male and 73 percent of female pensioners received less than $2,000 annually, with 16 percent and 41 percent, respectively, receiving less than $1,000. On the other hand, 13 percent of the men and only 2 percent of the women received $5,000 or more.[74]

Negotiated plans, prevalent among large firms, tend to base annuities on a flat amount per year of service, after some minimum service requirement, or, alternatively, on a combination of wage-related and flat benefit amounts. Most non-negotiated pensions are related to past earnings, as well as to age and length of employment with the firm. Approximately 80 percent of all wage-related plans base pensions on the worker's average earnings over the five years prior to retirement, and the remaining 20 percent utilize a career average.[75] Thus an employee covered by a defined benefit plan that provides 1 percent of final average wages for each year of service would receive 30 percent of such earnings after thirty years, but only 10 percent after ten years. In plans which define fixed employer contributions and where benefit levels are unspecified, total private sector retirement income depends on years of participation under the system, as well as the size of the trust fund itself.

Since a primary purpose of retirement systems is to discipline the labor force, annuities are most often "adequate" only when a worker has been employed with the sponsoring company for twenty-five or thirty years. Even if a worker is vested in several plans, according to Ball, "after fifteen years of service he does not take with him a deferred pension equal to one-half of what he would get after thirty years, but perhaps only 20 or 25 percent of that amount; and the amounts earned from several employers don't add up to a pension that is an adequate supplement to social security."[76] Employees who change jobs several times during their working lives are penalized by the retirement systems.

Moreover, as suggested earlier, significant differences characterize monopoly and competitive system benefit levels. In 1979, a newly retired worker covered under the United Auto Worker's-Chrysler system, with thirty years of continuous employment, was entitled to receive $8,400 annually, regardless of age, until becoming eligible for Social Security. At that time, although his private pension would drop to $3,960, his full worker and spouse Social Security annuities would bring his total retirement income as high as $11,400. On the other hand, an employee covered under the Amalgamated Clothing Workers' retirement system with a similarly long employment record would receive a private pension of only $1,890 at age sixty-five, on top of Social Security. The latter benefit would also tend to be substantially lower than that of the auto worker, given the probability of lesser preretirement wages.[77] Schulz has estimated that the median wage replacement rate for retired male workers with thirty years of continous employment in large single-employer plans (50,000 workers or more) is 26 percent of gross wages earned just prior to retirement. The median rates for small single-employer systems (1,000 employees or less), small multiemployer plans, and large multiemployer plans are 20 percent, 19 percent, and 10 percent, respectively.[78]

Private pension systems also offer substantially larger benefits to higher income than to lower income workers covered by the same plan. In addition, because of the integration of many private systems with Social Security, the greater the salary of the employee, the higher the wage replacement rate provided by the private plan. Integrated plans relate their benefit or contribution formulas to Social Security through either an "offset" or "excess" method. To receive favorable tax treatment for an integrated plan, an employer must comply with rules set by the Internal Revenue Service. However, current integration guidelines allow employers to deny, or reduce considerably, private pension benefits for workers with earnings below a specified "breakpoint." The Social Security taxable wage base is the highest allowable breakpoint level. In effect, integration methods neutralize Social Security's weighted benefit formula, the latter which is intended to aid low-income workers.

Under an excess plan, an employer can contribute into the private plan up to 7 percent of wages above the specified breakpoint without providing any contributions based on earnings under that level. Since the maximum differential is 7 percent, employers who contribute 12 percent of earnings above the breakpoint also must contribute 5 percent of earnings below it. In the case of an excess defined benefit plan, an employer can provide a benefit of up to 37.5 percent of a worker's average career earnings over the integration level without providing any benefit for an employee with average career earnings under that amount. Employers using an offset method can reduce the private annuity by up to 83.3 percent of an employee's Social Security pension. The offset, which is the most common integration method, also disproportionately benefits high income earners. Most offset plans reduce the private pension by 50 percent of the Social Security benefit.

In general, increases in the Social Security taxable wage base reduce private pensions for workers under excess plans, while increases in Social Security benefit levels reduce private pensions for workers under offset plans. If employers raise the breakpoint levels to the current Social Security taxable wage base ($29,700 in 1981), they potentially could deny private pensions entirely to the vast majority of employees covered by integrated plans. By 1981, 94 percent of all workers earned less than the Social Security taxable wage base. Approximately 30 percent of all private plan participants are affected by integration, primarily in non-unionized, competitive sector firms. As a recent report by the House Select Committee on Aging notes:

> The more frequent use of integrated plans by small employers may be caused in part by the fact that small employers have the opportunity to establish tax-qualified integrated plans that primarily benefit themselves by setting integration levels as high as possible and by providing as high a benefit as permitted in relation to excess earnings. Furthermore, integrated plans are popular among smaller employers since they are often sold to them by pension consultants on the basis of their exclusion of lower paid employees, or the provision of relatively smaller benefits for them.[79]

Third, unlike Social Security, most private systems do not provide cost-of-living adjustments, and therefore inflation erodes the purchasing power of benefits considerably. For example, Ball shows that, with a 5 percent annual inflation, even a preretirement wage replacement rate of 100 percent would be reduced to 78 percent in five years, 61 percent in ten years, and 48 percent in fifteen years. With 10 percent inflation per year, the replacement rate would drop to 62 percent, 39 percent, and 24 percent in five, ten, and fifteen years, respectively.[80] Although some employers have offered ad hoc pension adjustments, these have been far below increases in the CPI. A study of 425 pension plans in 1977 showed that only 7 percent had automatic cost-of-living adjustments and all of these had caps of 5 percent or lower.[81] A recent analysis of changes in private pension benefits between 1972 and 1974 by Gayle Thompson found that 56 percent of the pensioners studied had the same or lower benefit amounts at the end of the two years. Another 28 percent had obtained an increase that was lower than the growth of the CPI. Only 16 percent of the recipients had pension increases equivalent to or larger than the rise in prices over the two years studied.[82]

Fourth, most private plans do not provide adequate protection for the worker's family, especially if the employee dies before retirement or if his spouse is under age sixty-two. Many benefits cease or are reduced dramatically when the worker dies. Only about 10 percent of elderly widows of covered employees actually receive survivor benefits. ERISA requires employers to make available automatically, unless the employee chooses to cancel it, a 50 percent joint-and-survivor option at the time of retirement. Under most plans, however, no widow's benefit is available if the husband dies before reaching fifty-five, even if he is vested. Early widow's benefits after fifty-five are not automatic; the plan must have a provision allowing for "early retirement," and the husband must be vested, must have been working under the plan at the time of his death, and must have agreed to a reduction in his early retirement pension, if the widow is to receive any benefits. Since all of these various survivor options reduce the worker benefit levels, many employees with low annuities select the higher pension amounts, thus leaving their spouses unprotected. The consent of the wife is not required in these decisions. Plans also may withold early retirement survivor benefits if the worker dies during a period of up to two years after electing this option, except if the death results from an accidental cause. Consequently, widows usually are not protected by their husband's plans. Even if the surviving spouse is eligible for a benefit, it will be only a fraction of the worker's pension, and if the worker dies prior to retirement age, the total annuity is often miniscule. A divorced wife, on the other hand, has no claim whatsoever to her ex-husband's annuity. Most women tend to be affected adversely by the inadequate protection private retirement systems grant widows and divorcees. Due to their intermittent employment histories and, even more important, their concentration in the competitive sector labor market, even retired female workers usually do not have private pension income in their own right.

Since most monopoly sector corporations and unionized competitive sector firms already have retirement systems, it is highly unlikely that new coverage will spread substantially. Forecast estimates by several studies have indicated that the percentage of workers who participate in private pension plans probably will remain at the current level.[83] ERISA did not provide for the extension of private pension coverage to those workers currently outside the system. In fact, by setting some minimum requirements and standards, the act has actually discouraged the spread of new retirement systems. It has also been responsible, in part, for the termination of a substantial number of existing plans, particularly in competitive sector firms. Approximately 17 percent of employers who have abolished their retirement trusts since 1976 cited ERISA as the primary cause.[84] Most of these now defunct systems, however, were hopelessly underfunded and insubstantial. Any attempt by the government to aid workers materially by mandating immediate vesting, portability, higher benefit levels, more sufficient protection for dependents, and other changes that inevitably increase costs, would encourage even higher rates of plan dissolution.

Insurance for single-employer systems, administered by the Pension Benefit Guaranty Corporation (PBGC), is now mandatory under ERISA. Premiums are paid to PBGC by the participating plans. If a firm declares bankruptcy, the retirement systems have rights to up to 30 percent of the sponsoring company's net worth, and vested workers are guaranteed at least part of their annuities. However, the approximately one million older people who had lost their pension rights due to the bankruptcy of their employer prior to the enactment of ERISA were not aided.

The rapid rate of plan terminations threatens to outpace PBGC's available revenues and the collapse of a large system, such as Chrysler's, would probably bankrupt the agency. Since PBGC was scheduled to cover multiemployer plans in July 1980, public officials expected the problems of plan terminations and potential bankruptcy of the agency to intensify. PBGC estimated that the costs of assuming liabilities of multiemployer systems, which were to cover 100 percent of the employee's vested retirement benefits when their companies withdrew from the plans, could reach as high as $4 billion. Conseqeuntly, the recently enacted Multi-Employer Pension Plan legislation (1980) provides, among other things, some financial obligations by firms for vested pension benefits. However, the act fails to address fundamental issues underlying multiemployer systems and, at best, will avert only minimally both future PBGC costs and potentially high termination rates.

The Public Sector

The state has played an increasingly significant role in the American economy during the last several decades. Since governmental programs tend to be labor intensive and productivity per worker is relatively low, public sector employment at national, state, and local levels has been expanding. By 1979, nearly 20 percent of the nonagricultural work force was employed in the public sector. During the 1960s and 1970s, large numbers of jobs were filled by women and minorities who now "have a higher participation rate in the public sector than in the private sector."[85] Typically, these groups have been concentrated in the lower paid job categories.

Unlike the competitive sector, the public sector's demand for labor and mechanisms for determining wage levels are geared to political rather than market forces. Employment is relatively stable, while salaries at the national level tend to be commensurate with those in the monopoly sector. State and local government wages, though generally lower than federal wages, have risen in recent years, partly due to the expansion of collective bargaining. Nearly 35 percent of state and local employees are now unionized.

The rapid growth of public employee retirement systems (PERS) has mirrored the enormous expansion of the public sector. Public retirement plans have been viewed by government officials as a means of enhancing labor efficiency, lowering overall wage costs, and alleviating unemployment by serving simultaneously to attract and retain proficient workers and to force the retirement of older (and more highly paid) employees. Worker demands for higher salaries, on the one hand, and the political expediency of limiting current labor costs, on the other, also have fostered the expansion of PERS, the broadening of coverage to include more categories of public workers, a liberalization of eligibility requirements, and an increase in benefits. These changes have been made by mortgaging costs to future generations of taxpayers.

Slightly over 90 percent of all federal, state, and local workers, representing about 17 percent of the total labor force, are currently covered under PERS. By 1975, 10.4 million public employees and 2.4 million pensioners participated in 6,630 state and local retirement plans. Like private sector retirement plans, public sector plans have been highly concentrated: in 1975 less than 6 percent of the state and local systems covered nearly 95 percent of all active nonfederal public workers. Similarly, despite the existence of sixty-eight federal retirement systems, 94 percent of the federal workforce was covered under the Civil Service and Uniformed Services Retirement Systems. These two plans covered 2.8 million and 2.2 million active workers, respectively.[86]

In general, workers participating in PERS, particularly those having additional Social Security coverage, tend to receive higher pension incomes than those working for private industry, given comparable employment histories. Most of the difference can be accounted for by the absence of, or by very low, private pensions available to competitive sector workers as well as by their generally low wage levels. Moreover, although public sector retirement annuities increase with earnings and length of employment, just as they do under private plans, most PERS calculate pensions on the basis of final average salaries, as opposed to Social Security and some private plans, which base pensions on lifetime wage averages. PERS benefits are most often calculated by multiplying final average wages (for the three to five years prior to retirement) by a given percentage for each year of service, usually between 1 and 2 percent.[87]

Most nonuniform federal, and 30 percent of state and local employees participate in public retirement programs that do not offer additional coverage under the Social Security system. These employees are dependent on PERS exclusively for their work-related retirement income. According to a 1979 senate report on aging, the federal civil service system is designed "to provide adequate sole support for former Federal workers. It is a defined-benefit, fixed-rate system, which means one's annuity is based directly on length of service and size of contributions."[88] The average federal civil service employee who retired in 1975 after thirty years of service received a pension of 54 percent of his preretirement salary.[89] However, the benefit formula utilizes a greater percentage of wages for each year of service after five years, and raises the percentage again after ten years. As Greenough and King observe, "the aim and effect is to provide a benefit weighted in favor of long-service employees."[90] Moreover, the pension for those who are employed under this system for thirty-five to forty years reaches between 65 and 80 percent of final salaries. For state and local workers retiring in 1975 with earnings of $13,200 (the median wage level at the time), and thirty years of participation under PERS not offering additional Social Security coverage, the average pension was 58 percent of final gross earnings.[91]

Not only are total retirement benefit levels higher in absolute dollar amounts for higher paid workers under these systems, but in addition they are not weighted (as they are under the Social Security system) in favor of lower income employees; wage replacement rates tend to remain constant as income rises. A low-income worker ($6,000) with thirty years of service under state and local systems not offering additional Social Security coverage averaged, in 1975, approximately $3,480 annually in retirement benefits, compared with $10,440 received by high-income earners ($18,000). Moreover, since benefit levels are higher than those provided through the Social Security system, particularly at the middle and upper wage levels, and are based on final average earnings, these public employees not enrolled tend to receive substantially higher pensions than comparably paid competitive sector workers who depend exclusively on Social Security.

Public sector workers are also eligible for benefits at any normal retirement age without actuarial reductions, with some systems allowing retirement at full benefits as early as age fifty or fifty-five. Under the federal civil service plan, full benefits are available at age fifty-five after thirty years of coverage, and at age sixty after twenty years. Employees may also become eligible for additional Social Security pensions through private sector employment prior or subsequent to their public sector jobs. These retired workers—labeled "double dippers" by social analysts—typically earn just enough to qualify them for Social Security at the lowest benefit levels. The latter are based on weighted formulas intended to aid low-paid private sector workers. A "double-dipper" who retired at age sixty-five in 1975 with final earnings of $18,000 was able to increase his PERS pension income by at least 9 percent with additional Social Security benefits. Similarly situated retired public sector workers with earnings of $13,200 and $8,400 augmented their PERS benefits by at least 12 percent and 18 percent, respectively.[92] Over 40 percent of federal civil service employees manage to receive both PERS and Social Security annuities.

On the other hand, 70 percent of state and local workers receive automatic coverage under both PERS and Social Security. Under nonintegrated dual systems, the average wage replacement rate for employees retiring in 1975 with median earnings and thirty years of coverage was 46 percent of final annual earnings on top of their regular Social Security benefits.[93] In fact, most long-service workers participating in such nonintegrated dual systems receive substantial total retirement income, reaching as high as 100 percent or more of their final wages. Although the replacement *rate* of the PERS portion is not related to income level, the weighted Social Security annuity favors low-income employees. However, this is not the case where PERS and Social Security are integrated, as is true for 15 percent of state and local workers.

All military personnel are similarly covered under dual programs—in this case both the Social Security and uniformed services retirement systems. The latter offers its participants one-half of their final preretirement wages after twenty years of employment, and a whopping 75 percent after thirty years. Most military "retirees" leave the service between the ages of forty and forty-five and receive full inflation protected pensions for the remainder of their lives. In 1979 the benefit was approximately $6,118 annually after twenty years for enlisted men, and $13,324 for officers. When annuitants reach age sixty-two, they become eligible for their Social Security pensions which, together with military benefits, replace 100 percent or more of their preretirement wages.[94] Moreover, they can work for private industry after retiring from the armed services and thus become eligible for a third pension, as well. In these cases, ex-military personnel receive annual retirement income greater than their military preretirement wages.

Despite nearly universal coverage of public sector employees, who comprise nearly one-fifth of the work force in the United States, only 13 percent of all men and 9 percent of all women age sixty-five and over received a PERS pension in 1976.[95] One study estimates that in 1976, only 1 percent of older people were receiving a military pension; 4 percent received a federal civil service pension; and 5 percent received a state or local system pension. Minorities, particularly single black women, were less likely than whites to receive retirement income from these public sector plans. Seven percent of blacks (compared with 11 percent of whites and 8 percent of single, white women) were estimated to be receiving annuities from the military, federal, state, and local retirement systems together.[96]

Moreover, the provision of relatively high benefits to public sector workers with long service under a given plan does not guarantee adequate retirement incomes for most PERS participants. Since many employees change jobs frequently, they may receive a low pension based on only five or ten years of coverage. In 1976 the median PERS pension actually received by the 65-and-over population was $4,990 for couples, $4,250 for unmarried men, and only $2,660 for unmarried women.[97] These figures, of course, do not reveal the total retirement income received by retirees with additional pensions, nor the differences among workers participating in the various public sector systems.

The limited number of annuitants, and low pension income received by most public sector retirees, and their dependents, are due to a number of factors. Public sector employees often are ineligible for their pensions because of prohibitive vesting requirements and other restrictive regulations. The armed services retirement system has the most severe vesting requirements; military personnel must serve in the armed forces for a minimum of twenty years before becoming eligible for a pension. Although all workers participating in the federal civil service retirement system are vested after five years of service, 20 percent of state and local employees are covered by plans having even later vesting than the maximum ten years mandated by ERISA for private sector workers. Another 40 percent participate in systems with requirements equivalent to those of private systems. Only 38 percent of state and local workers become vested in five years or less.[98] Approximately half of all covered state and local employees ever become vested in a public sector plan.

Moreover, there is a conspicuous absence of interstate reciprocity or of reciprocity between states and the federal government; workers who move frequently around the country often fail to become vested in any one system and cannot transfer their service credits.[99] Fewer than 13 percent of employees covered under state and local systems are eligible to receive pension credits for out-of-state government service. This is particularly restrictive for those public sector workers not covered by Social Security.

Significantly, a large number of public sector employers, particularly at the state and local levels, have a low percentage of terminated vested workers on their deferred pension rolls. According to a recent government report,

> This suggests that the withdrawal of employee contributions by terminated vested participants is a practice that is widespread among public pension plans. Because accrued benefits related to employer contributions are forfeited in nearly all such cases, hundreds of thousands, perhaps millions, of public employees have lost valuable benefits by withdrawing their own contributions. This unfortunate situation exists because most public employees are not told that they may be forfeiting benefits of much greater value when they elect to withdraw their own contributions.[100]

Nearly 18 percent of state and local workers, and employees with five years of service or less under the federal civil service retirement system, are not even eligible for interest on their portion of pension contributions when they withdraw them.[101]

Although most public plans offer joint and survivor annuities, these are not automatic. At retirement age a participating employee must agree to a reduction in his retirement pay in order to protect the surviving spouse. Fourteen percent of federal civil service workers and 51 percent of military personnel retiring in 1980 opted out of survivor protection entirely.[102] Under the federal retirement system, the spouse's benefit equals 55 percent of the worker's annuity earned at the time of death, or the portion elected as a base for the survivor's annuity. Most state and local systems return the worker's contributions in the form of a lump sum, or through very low annual benefits if the worker dies before retirement age. Surviving spouses of military personnel who elect to participate in the survivor benefit plan (SBP) are assured only a minimum income from the system until they reach sixty-two. When a widow becomes eligible for Social Security benefits, the military SBP mandates a full dollar-for-dollar reduction of benefits for each dollar of Social Security she receives, although the maximum amount of the offset was limited to 40 percent of the SBP benefit in 1980.

Divorced spouses of public sector employees are not eligible for survivor benefits at all. Where there are community property laws, former spouses of retired workers must rely on the courts to allocate a portion of their former mate's pension in the property settlement—if they are willing to go to court, and then prove successful.[103] However the U.S. Supreme Court, in 1981, held that military retirement benefits cannot be divided by a state court as part of a property settlement in a divorce proceeding (Mc Carty v. Mc Carty).

Both the civil service and armed services retirement systems fully protect retired workers from inflation with cost-of-living adjustments. Although over 90 percent of state and local workers participate in plans that provide some inflation-related increases, most pensions are adjusted upward only on an ad hoc basis. Nearly half of these retired workers are covered by systems that increase pensions annually, usually at rates below the CPI. Some other plans link benefits partially to the growth in prices. Less than 5 percent of state and local workers participate in plans that automatically and fully protect pensions against inflation.[104] Consequently, not only wide initial pension income variations, but also growing monetary differences over their retirement spans, characterize PERS pensioners.

INDIVIDUAL RETIREMENT ACCOUNTS

In 1974, the federal government encouraged supplementary retirement income through Individual Retirement Accounts (IRAs) and Keogh plans for workers and the self-employed who are not covered under a private or publicly sponsored retirement system. Prior to 1982, Keogh plans allowed up to $7,500 annually in tax deductible contributions; a self-employed person could tax defer the lesser of $7,500 or 15 percent of his or her gross earnings. Under IRAs employees could tax defer annually up to $1,500, $1,750, and $3,000 for single workers, one-earner couples, and two-earner couples, respectively. In order to stimulate private savings, Congress revised these provisions in 1981. Under the Economic Recovery

Tax Act the maximum deductible amount for Keogh plans will be the lesser of $15,000 or 15 percent of total compensation beginning in January 1982. The maximum amounts deductible for IRAs will be increased to $2,000 for single workers, $2,250 for one-earner couples, and $4,000 for two-earner couples. Moreover, in contrast with the earlier law, all employees, even those who are already covered by a company plan, can participate.

However, the primary beneficiaries of these plans tend to be higher paid workers. Under Keogh plans, deductions of up to $15,000 are allowed for the $100,000 a year earner and only $1,125 for the $7,500 a year earner. Moreover, the tax break under IRAs for lower income groups most in need of supplementary retirement income is relatively small. They are also unlikely to have sufficient wages to provide for current needs, let alone to pay money into an IRA. The Treasury Department has estimated that 52 percent of eligible employees with incomes of $50,000 or more per year and only 5 percent with incomes of $20,000 or less have taken advantage of IRAs.[105] Participation rates of workers earning the minimum wage have been negligible.

SAVINGS AND OTHER ASSETS

Substantial savings and earnings from other income-producing assets, an additional tier of retirement income, are highly concentrated among a relatively small number of older households. The lowest wage earners, on the other hand, tend to have negligible savings available for their old age. As Kolko writes:

This is the logical result of the necessity for the lower-income segments to spend all their income—or more—to obtain the basic essentials of life. In each postwar year, one-third of all families and unattached individuals have been spending more than they earn . . . and even though lower- and middle-income spending units may save at some time, by the end of their earning career, they generally have accumulated very little. . . . There can be little dispute over which income classes have the highest savings-to-income ratio. Clearly, the higher the income the greater the savings.[106]

While 52 percent of older Americans received some interest income in 1976, the median amounted to only $590 for couples and $340 for unrelated individuals.[107]

The small minority of capitalists who own the means of production, and whose advantageous economic position consequently has been derived from producing, circulating, and appropriating surplus value from employees in the form of profits, rent, interest, dividends, and capital gains, can continue to rely on the labor of others indefinitely. The major source of income for the upper class is not affected considerably by age or retirement.

In 1966, the bottom 59 percent of working families relied almost exclusively on income from wages and salaries. Slightly more than half of total income for employees earning between $20,000 and $50,000 was derived from their own labor. Individuals with wages between $50,000 and $100,000 received about one-third of their total income from salaries and two-thirds from income-producing wealth. The highest income households, with earnings over $100,000, accrued only 15 percent of their total resources through salaries and the remainder from assets, predominantly stocks and bonds.[108] In 1979 only 16 percent of older people had income from dividends, 10 percent from rent and royalties, and another 1 percent from estates or trusts.[109] Friedman and Sjogren, in their analysis of the Social Security Administration's Retirement History Study, found that out of 11,153 respondents aged sixty-four or over in 1975, approximately 28 percent of the married men, 14 percent of the single men, and 10 percent of the single women had total assests of $50,000 or more. In contrast, 13 percent, 39 percent, and 40 percent, respectively, had less than $3,000 in total assets. About 6 percent of married men, and 20 percent of single persons in the sample had no assets at all.[110] The highest wage earners who retire with maximum Social Security benefits in addition to large supplementary pensions also have extensive asset holdings.

OLDER WAGE EARNERS VS. RETIREES

Regardless of its form of political economy, every society organizes the mode of production with work as the central activity for the vast majority of its population. Since, in the modern capitalist system, workers have become dependent on the paid labor market for subsistence, forced retirement (whether formal or informal) without adequate pensions deprives them of their primary means of support. Indeed, those older people who continue to work after age sixty-five, despite low paying, often part-time employment, tend to be somewhat better off than their cohorts who do not participate in the paid labor market. For those who do not constitute the "pension elite" (i.e., who were not highly paid, long-term, continuously employed workers protected by a public or monopoly sector retirement system during their working years), or do not hold significant assets, the choice is often either poverty or continuing (and, in some cases, entering) low paying competitive sector employment.

In 1976, 41 percent of older couples, who tend to be financially better off than single older people, had at least one member working. Only 14 percent of single women and 21 percent of single men sixty-five and over derived income from earnings. Most importantly, about 48 percent of all employed males and 59 percent of all employed females sixty-five and over worked part time, usually in low-paying jobs. Thus the median wages of 65-and-over married couples, nonmarried women, and nonmarried men were $4,065, $2,040, and $2,300, respectively. For many part-time employees, low annual wages were supplements to their pension compensations.[111]

Whether working part time or full time, a large percentage of older wage earners with low but "adequate" incomes may suddenly find themselves or their survivors within the ranks of the officially defined poor or near-poor categories. A sudden illness, unemployment, divorce, or the death of a spouse will leave them fully dependent on whatever pension income they might have accrued. Women, of course, are particularly vulnerable to such catastrophes since most supplementary resources available to them tend to be related to their husband's earnings or only fractionally to their husband's pensions.

CONCLUSION

Distribution of income among the elderly, whether measured by wages, assets, or retirement benefits, as Talley and Burkhauser note, "has a greater variance than that of any other age group, indicating that differences in relative income positions are greatest within the oldest group."[112] While income and other economic resources are concentrated among a small segment of the aged, older people are disproportionately represented at the lower end of the income and wealth distributions in American society. Economic inequality, inherent under capitalism, is intensified by age. Consequently, any meaningful assessment of income maintenance programs and their impact on the elderly's economic situation must focus on distinct and widely varying subgroups within the older population. Elderly blacks and older single women tend to suffer more substantial economic deprivation than either older white males or couples. The latter two groups are relatively more likely to receive high and multiple sources of retirement compensation.

According to Ball, in 1976 approximately 20 percent of older Americans had incomes equivalent to or even greater than those they received prior to attaining age sixty-five.[113] At the end of 1978, 6.5 percent of older families had incomes between $20,000 and $25,000; 9.6 percent, between $25,000 and $50,000; and 2 percent, over $50,000. In other words, more than 18 percent of older families received an income greater than the median $19,310 received by younger families. Of older unmarried individuals, 13 percent had incomes in excess of $10,000 and 1.5 percent received $25,000 or more.[114]

At the other end of the scale, those older people who are not part of the "pension elite" have only one annuity, usually Social Security, as their sole means of support. Twenty-two percent of couples, 30 percent of single men, and 40 percent of single women sixty-five and over who received SSI or Social Security in 1978 relied on these sources for all of their retirement income.[115] About 14 percent of all retired Social Security beneficiaries were living in abject poverty.

Of the 65-and-over population officially classified as poor, 72 percent are unmarried women.[116] Couples and single men account for another 13 and 15 percent, respectively, of the poverty population. Moreover, 38 percent of all widows and 43 percent of divorced or separated women, compared with 27 percent of unmarried men and 9 percent of married couples, live at or below the "official" poverty level. Nearly 25 percent of the older males living in poverty are black, representing about one-third of the elderly black population. Of older black women, 41 percent have incomes below the "official" poverty threshold. In 1976 the median income of older white married couples, unmarried men, and unmarried women was $8,150, $4,090, and $3,370, respectively. By contrast, the median income of the older black population was $5,460 for married couples, $2,930 for single men, and $2,480 for single women.[117]

Obviously, old age income support programs do not adequately serve the needs of the vast majority of older Americans. Rather they maintain extremes of wealth and poverty, reinforce preretirement sexual and racial stratifications, and strengthen work norms. They also perpetuate inequalities between the generations, since most older people, who tend to rely on fixed incomes, do not share in the fruits of economic growth. As the next chapter will show, public and private retirement systems primarily serve the needs of capital.

Chapter 4
Investment Capital and Pension Power

Private and public pension systems produce forced savings and investment capital essential to the capitalist economy. Rather than assuring adequate retirement income and economic security for the vast majority of older people, a major goal of private, state, and local trusts is capital formation. By the early 1960s these retirement systems had accrued approximately $73 billion and held 4 percent of outstanding stock in the United States. Since that time their assets have grown dramatically, reaching $653 billion by 1980, at which time they also held between 20 and 25 percent of total stocks of companies listed on the New York and American exchanges. Together with the federal retirement systems and the Social Security trust, public and private pension assets totaled over $700 billion.[1]

The enormous and growing impact of pension assets on the economy has been recognized by the financial community for years. But, until recently, the economic, political, and social implications of retirement trust funds were neglected by political leaders, union officials, and public interest groups. Even the President's Committee on Corporate Pension Funds, in the early 1960s, and later congressional studies and hearings culminating with the Employee Retirement Income Security Act (ERISA), failed to address ade-

Portions of this chapter originally appeared in Union of Radical Political Economists, ed., *The Public Sector Crisis Reader* (New York: Monthly Review Press, 1981); copyright © 1981 URPE/MR; reprinted by permission. And in Charles Bulmer and John L. Carmichael, Jr., eds., *Employment and Labor-Relations Policy* (Lexington, Mass.: Lexington Books, D. C. Heath, 1980); copyright © 1980 D. C. Heath; reprinted by permission.

quately the capital accumulation role of pension trusts. Significantly, however, the newly formed 1979 President's Commission on Pension Policy, several recent congressional investigations and reports, organized labor, public interest groups, and various other organizations, have all shown increasing awareness of workers' funds as a rapidly expanding source of capital and economic power.

In this chapter, I argue that public and private retirement assets have been used to help in the creation of, or to sustain, practices that adversely affect working class and community interests. They contribute, among other things, to (a) the increasing power of financial institutions; (b) the growth and concentration of monopoly capitalism; (c) a shortage of capital for "socially useful" investments; (d) the fiscal crisis facing, particularly, state and local governments; and (e) the support of corporations whose activities are antithetical to working class interests and socially desirable goals. Clearly, however, these funds have the potential to serve alternative political, social, and economic objectives, to enhance the power of labor, and to promote fundamental changes in society.

THE GROWTH AND INVESTMENT OF RETIREMENT
TRUST ASSETS

Most state and local retirement systems either have been vastly underfunded or have utilized a pay-as-you-go financial approach. In recent years, however, the retirement trusts have moved in the direction of funded systems. By 1978 over 83 percent were at least partially funded.[2] The growth in public sector employment and expanded coverage have further promoted the rapid accumulation of capital, a large percentage of which derives directly from worker contributions into the systems. Total assets of state and local trusts have steadily increased, from less than $2 billion in 1940 and $20 billion in 1960, to $58 billion by 1970. Since that time assets have grown by approximately 12 to 15 percent annually. At the end of 1980, these public systems had amassed over $203 billion (see table 3).

During the 1950s and 1960s, the investments of state and local systems tended to be legally restricted to certain types of fixed-income securities, such as U.S. government obligations and state and local bonds. As late as 1961 corporate stocks accounted for only

Table 3. State, Local, and Private Pension Fund Assets, 1940–1980 ($ billion)

	1940	1950	1955	1960	1965	1970	1973	1974	1975	1976	1980*
State and local	†	$5.2	$10.6	$19.7	$33.1	$58.2	$82.7	$92.4	$103.4	$117.2	$202.7
Private noninsured	†	6.1	15.3	33.0	58.1	97.0	126.5	133.7	145.2	160.4	286.1
Private insured	†	5.6	11.2	20.2	27.3	41.2	56.1	60.8	71.7	80.1	164.6
Total pension fund assets	$4.0	$16.9	$37.1	$72.9	$118.5	$196.4	$265.3	$286.9	$320.3	$357.7	$653.4

SOURCE: U.S. Securities and Exchange Commission, *Statistical Bulletin* (various).
NOTE: Amounts are at book value.
* 1980 figures are at market value.
† Represents less than $2 billion.

3 percent ($.6 billion) and corporate bonds for 39 percent ($8.5 billion) of investments, while public sector securities represented nearly half ($10 billion) of the total. However, in the mid-1960s, investment in corporate stocks and bonds surpassed that in public issues. By 1976 corporate stocks and bonds accounted for about 74 percent, and public sector obligations represented only 11 percent, of state and local retirement trust portfolios. As of 1979 the breakdown of such retirement trust investments is as follows: equities, 22 percent; corporate bonds, 52 percent; state and local securities, 2.8 percent; federal securities, 8.3 percent; mortgages, 7.1 percent; cash and deposits, 1.3 percent; real estate, 1.3 percent; and foreign and other investments, 5.7 percent. Moreover, state and local retirement systems have been increasing holdings of equities at a faster rate than other institutional investors. From 1970 to 1978, their equity investments alone grew from 13 to 22 percent of total investments.

For example, the $18 billion California State Public Employes and Teacher Retirement Systems, which are allowed to maintain 25 percent of total assets in common stocks, have been directing about 30 percent of new investments there. In Connecticut, the public employes' fund invested heavily in certificates of deposit and U.S. Treasury notes until the early 1970s. Since 1972, the system, which holds $1.6 billion, has moved toward an equity orientation. The overall investment strategy of the Illinois public retirement systems, Florida State Retirement Fund, and other state and local pension trusts have also shifted toward corporate stocks. In 1980 the $1 billion Mississippi Public Retirement System received legislative approval to invest up to 20 percent of its pension assets in stocks. The system, which has not acquired stocks previously, intends to reach the maximum in two years. The $250 million Wyoming Retirement System is seeking legislative approval to purchase equities, as well.

Private pension assets have also experienced spectacular growth. As table 3 shows, while the assets of noninsured funds rose from less than $2 billion in 1940 to only $6 billion ten years later, from 1955 on they began vastly to outpace state and local systems. Holding $33 billion in 1960, private noninsured trusts amased $97 billion by 1970 and approached $286 billion in 1980. In combination with the insured pension systems, private trusts held a whopping $451 billion at the end of 1980.

Prior to the 1950s, private pension funds had divergent investment priorities. In fact, until 1939, private pension assets were invested primarily in the fund's parent corporation, thus providing in-house capital for expansion.[3] In 1939 corporate stocks represented approximately 20 percent of the total assets of private funds, while 15 percent was invested in federal securities. However, by 1945, federal securities represented nearly half of their reserves. Although Greenough and King note that "the emphasis on federal securities was due to a desire to assist in the financing of the government's mobilization and war costs, and to a dearth of alternative investments available during wartime,"[4] the latter explanation appears more plausible.

Table 4 shows the investment pattern of private funds from 1951 to 1976. Moving away from U.S. government securities after 1945, the retirement trusts increasingly began to acquire corporate equities and, according to Roger Murray, "provided a major remedy to the shortage of equity capital in the period immediately following World War II."[5] During the 1950s, pension funds, along with insurance companies, supplied 10 to 15 percent of industry's new capital.[6] In 1961, approximately half the assets of private funds were invested in corporate stocks and over 85 percent in corporate stocks and bonds together. By 1966, "[private] pension funds had become the largest buyer of common stock, accounting for 10 percent of all transactions."[7] Investment priorities continue to emphasize corporate securities, although, during 1978, private pensions acquired equities at the lowest rate in thirty years. By the end of that year, 52 percent of their assets were invested in stock, 39 percent in debt securities, primarily corporate bonds, 6 percent in liquid assets, and the remainder in mortgages, real estate, and foreign markets. Consequently, both private and public worker retirement systems, which are the single largest holders of corporate stocks and bonds in the United States, contribute substantially to corporate capital markets.

WHO CONTROLS PENSION FUNDS?

It is a significant but unquestioned aspect of employer-initiated noninsured private plans that workers are provided no role whatsoever in the administration of the funds. Trustees are appointed

Table 4. Investment Areas of Private Noninsured Pension Funds, 1951–1976 ($ billion)

Asset Classes	1951 Amount	(%)	1961 Amount	(%)	1965 Amount	(%)	1970 Amount	(%)	1974 Amount	(%)	1976 Amount	(%)
Corporate bonds	$3.5	(44)	$15.9	(35)	$22.7	(39)	$24.9	(24)	$30.8	(28)	$37.9	(22)
Corporate stock	1.4	(17)	22.8	(50)	25.3	(43)	67.1	(64)	63.3	(57)	109.7	(63)
U.S. government securities	2.4	(31)	2.7	(.06)	3.1	(.05)	3.0	(3)	5.6	(5)	14.9	(9)
Mortgages	.1	(2)	1.6	(.04)	3.3	(6)	3.5	(3)	2.1	(2)	2.2	(1)
Cash and deposits	.3	(4)	.7	(2)	.9	(2)	1.8	(2)	4.3	(4)	2.2	(1)
Other	.2	(3)	1.6	(4)	2.8	(5)	4.4	(4)	5.7	(5)	7.1	(4)
Totals*	$8.0	(101)	$45.3	(101)	$58.1	(100)	$104.7	(100)	$111.7	(101)	$173.9	(100)

SOURCE: Data computed from U.S. Securities and Exchange Commission, *Statistical Bulletin* (various).
Note: Amounts are computed market value.
*Certain totals do not add to 100 percent because of rounding.

exclusively by the corporations. Similarly, management tends to appoint representatives to oversee collectively bargained single-employer funds. Multiemployer and most union plans are trusteed jointly by management and union representatives. The Taft-Hartley Act requires joint administration of all union plans instituted after January 1946; those few plans initiated prior to that time are administered solely by the unions. Under insured private plans, the employer pays premiums to an insurance company which is then responsible for retirement benefits and investment decisions. Regardless of the formal arrangement for trusteeship, however, nearly all private pension assets are turned over to institutional money managers, usually with full investment authority and stock voting rights.

ERISA has tended to strengthen, and even to expand, the control financial institutions exert over private retirement funds. The act mandates fiduciary responsibility for investment decisions and states that asset managers must personally assume any losses resulting from a violation of the "prudent man" rule.[8] Burt Seidman, Social Security director of the AFL-CIO, suggests that this provision of the act has encouraged trustees to turn over even more funds to institutional managers in order to protect themselves.[9]

On the other hand, both employee and consumer representatives often influence investment practices of state and local pension systems. About 50 percent of the nearly $37 billion in state and local equity portfolios is managed internally. Most of the larger state and local plans place full control over trust assets in retirement or investment boards; employee representatives constitute a majority in 25 percent, and a near majority in another 34 percent of such boards. In nearly 75 percent of all state and local retirement systems, at least some employee representatives are elected by covered workers.[10] For example, the trustees of the three major Wisconsin pension funds, holding $5 billion in assets, are a seven-member state investment board, four of whose members represent the general public and two plan participants. Although professional staff make specific investment decisions, they do so within general guidelines established by the board and, as with most other public pension trusts, within the limits of constitutional or legislative directives, as well.

Banks and insurance companies serve as custodians or outside advisors for a substantial number of public pension systems.

Twenty-one percent of all plans rely on the services of banks; 24 percent on insurance companies. While the power of these outside custodians/managers/advisors varies widely, they often obtain full or partial control over the assets. Furthermore, "in some cases, one-half of the members of the investment committees [of state and local pension boards] represent financial institutions."[11] Therefore, in addition to exercising authority over substantial portions of private pension assets, financial institutions influence the usage of public sector retirement funds, as well. Some observers have even suggested that there is a growing trend among public systems toward hiring outside equity managers and allowing them a high degree of investment discretion and stock voting rights similar to powers provided through the private pension systems. For example, in the early 1970s, Oregon, Virginia, and Connecticut gave their respective equity managers nearly full authority over investments.[12] In 1977 the $600 million Utah retirement system made similar changes.

RETIREMENT SYSTEMS AND THE GROWING POWER OF FINANCIAL INSTITUTIONS

The rapid expansion of monopoly capitalism in recent years has been encouraged by and largely funded through the investment community, particularly commercial banks and insurance companies. The growing domination of the economy by large financial institutions, which has intensified considerably over the last several decades, is due primarily to their control of major sources of capital and their increasing control over corporate stocks and bonds. Linkages between large corporations and financial institutions through stock voting rights as well as interlocking directorships have strengthened the concentration of power within the private sector.[13]

In January 1978 the late Senator Lee Metcalf's Subcommittee on Reports, Accounting, and Management revealed that "power to vote stock in 122 of the largest organizations in America, whose common stock represents 41 percent of total market value of all outstanding, is concentrated in 21 institutional investors."[14] Table 5 shows the number of corporations in which each of the twenty-one major investors is one of the five largest stockholders and the number of times they are the major stock voter. The most influential is Morgan

Table 5. Stock Voter Interests of 21 Major Investors in 122 Corporations

Investors	Number of companies in which investor is one of five largest stockholders	Number of times investor is stock voter number one
Morgan Guaranty Trust Co. of N.Y.	56	27
Citibank	25	7
TIAA-CREF	24	2
Capital Research and Management Co.	19	2
Prudential Insurance Co.	18	4
Dreyfus Corp.	17	4
National Bank of Detroit	17	5
Kirby Family Group-Allegheny Corp.	16	4
Bankamerica Corp.	15	1
Fidelty Management and Research Corp.	13	2
Manufacturers Hanover Trust Co.	12	1
Bankers Trust Co.	11	0
First National Bank of Chicago	11	2
Lord Abbett and Co.	11	2
Equitable Life Assurance Society of U.S.	10	2
First National Bank of Boston	10	0
Harris Trust and Savings Bank	10	2
Chase Manhattan Corp.	8	3
Continental Illinois National Bank & Trust	8	3
Marlennan Corp. (March & Mclennan Co., Inc.)	7	0
Massachusetts Financial Services Inc.	7	2

Source: U.S. Senate, Committee on Governmental Affairs, Subcommittee on Reports, Accounting, and Management, *Voting Rights in Major Corporations*, 95th Cong., 1st sess., January 1978, p. 258.

Guaranty Trust Company of New York (the major identified stockholder in twenty-seven corporations, and among the top five in fifty-six), followed by Citibank (the major identified stockholder in seven corporations, and among the top five in twenty-five). Noting that diverse authorities tend to agree that stock holdings of 5 percent or more can constitute significant power over a corporation, the subcommittee staff identified thirteen corporations in which family interests controlled 10 percent or more of the stock, nineteen companies in which a single institutional investor controlled 5 percent or more, and twenty-four firms in which a combination of five or fewer investors controlled at least 10 percent.[15] These figures probably underestimate the extent of power since, as a 1968 congressional report pointed out, stock ownership (or control) of only 1 or 2 percent of a company's equities may be sufficient for influencing its policies.[16]

Similarly, in a study of the 200 largest nonfinancial corporations, David Kotz found that financial institutions exercised predominant control over U.S. firms. Kotz defined control as participation in the selection of management, the ability to pressure successfully for key policies, and direct service in a decision-making capacity. He discovered that financial institutions dominated nearly 40 percent of the corporations analyzed. He concluded that "leading bankers have the power to determine or influence the allocation of capital over a significant portion of the economy, and to influence many other aspects of corporate behavior as well."[17]

Since the ten largest banking institutions hold over one-third of total trust department assets, power is concentrated even further. In addition, as shown by the Senate subcommittee report, *Voting Rights in Major Corporations*:

> the principal stockvoters in large banks are—large banks. Morgan Guaranty is Stockvoter Number 1 in four of its New York sister banks—Citicorp, Manufacturers Hanover Corp., Chemical New York Corp. and Bankers Trust New York Corp.—as well as Bankamerica Corp. In turn, Citicorp is Stockvoter No. 1 in Morgan Guaranty's parent holding company, J. P. Morgan and Co. Stockvoter No. 2 in J. P. Morgan and Co. is Chase Manhattan. Stockvoters No. 3 and 4 in J. P. Morgan & Co. are Manufacturers Hanover and Bankers Trust, in whose parent holding companies Morgan Guaranty Trust is Stockvoter No. 1.[18]

Existing administrative arrangements for pension funds have buttressed the growth and power of financial institutions considerably. Pension funds often represent the second and sometimes the primary source of economic power for institutional investors. A 1980 study by the periodical *Pensions and Investments* of the top 413 financial institutions overseeing pension funds showed that tax-exempt assets, consisting mostly of employee retirement funds, represented 53 percent of all assets administered by these financial institutions. Of the $442 billion in worker funds held by these institutions, bank trust departments, investment counseling firms, and insurance companies controlled 43 percent, 30 percent, and 27 percent, respectively.[19] The total amount of worker benefit funds under institutional control increases steadily every year.

Significantly, financial institutions have complete discretionary power over investments for 81 percent of the worker benefit funds they hold. Full discretionary power increased 10 percent during 1977 and 5 percent over 1978, indicating that pension trustees are delegating more power to institutional investors.[20] At the same time, the institutional managers tend to acquire full voting rights over the stocks they purchase for the retirement trusts. For example, Morgan Guaranty exercises proxy voting rights for 98 percent of the retirement fund stocks it manages. What this means, of course, is that pension assets managed by institutional investors will continue to increase their control over major corporations and the economy. Moreover, the largest institutions all had at least some state and local funds, mostly with either full or partial discretion over investment decisions. Since these funds are partially derived from taxpayers, government officials are relinquishing their control over public money.

Worker pension funds are concentrated in the hands of a few elite institutions. According to *Pensions and Investments*, one hundred large-scale financial institutions "oversee the investment of more than 65 percent of the approximately $560 billion in tax-exempt assets in the U.S.,"[21] or $364 billion. The leading ten managers alone (Equitable Life, Prudential Insurance, Morgan Guaranty, Metropolitan Life, Aetna Life, Bankers Trust, Mellon Bank, Connecticul General, Harris Trust, and Scudder, Stevens and Clark) managed $128.1 billion at the end of 1979. The great bulk of noninsured pension funds are controlled by approximately twenty-five banks, the latter holding $124.6 billion in tax-exempt assets. This represents 65 percent of the $191 billion held by the top 151 banks profiled by *Pensions and Investments*. Tax-exempt assets administered by the ten most prominent banks include: Morgan Guaranty Trust, $16 billion; Bankers Trust, $10.8 billion; Mellon Bank, $9.2 billion; Harris Trust, $7.9 billion; Citibank, $7.2 billion; Manufacturers Hanover, $6.5 billion; National Bank of Detroit, $5.4 billion; Capital Guardian Trust, $5.1 billion; Old Colony Trust (First National Bank of Boston), $4.9 billion; and Chase Investors Mgt., $4.5 billion.[22]

CURRENT INVESTMENT PRACTICES: WHO GAINS?

The emergence of financial institutions as a leading economic power has been aided and abetted by pension funds, but this trend has had negative consequences for workers and society as a whole. As Kotz argues, "The significant and growing power of bankers today is an important force for collusion and against competition. The leading financial institutions control many competing, or potentially competing, companies."[23] For example, Bankers Trust is the fourth largest stock voter of U.S. Steel, and the fifth largest of Bethlehem Steel, with .9 percent and 1.2 percent of their totals, respectively. Chase Manhattan has acquired voting rights over Exxon (1.3 percent), Standard Oil of California (1.6 percent), and Mobil (1.5 percent). Morgan Guaranty votes stock on American Airlines (6.1 percent) and Northwest Airlines (3.7 percent), General Motors (1.1 percent) and Ford Motor (1.7 percent), and U.S. Steel (2.4 percent) and Bethlehem Steel (1.9 percent).[24]

Moreover, pension investments in corporate stocks and bonds have produced extremely poor financial returns. Between 1965 and 1975, Treasury securities yielded higher returns on investment than either corporate bonds or equities.[25] According to several studies, between 1962 and 1978 87 percent of pension managers underperformed the Standard and Poor's (S&P) 500 index. From 1972 to 1976 alone, while the S&P index rose by 4.9 percent, the top 183 banks and 51 insurance companies averaged retirement trust investment returns of only .8 percent and 1 percent, respectively.[26] Only 4 percent of all pension equity portfolios were able to outperform the S&P index during the last fifteen years.[27] As pointed out in a *Pensions and Investments* editorial, "some large banks have maintained their pension clients" despite poor performance "mainly because they have commercial ties with those clients. . . . Clients fear corporate relations will be jeopardized if they fire the banks as pension fund managers."[28]

There are strong interlocking interests between the plan-sponsoring company and the institutional investors of pension funds. A Nader study group report on First National City Bank (FNCB or Citibank) argues that "banks like to focus on what they call the 'total account relationship.'" For example, a corporation will select a bank to manage their pension funds in return for prime rate loans and other benefits. "Pension fund business is an important source of deposit growth for a commercial bank and this might be one reason why Boeing, Pan Am, and American Airlines—these troubled companies whose pension funds have been managed by FNCB in recent years—all borrow from FNCB at the prime rate." Similarly, a 1971 congressional report noted that when large banks serve as pension managers for major enterprises, they almost invariably have other commercial ties with the firm. The Nader group found that when Citibank managed a large company's pension trust, the bank either had a director interlock with the company, held the company's stock in its portfolio, or made substantial loans to the firm.[29]

Poor investment performance, of course, tends to curtail increases in private pension benefits and to prevent liberalization of provisions that would enhance the economic situation of retired workers and their dependents. Employers take into account the health of the trust funds, particularly investment returns, when deciding upon or agreeing to plan improvements. Benefit levels provided to employees participating in multiemployer and union systems depend on the size of the trust fund directly. Thus the losses from poor portfolio performance are often borne by the workers themselves.

Moreover, since money managers invest nearly all pension assets in the largest corporate firms traded on the New York and American Stock Exchanges, they profoundly and adversely affect financial markets by creating a shortage of capital for small and emerging firms in the competitive sector.[30] Such firms tend to be labor intensive and have been responsible for a large percentage of gains in employment opportunities. Their inability to attract capital further exacerbates unemployment in the United States.

Additionally, decisions made by large institutional investors contribute to the sustenance of corporations that thwart union goals and community interests, including firms that pollute the environment, flagrantly violate civil rights and labor relations laws, provide unhealthy industrial working environments, and engage in other socially injurious practices. Senator Metcalf noted that the present practice of pension administration and control results "in the use of pension money to assist 'notoriously antiunion companies.'"[31] The Ford-UAW retirement plan, one of three United Auto Workers funds, holds a stock portfolio of approximately $873 million. These assets, controlled by large banks, are invested primarily in twenty-four major corporations. Eleven of these firms are among sixteen categorized by the AFL-CIO as leading antiunion or nonunion corporations.[32]

A 1979 study by Corporate Data Exchange reviewed the stock portfolios of the 20 largest public and 122 major private pension trusts. This study assessed the trusts's investments in 99 companies that (a) are predominantly nonunionized; (b) have a poor record in the field of occupational health and safety; (c) fail to meet equal employment guidelines; or (d) are major investors in South Africa. Out of $44.6 billion in common stock held by the private plans studied, 30 percent was invested in nonunionized companies; 5 percent in firms with serious health and other hazards; 9 percent in firms violating equal employment opportunity standards; and 19 percent in companies with significant activities in South Africa. The percentages for the $16.6 billion held by public plans are 26, 7, 8, and 20 percent, respectively. Forty-six percent of the total equities held by the private pension systems, and 44 percent of those held by the state and local employee systems, goes to support 99 firms whose activities are counter to the interests of plan beneficiaries, workers, and the public interest.[33]

As persuasively argued by Jeremy Rifkin and Randy Barber in *The North Will Rise Again*, workers' pension funds have also supported the movement of firms and capital from the North and Midwest to the Sunbelt region, and to other nations, thus contributing to the fiscal crisis, dearth of employment opportunities, and pressures on services in the industrial northern states and localities.[34] Rifkin has pointed out that over 90 percent of the equities held by the Ohio public funds are "out of state, out of the region and out of the country."[35] After studying the pension funds of ten major corporations, the Industrial Union Department (IUD) of the AFL-CIO found that five of these companies had 50 percent or more of their largest pension fund investments in firms employing over one-third of their workers abroad.[36]

The poor performance of the American economy in recent years, coupled with corporate concern over low rates of return on retirement trust investments, has prompted money managers to seek new and expanded worker pension investments abroad. In 1979, Morgan Guaranty, the largest institutional investor of worker benefit funds, had over $609 million in pension assets invested in foreign securities, an increase of approximately 5 percent during 1978 alone.

Over 80 percent of its pension fund clients participated in either its commingled international equity fund (instituted in 1974) or its commingled international bond fund (instituted in 1977). Another large pension manager, Scudder, Stevens and Clark, has $220 million in tax-exempt funds invested in foreign markets. By 1979, seventeen of the top one hundred pension trusts were investing at least some of their assets overseas, and six others were considering it. At the end of 1980, private retirement trusts had invested over $4 billion in foreign securities. International investment of private and public pension assets will increase considerably during the 1980s, with a substanital negative impact on American labor, industrially based communities, and the economy overall.

THE FISCAL CRISIS AND STATE AND LOCAL RETIREMENT TRUSTS

The contradictions of monopoly capitalism have required states and localities to budget increasing expenditures for welfare, unemployment insurance, the health needs of the poor and dependent aged, public housing, and a wide range of social services, as well as urban redevelopment projects, transportation, and other infrastructural services. The corresponding growth of public sector employment at the state and local levels, which increased by 20 percent from 1970 to 1976 alone, has also had a substantial impact on public budgets. Since state and local governments increasingly cover needs generated by monopoly capitalism, while profits continue to be expropriated privately and traditional means for increasing revenues have become politically and economically inaccessible, these public entities are faced with a potential (and, in some cases, real) fiscal crisis. However, figures for budgets, revenues, and deficits reveal only the more visible aspects of government activities. These indicators fail to expose the hidden dimension of public pension obligations, without which the extent of the crisis cannot be appreciated fully. Even though state and local retirement trusts have amassed enormous assets since the 1960s, state and local governments simultaneously face growing pension obligations and pressing social needs that increasingly outpace available or projected revenues.

A combination of rising public sector employment, improved

benefit and eligibility provisions, rampant inflation, and an increasing percentage of retirees relative to active workers in the 1970s has resulted in both higher current pension costs and growing accrued liabilities. The major component of such liabilities is the expected cost of pensions already promised but which cannot be met through current contribution rates. State and local governments must raise sufficient revenues to fulfill pension obligations that reached $7.3 billion a year by 1975 and are rising by 16 percent annually. These units of government also face an enormous growth of unfunded accrued pension liabilities (future obligations for which no money has been set aside) that are estimated at between $150 and $175 billion.[37] In the Illinois Public Retirement System, for example, the unfunded liability rose 10 percent over the last two years, reaching $7.7 billion in 1979. California's aggregate unfunded liability of $4.5 billion is considerably greater than its general obligation debt.[38] Only about 20 to 25 percent of public plans technically meet ERISA's minimum funding requirements.[39]

Local governments already relegate a high proportion of the property taxes they receive toward payment of fringe benefits. Nearly 30 percent of Chicago's and 46 percent of Los Angeles' property taxes have been used to fund pensions and pension systems. In 1977, for every dollar paid their workers, municipalities provided 42.7 cents for fringe benefits, with retirement systems accounting for the greatest percentage of that additional expense. Raising taxes at state and local levels, where tax structures tend to be highly regressive, would place growing public pension burdens primarily on low- and middle-income families who already provide substantial and increasing payroll tax support for federal Social Security programs. Since raising either state and local taxes or general debt obligations, or both, is not a viable prospect, particularly given the current political climate, mounting pension obligations compete increasingly with scarce revenues for social programs and projects. Significantly, many states and localities even utilize revenue sharing funds to meet retirement obligations rather than to enhance services or to develop local economies.[40] The General Accounting Office has found federal revenue sharing funds used increasingly to fund pension systems. In 1977, for example, Delaware placed its entire revenue sharing money into the state employee's system.[41] The proposed elimination of these funds by the executive branch, and their actual reduction in 1981, will leave less capital available for rising pension costs and postpone lowering the vast unfunded retirement trust liabilities of many states and localities.

Two important methods of cutting the public share of pension costs are now being tried. First, a number of state and local governments have begun to lower present or future benefit levels while simultaneously increasing mandatory employee contribution levels. As the 1978 congressional study of public pension systems notes, "it is clear that even state governments can and will renege on present or future pension commitments when pension costs become too burdensome or threaten the governmental unit's fiscal stability."[42] In fact, *Pensions and Investments* reported in the same year that thirty-five states permitted legal reduction of benefit accruals based on prospective service, even for present plan participants.[43] According to the congressional report, approximately 8 percent of public sector plans, covering 18 percent of active participants, have been amended to reduce the value of past or future benefits in the last ten years.[44] The $946 million San Francisco City and County Retirement System recently initiated a new pension plan offering lower benefits and providing for greater employee payroll taxes. In Los Angeles, revised pension provisions for new workers raised employee contributions by 50 percent while at the same time lowering early retirement benefits by 23 percent and annual cost-of-living adjustments for retirees from 3 to 2 percent. In March 1979, Maryland's new pension scheme for all future teachers and state employees reduced benefits by approximately 20 percent and placed a 3 percent maximum on cost-of-living increases for retirees. Massachusetts enacted a five-year program to fund its retirement systems, and increased employee contributions from 5 to 7 percent of wages.

A second method of restoring fiscal solvency has been the gradual shift from pay-as-you-go to partially funded systems, along with new investment priorities focused on corporate equities and bonds. A primary impetus for these changes is the desire to reduce government costs by covering larger amounts of current pension obligations through investment earnings. However, the acquisition of corporate stocks and bonds has produced extremely poor financial returns. According to a report by the Conference on Alternative State and Local Policies, "public pension funds are earning overall far less on their monies than either a passbook savings account, Treasury securities, or the average home mortgage."[45] Moreover, the movement of state and local funds into corporate securities diverts capital which might have been potentially available for investment in state and local programs of direct and indirect benefit to plan participants and public treasuries. Instead of promoting job creation, neighborhood revitalization, and other socially desirable projects, these growing assets are instead funding capital markets and private accumulation. Despite the shortage of revenues available for pressing state and local needs, and despite the availability of huge pools of potential investment capital through public pension trusts, public employee retirement systems are investing increasingly in major corporate enterprises.

INVESTMENT ALTERNATIVES: THE ISSUE OF SOCIAL INVESTING

Workers have the potential to gain some control over their trust assets. Employees in the private sector can influence investment decisions of jointly trusteed (multiemployer) and union-sponsored plans. Together with the pension systems of nonprofit organizations, these funds represent approximately 16 percent of all pension assets. If one adds state and local retirement systems, where workers tend to be represented on investment boards, employees can exercise a substantial influence over another 32 percent of total pension trust assets in the United States. Additional power could be exerted over those single-employer plans subject to collective bargaining. About half of all single-employer benefit funds, which amounted to $320 billion in 1980, are subject to collective bargaining.[46]

A strong case can be made, moreover, for worker ownership of and control over all pension assets. Although employers contribute to the systems, these monies are paid in lieu of wages, a factor taken into account in determining salary levels during collective bargaining. Since the costs of employer contributions are borne by employees, there appears to be substantial justification for arguing that pension funds should be under their exclusive control. In addition, 85 percent of state and local workers are required to contribute to their plans; thus a significant percentage of the accumulated assets of these systems accrues directly from the workers themselves.

The high concentration of participants and assets in a few state-administered and private sector systems enhances possibilities for efficiently coalescing efforts aimed at attaining employee pension power. At the end of 1980, the assets of the top one hundred funds represented $310.9 billion, an increase of 11.5 percent since 1979. Forty-two state and local retirement trusts are among the one hundred largest pension systems in the United States. The California Public Employee Trust held $18.1 billion, followed by New York City Employees ($13.5 billion), New York State Common Fund ($13.3 billion), New York State Teachers ($7.9 billion), New Jersey Division of Investment ($7.6 billion), Texas Teachers ($5.3 billion), Wisconsin Investment Board ($5 billion), Ohio Teachers ($4.7 billion), Ohio Public Employees ($4.6 billion), and Michigan State Employees ($4.6 billion). These ten funds alone held $84.6 billion.[47] The ten largest multiemployer and union plans held over one-third of these assets. Similarly, the top twenty-five corporate sponsors have accrued nearly 25 percent of total single-employer funds. The twenty-five largest corporate funds had assets totaling $119.9 billion in 1980. AT&T Bell System held $31.1 billion, followed by General Motors ($14.1 billion), General Electric ($7.2 billion), Ford Motor ($6.4 billion), U.S. Steel and Carnegie ($5.5 billion), International Business Machines ($5.2 billion), Dupont ($4.9 billion), Exxon ($4.3 billion), General Telephone and Electronics ($3 billion), and Sears ($3 billion). Further, the Teachers' Insurance and Annuity Association/College Retirement Equity Fund (TIAA-CREF), one of the largest pension funds in the United States, controlled over $14 billion.[48]

One can envisage several alternative means for advancing institutional change through worker pension power. First, pension investments could be restricted to "socially desirable" programs and projects, as well as to firms that provide heightened employment opportunities, are unionized, and adhere to socially desirable guidelines developed by fund members. The authors of a report by the Conference on Alternative State and Local Policies provided myriad innovative investment possibilities for constructive social change. These include neighborhood revitalization; enhanced old age homes and retirement communities; development of community-controlled services such as health care and day care; expansion and rehabilitation of low- and moderate-income housing; employee purchase of factories facing shutdown; energy conservation and development of alternative energy sources; pollution control; college tuition loans for low- and moderate-income students; and the purchase of small as well as minority-owned businesses.[49] Although public pension funds could be made available for private development of desirable projects, they present an opportunity to establish community owned enterprises with profits accumulated publicly.

Second, workers could pressure corporations and financial institutions to move toward desirable social and economic goals by threatening to withdraw pension capital from current commitments. For example, Parker and Taylor suggest that "the investor should put short-term funds deposits in banks which agree to increase (by an agreed-upon amount) their mortgage activity in low-income areas, improve women and minority hiring, or expand lending to small and minority-owned businesses."[50] Furthermore, since massive withdrawals of funds from selected large-scale enterprises would depress stock values considerably, the threat of divestiture places enormous pressure on corporate boards to alter their policies and priorities.[51] Enhanced working conditions, unionization, and other employee goals could become the foci of such tactics.

Third, stock voting rights could be utilized to promote significant changes in corporate activities as well as to place employee representatives on corporate boards. The Corporate Data Exchange study discussed earlier notes that private and public retirement funds together account for 5 percent or more of the outstanding stock of over 50 percent of the ninety-nine "target" companies analyzed. The study points out, for instance, that "UAW-related funds have a major investment in Texas Instruments (TI), an antiunion company which the UAW has tried to organize without success. These holdings have not been utilized for gaining leverage over Texas Instruments. In fact, 55 union-related plans were identified as owning more than 8 percent of TI's common stock, a potentially powerful weapon in any union drive." The authors define a union-related plan as any pension system which is subject to collective bargaining, whether trusteed by employers alone or by unions and employers jointly. The Communication Workers of America (CWA), which collectively bargains for employees of telephone companies, has over $2 billion invested in predominantly nonunionized companies through sixteen telephone company plans. Its stock holdings provide potential leverage over a number of nonunionized companies, including Texas Instruments (holdings of 2.6 percent of the firm's common stock), K-Mart (2.8 percent), Halliburton (2.1 percent), McDonald's (1.9 percent), J. C. Penney (1.4 percent), Eastman Kodak (1.1 percent), and Sears (1.1 percent).[52] Moreover, *Pensions and Investments* reported in 1978 that state pension funds alone held over 5 percent of the stock of at least eighteen major companies.[53]

In the past, unions made only limited efforts to establish their own administration of pension funds, to encourage socially desirable investments, or to promote worker-oriented investment goals. In the mid-1940s, the CIO sought full participation with management in all administrative functions related to their pension funds. According to Dearing, "this claim included a full voice in selecting the method of financing the program as well as decisions with respect to investing the pension funds." [54] When John L. Lewis, President of the United Mine Workers, demanded a welfare and retirement fund during 1945–1946, he also proposed—but failed to secure—total union control over the assets of the fund. Similarly, in 1949 Walter Reuther, President of the United Auto Workers, sought joint union-employer control over pension plans. The eventual settlement provided for a joint board to oversee benefit structures, but the automobile companies controlled investment of the funds.[55] In the ensuing year, Reuther attempted, but failed, to influence the fund managers to invest in housing, day care, and other socially beneficial projects.[56]

H. Robert Bartell's study of pension investment patterns from 1959 to 1964 found some differences between funds trusteed exclusively by employers and those where unions had some influence. He noted that 42 percent of the company-controlled assets, as compared to 24 percent of multiemployer and union trusts, were in common stock. Mortgages and government bonds were more favored by the latter systems. A closer look, however, revealed that the divergent investment patterns were predominantly due to the activities of eight funds covering members of five unions. These include the Teamsters, International Ladies' Garment Workers, International Brotherhood of Electrical Workers, Amalgamated Clothing and Textile Workers, and the United Mine Workers.[57]

In general, unions have been concerned primarily with maximizing retirement benefits, easing restrictive qualifying provisions, and ensuring that the sponsoring companies are financially capable of fulfilling pension obligations when they come due, rather than with influencing investment decisions. However, workers, political leaders, and community activists have become increasingly aware of the adverse social, economic, and political impacts of current uses of pension funds, as well as their potential for moving the economy in new directions. Partly in response to the attention paid to questionable pension fund investment practices, by Rifkin and Barber in *The North Will Rise Again*, (above, n. 34), an increasing number of public leaders and labor unions have begun seriously to consider alternative investment opportunities for retirement trust assets.

Organized labor, for one, has been reevaluating its generally neutral position on investments.[58] At the end of 1977, the AFL-CIO convention evidenced a strong interest in pension assets and investment practices by adopting a key convention resolution proposing that

> union funds be entrusted to financial institutions whose investment policies are not inimical to the welfare of working people, and that a portion of union funds be invested in national programs that meet public needs and provide construction jobs, such as houses, schools, hospitals, factories and stores.

A general review of investment portfolios for antiunion practices was urged.[59] More recently, the AFL-CIO executive council, at its August 1980 meeting, addressed several specific issues related to union participation in the management of collectively bargained pension funds. The executive council set broad policy investment goals for these trusts; urged the establishment of an antiunion investment file, consisting of firms whose policies adversely affect labor; encouraged fund trustees to exercise stockholder voting rights to promote worker and community interests; and endorsed union representation on pension fund boards. It also recommended that Congress establish an independent institution to manage collectively bargained retirement funds, with a board of directors comprised of union, employer, and consumer representatives.[60]

Throughout the country there has been a new and growing recognition by individual unions of pension funds as a significant political and economic tool. In November 1977, William Winpsinger, President of the International Association of Machinists, proposed that his union's retirement assets (over $80 million) be withdrawn from their present managers, Manufacturers Hanover Trust, since James D. Finley, board chairman of J. P. Stevens, is a member of the bank's board of directors.[61] As is well known, J. P. Stevens and organized labor have been at odds over a number of critical issues, including unionization itself. Encouraged by Ray Rogers, director of the Amalgamated Clothing and Textile Workers' corporate campaign, other unions with trusts managed by Manufacturers Hanover also protested Finley's presence on the board and threatened to withdraw their funds. By March 1978, Finley had been forced to resign from Manufacturers Hanover. A second Stevens director, David W. Mitchell, President of Avon Products, was similarly pressured into leaving his positions as director of both Manufacturers Hanover and J. P. Stevens. The Amalgamated Clothing and Textile Workers also drew attention to other institutional investors having ties to J. P. Stevens, including New York Life Insurance (which manages about $1.3 billion in pension assets). The union was unsuccessful, however, in its attempt to oust Finley from the board of Sperry Corporation in 1980. In addition, the Retail Clerks International Union (RCIU) has urged labor organizations to withdraw pension funds from the Seattle First National Bank, since the bank refuses to bargain with the Financial Institution Employees of America. Since this campaign began in May 1979, over fifty of the two hundred unions with funds in the bank have withdrawn them.

Demonstrating a new interest in the potential power of pension trusts for workers, Lloyd McBride, president of the Steelworkers Union, indicated at the union's 1978 annual convention that control over benefit-fund investments would become a critical issue during collective bargaining with the steel industry in the near future. Furthermore, in 1978 the construction industry pension funds contributed a share of their total assets (about $5 million) to a Union Labor Life Insurance Company that can invest only in construction projects using union labor.[62] The National Union of Hospital and Health Care Employes pension fund, in the same year, resolved that a portion of its $236 million assets be utilized to support socially useful programs.[63] Similarly, the Plumbing, Heating and Piping Industry of Southern California benefit fund, the largest plumbing pension fund, with assets over $181 million, decided to remove its money from the stock market entirely and redirect fund assets into new construction projects, in order to enhance employment opportunities for its members.[64] The United Auto Workers urged the managers of its pension funds not to agree to United Technologies' tender offer for Carrier Corporation stock, due to United Technologies' antilabor record. The union also successfully bargained with Chrysler Corporation for the right to invest up to 10 percent of all new pension money in worker housing, health care facilities, day care centers, and affordable retirement villages.

In 1980, the International Chemical Workers Union (ICWU) voted to withdraw its staff pension funds from the current manager, an insurance company. According to ICWU president Frank D. Martino, the insurance company "refused to agree to our demand for assurances that the monies would not be invested against our own or other workers' interests."[65] The union intends to manage its staff pension fund in house. The new periodical *Labor and Investments* notes, "The ICWU move with its staff pension fund is part of a broader strategy by the union to gain a stronger voice in the management of its members' pension funds."[66] A social investment position was also taken that year by local 675 of the International Union of Operating Engineers. The Fort Lauderdale-based local intends to offer home mortgages to its members, and invest its funds in stocks of south Florida construction firms that hire only union labor. Paul M. Whalen, research director for the local, argued, "the fatuous dichotomy, established by labor law in this country, which separates the interests of workers as workers from the interests of workers as plan participants is an impediment to real economic progress."[67] A number of other unions have either begun—or are discussing alternative possibilities for—using pension funds to benefit workers and their communities.

Attempts to invest pension trust assets to achieve social goals have also been made by a number of public systems. State and local pension funds have become increasingly explicit about making social criteria part of their investment decision-making process. Although most public sector efforts aimed at encouraging social investing and promoting employee interests are only in preliminary stages—and many of these activities have not been immediately successful—they are indicative of potential pension power in the near future.

Since the late 1970s a number of states and localities have begun to consider new investment options based on socially responsible criteria. For instance, the Massachusetts Social and Economic

Council has assessed the feasibility of investing some of its $1.4 billion state employee and teachers' funds in ways intended to promote economic growth in the commonwealth. Similarly, the state treasurer of Rhode Island has indicated that a portion of the Rhode Island retirement funds will be made available for middle-income housing mortgages exclusively within the state. In 1980, the Kansas Public Employes Retirement System expanded its policy of investing locally. Furthermore, the Wisconsin Center for Public Policy has been studying potential investment alternatives, based on social criteria, for the state's $5 billion in pension money without increasing risk or lowering yield.

Political leaders held a public hearing in Hartford, Connecticut, at the end of 1978 to consider the issue of socially responsible investment of its pension assets. Questions were raised about investments in corporations that violate the National Labor Relations Act, thwart affirmative action programs, and pollute the environment. By 1980, the managers of the $105 million city fund were "instructed to submit to the treasurer all proxy solicitations that have socially related issues for voting at annual meetings."[68] Furthermore, Lee Van Meter, deputy treasurer in charge of investments for the state's retirement funds ($1.4 billion), indicated that he intends to address such social responsibility questions, as well. He also noted, "Maybe we'll get to the point where we'll say social responsibility is as important as expected investment returns."[69]

In the spring of 1979, legislation was introduced in the Illinois state legislature which, if enacted, would have required the pension board to consider social dividends as well as profitability in making investment decisions; to provide venture capital, including loans for family farms and small businesses; and to construct quasi-public and senior citizen housing. Similar bills were proposed again during the 1981 legislative session. Moreover, the governor has established the Illinois Study Commission on Public Pension Investment Policies to assess whether the state's pension funds should be used for internal economic development. The group is expected to complete its report in January 1982.[70] The state (and city of Chicago) is under pressure from a Chicago-based public interest group, Trust, Inc., to move toward socially responsible investments. The group already has established guidelines for the $2 billion Chicago pension funds. It recommended that retirement trust boards deposit their assets in banks demonstrating a commitment to neighborhood revitalization; invest in companies operating in Chicago; and support small businesses in the city.[71] City officials have indicated they will seek state approval for investing a portion of the funds' assets in low-interest home mortgages. Retirement trust boards would also have to agree to such investments.

The California legislature recently considered a bill that attempted to establish "minimum social responsibility criteria" and to encourage pension fund trustees to vote proxies on social issues. Both the California Public Employes Retirement System (PERS) and the California State Teachers' Retirement System (STRS) already "follow an ethical tenet regarding their investments."[72] In 1980, state legislation was enacted allowing PERS to establish a home mortgage program for plan participants. Further, the California Governor's Public Investment Task Force recommended at the end of 1981 that public funds in California invest in areas that benefit the state, seek out investment opportunities in small businesses and new technology, and adopt specific guidelines for social investing. Nathan Gardels, executive secretary of the task force, indicated that "the task force will recommend that pension funds seek positions on boards of directors of companies in which they hold large blocks of stock."[73] With over $18 billion in assets, the California Retirement System is one of the largest pension investors in the United States.

In New York, public sector unions have successfully proposed the creation of a stock proxy voting committee for the state's retirement funds which, in 1980, amounted to $13 billion. Chaired by the president of New York's fire fighters' union, the committee has utilized its pension-owned stocks—if only symbolically—to promote worker and community interests. For example, it voted against management in 50 percent of the 204 corporate resolutions the committee considered during 1980. It also used its 500,000 pension fund equity shares in Sperry Rand to vote against the candidacy of James Finley for a seat on the company's board of directors. Holding one percent of Halliburton's outstanding corporate equities, the stock proxy committee voted against that firm's entire management-supported board because of its poor labor record. Public sector employees are also pressuring New York State legislators to establish a board of trustees (with representation for unions) to manage the state's benefit funds. Currently, the pension trusts are controlled by New York State's comptroller.[74]

There are indications that plan participants themselves are vitally interested in all aspects of their retirement trusts, including investment practices. A 1979 Harris poll, *American Attitudes Toward Pensions and Retirement,* disclosed that most workers would highly value receiving information on the financial status of their plans, where funds are invested, and who is managing the trusts. The survey also asked employees covered under private pension plans whether they believed "that pension funds should not be invested in companies or countries with socially undesirable policies, or funds should be invested wherever they bring the largest return." Forty-seven percent of the respondents opposed investments in firms whose activities are counter to the public interest, while 41 percent opted for the largest return. Eighty-four percent of the former respondents continued to favor socially responsible investing even if it meant lower investment returns and thus lower pension benefits.[75]

A study of 400 participants in the Wisconsin public retirement system, jointly financed through the Wisconsin State Employees Union and the American Federation of State, County, and Municipal Employees, found that two-thirds of the respondents were concerned with how fund investments affected both their jobs and unions in general, as well as other public policy issues. The study concluded that, "by sizable margins, the employees want to be involved in the investment policy particularly from the standpoint of social and economic matters."[76]

WORKER UNITY: NEW ISSUES

Threats of higher employee pension burdens and lower retirement income, severe pressures to limit wage increases and lower available public services, and rampant inflation all combine to undermine the stake of state and local workers in the current economic system. These factors provide incentives for the growth of militant public sector organizations and unions. Organized labor may have achieved extensive pension coverage for workers, yet not only do workers and their dependents receive inadequate supplementary retirement income, but also they do not appear to be the primary beneficiaries of the trusts. Current private and public pension investment practices which adversely affect basic community and worker interests and state and local economies provide an opportunity for developing a progressive consciousness among public and private sector employees as well as for forging a coalition between them.

Both share substantial mutual concerns with regard to current and alternative uses of pension power. Increasing the capital available for social needs and economic growth in depressed areas will enhance everyone's communities, all workers, and the poor. Funds targeted for union labor and diverted from runaway firms,[77] pressures on corporations for social responsibility, and community ownership and control of productive activities will benefit the vast majority of citizens.

Private, state, and local trusts together accounted for $653 billion and held from 20 to 25 percent of total equities in the United States at the end of 1980. They pose a potentially formidable challenge to monopoly capitalism and existing institutional arrangements. Ray Rogers, of the Amalgamated Clothing and Textile Workers' Corporate Campaign, cogently concludes his assessment of pension systems by remarking:

> Once organized labor begins to use its own vast economic and political power and begins to understand how to pit one part of Corporate America against another part, the way it has pitted the workers against themselves and the poor—there is going to be a social, political and economic revolution in this country.[78]

To further worker and community goals, employees will have to seek control over their retirement trusts, regain participation in decision making concerning those funds that have been turned over to banks and other investment managers, and urge Congress to liberalize selective investment restrictions incorporated in ERISA. New awareness of pension trust potentials by unions and public leaders encourage them to seek alternative uses of pension assets in the interests of workers and the communities in which they reside.

Chapter 5

The Graying of the Medical-Industrial Complex

The American health care system has been shaped predominantly by economic and political interests whose primary goals were (and are) to increase profits, enhance the status and income of medical professionals, and conform health care to the needs of capital. As documented by E. Richard Brown, corporate leaders, through "philanthropic" foundations, initially funded and consequently were a leading force in the development and direction of medical education, research, and practice from the early 1900s to World War II.[1] Although the state began to assume a significant portion of financial support for medical education, biomedical research, and hospital construction by the mid-1940s and later for categorical health care programs aimed at the elderly, disabled, and indigent, it did so within the narrow parameters of health care established by the foundations, hospitals, doctors, and other special interests benefiting from the privately controlled medical network.

THE RISE OF THE PRIVATELY CONTROLLED MEDICAL MARKET

The Ascent of the American Medical Association

Before the turn of the century medicine "was pluralistic in its theories of disease, technically ineffective in preventing or curing sickness, and divided into several warring sects."[2] Lacking public support for its methods, and facing intense competition from an expanding output of medical school graduates, differing medical perspectives, and lay health providers, physicians had relatively low incomes, status, and power. Similar to the emerging large corporations, which turned to and received state support for stabilizing markets and competition, and increasing profits, the American Medical Association (AMA) achieved monopoly status over physician care by the 1930s. The strengthening of the AMA in 1901 and its successful "reform" strategy, aided through foundations emphasizing scientific and technological medicine, placed state licensing of doctors, medical education, physician output, and drug utilization firmly under the control of organized medicine. Consequently, physicians were able to elevate their status, reduce their number, deny the legitimacy of paramedical and other health care providers, and increase their incomes considerably. With the growth of medical specialization and physician researchers the number of primary care doctors steadily decreased.

Having secured control over medical care, the AMA fought adamantly and successfully against any governmental controls, funding, or intervention. Attempts by "reformist" groups such as the American Association for Labor Legislation to institute compulsory medical insurance in the states were defeated by the medical lobby, which had initially supported the measures. After preventing potential inclusion of health care provisions in the Social Security legislation in 1935, the AMA continued its successful battle against national health insurance proposals throughout the 1930s and 1940s. Moreover, as a result of its eventual support for Blue Cross and commercial hospital insurance, and its direct sponsorship of Blue Shield Plans for physician services, the AMA and its affiliate state medical societies were able to increase revenues for doctors while simultaneously deflecting popular support for governmental intervention in their monopoly. Between 1953 and 1963 alone physician fees rose by 37 percent and by 1964 the median income of doctors grew to over $34,000 annually.[3]

The Expansion of Power: Hospitals, Blue Cross, and the Medical Commodities Market

The high costs of capital intensive medicine fostered the growth and expansion of hospitals and hospital-based medical care. In turn, hospitals required massive outside economic support for their rising capital needs, a problem that became increasingly acute with reduced patient revenues during the depression. Consequently, as Davis and others point out, Blue Cross hospital insurance was initiated by and designed to serve the hospital industry, which became the recipients of "an assured source of revenue."[4] Since these plans provided income on a cost-plus basis, hospitals were able to expand their facilities, purchase expensive medical equipment, and increase administrative salaries. Funds made available by the state further enhanced the position of the hospital industry.

Consumers were confronted with rapidly increasing hospital costs which were particularly devastating for the elderly, who tended to lack hospital insurance coverage. Between 1953 and 1963 the cost of a hospital bed increased by 90 percent.[5] Hospital revenues, which were $3.8 billion in 1950, rose to $13.8 billion annually by 1965.[6] Not only did the income and power of hospitals increase dramatically, which led to their further expansion and growth, but also physicans soon became dependent on hospital-based facilities and equipment for patient care. At the same time, the medical supply industry and other private interests associated with the growing medical-industrial complex profited enormously.

Organized Labor and the Expansion of Private Health Insurance

During the period of rapid industrialization, employers were concerned with increased productivity rather than with the health of their employees. Hazardous and unhealthy working and living environments contributed to the prevalence of illness, accidents, and early death among industrial workers. In a few large corporations, employer-sponsored medical care emerged, along with pension plans, to enhance labor productivity and to reduce the appeal of unionism. By 1930 over a million workers were covered by employer health plans in railroads, mining, and lumbering.[7] Many union leaders, who were concerned with retaining and expanding union membership, initiated their own health and welfare systems. They tended to oppose both company-controlled medical plans (on the grounds that they tied labor to the corporation and curtailed the growth of unions) and governmental health insurance proposals. The AFL in particular argued that the latter efforts would decrease worker dependency on unions, reduce salaries and "divert workers from the 'real goal' of higher wages and shorter hours."[8]

After the depression, and the collapse of union health and welfare systems, unions strongly began to support national health insurance. However, due to the vigorous opposition of the AMA and other medical interests they were unable to secure its passage. When welfare and health issues became subjects of collective bargaining, and since national health insurance appeared to be an increasingly unlikely alternative, unions fought for and won diverse packages of private health care insurance during the 1940s and 1950s. As a result, the hospital-supported health insurance industry expanded rapidly. By the early 1960s, the American Hospital Association, the National Blue Cross, and the health commodities and equipment industries had become dominant forces in and beneficiaries of health care practices in the United States.

The State, Capital, and the Growth of Technological Medicine

The eventual triumph of scientific and technological medicine in the early twentieth century was funded by and served the needs of the capitalist class. Supported primarily by the corporation-controlled foundations until World War II, and since that time by the state, biomedical research, along with its scientific and reductionist health care practice, helped to "legitimize capitalism by diverting attention from structural and other environmental causes of disease."[9]

Though the federal government emerged as a major source of economic support for health-related costs in the mid-1940s, "from about 1946 to 1963 . . . the major thrust of federal involvement in health was not the provision or subsidy of services but the less direct function of long-term investment in hospital construction, biomedical research and funding of health manpower programs." Medical research outlays for the National Institute of Health alone rose steadily from $2.5 million annually in 1945 to $1.6 billion per year by 1968.[10] Government funds, which were funneled primarily to medical school researchers, were utilized to expand scientific and technological medicine. With an almost exclusive focus on "the disease process *within* the body," research and its utilization continued to flagrantly disregard economic deprivation, inequalities of wealth and income, unhealthy occupational environments, and industrial pollution as major causes of ill health in society.[11] By 1965, medical schools had become highly scientific research institutions which, in turn, affected the education and training of physicians themselves. Moreover, the American Association of Medical

Colleges took its place as a leading force within the medical-industrial complex.

With the passage of the Hill-Burton Act, the federal government also began to subsidize hospital construction and growth, initially in rural areas, and later in some urban communities as well. Between 1946 and 1968 the hospital industry received nearly $3.2 billion through the program. By 1966, Hill-Burton funds accounted for 10 percent of total capital available to hospitals.[12] In addition, the state expanded its massive and well-developed health programs for the armed services and veterans, including the growth of costly government-supported veterans' hospitals.

Welfare Medicine and the Aged

Until 1950, the federal government avoided any responsibility for the direct health service needs of the population. Care for the indigent fell to state and local governments, which supported overcrowded and understaffed public hospitals in some areas or reimbursed proprietary institutions and doctors, usually at a fee well below actual costs. The poor generally received inadequate levels of health care. Although the 1950 Social Security amendment introduced federal involvement in health services by providing funds to the states for public assistance recipients, the two-class system of medical care was not affected. Moreover, not only were federal grants-in-aid limited to vendor payments on behalf of the indigent population exclusively, but also ten states did not even take advantage of the program, the funds available and services covered were severely limited, and benefits varied widely among the states and localities.

For the unemployed, most nonunionized competitive sector workers, and the elderly, health care insurance was either unavailable, costly, or vastly inadequate. Moreover, upon retirement even workers and their families who had been covered through the work place often found themselves cut off from their former group health insurance policies, as did spouses of employees who died prior to retirement. Other plans, while allowing continued coverage for retirees, offered reduced benefits at higher premium costs, which were usually borne by the individual. In the main, the aged who were no longer contributing to the productive order were unable to obtain or afford insurance, had to pay relatively expensive premium rates when policies were available, and were burdened with the major portion of their health care costs.

In 1962, for example, 62 percent of retired workers were without any form of health insurance and those with coverage were reimbursed for only about 7 percent of their total health care bills.[13] Those older people who were not eligible for the restrictive needs-tested state public assistance programs faced rising costs that "were pricing vital health services out of reach."[14] During a prolonged illness any savings which had been accrued during the working years were rapidly depleted. Consequently, a large percentage of the aged population continued to be or became newly dependent on demeaning and inadequate publicly supported or charity services, while others were forced to forgo health care entirely.

By the 1950s the crisis in medical care for older people, which was widely acknowledged, had become a focus of political attention and controversy. However, the passage of the Kerr-Mills legislation in 1960 was primarily an attempt by the powerful health groups to defuse efforts for more comprehensive old age national health insurance. Although Kerr-Mills established a new category of "medically needy" aged through its Medical Assistance to the Aged (MAA) program, the act merely expanded the existing and inadequate welfare medical system of vendor payments and shifted more of the medical costs for the poor from states, localities, hospitals, and doctors to the federal government.[15] It retained the means-tested stigmatized approach of welfare medicine and failed to provide for uniform national standards or requirements. It also continued to force dependency; in order to receive any benefits under MAA, older people were required to spend their own limited assets until they reached the low eligibility levels set by the states. Moreover, the bulk of the Kerr-Mills program was concentrated in only a few states and nearly all of the outlays accrued to (and enriched) hospitals and nursing homes.[16]

Even before the act was fully implemented it became clear that support for compulsory wage-supported old age health insurance had not abated. The potentially mounting costs of the Kerr-Mills program, which the states and national government were unwilling to fund indefinitely, the act's apparent inadequacies, and its welfare orientation encouraged new proposals for Social Security based health insurance for the elderly.

MEDICARE AND MEDICAID

The emergence, between 1957 and 1965, of national health insurance proposals restricted to the needs of aged recipients of Social Security, and the eventual passage of Medicare and Medicaid in the latter year, represented the failure of the state to support even a modest health care program for the general population. The debate surrounding Medicare itself, and the final compromise legislation also exemplified the limited parameters of and approaches to health care that had been defined and developed by medical and corporate interests. Aiming exclusively to remove some financial barriers to health services for the aged and indigent populations, Medicare and Medicaid were superimposed on the existing ineffective and unresponsive privately controlled medical care market. The programs, among other things: (a) emphasized technological and hospital-based medical services rather than prevention, rehabilitation, or home-health care; (b) fostered even greater inflation in health costs without increasing appreciably the quality of or access to care; (c) encouraged the exploitation of illness for profit thereby enhancing the prestige, power, and profit of providers; (d) failed to alter the inequitable distribution and allocation of health services and facilities among income and social classes as well as among geographic areas; (e) avoided full governmental responsibility for the health needs of older people; (f) promoted increased institutionalization of the elderly; and (g) focused on medical services, thus deflecting attention from social and environmental causes of disease and ill health in society.

General Characteristics

Medicare is a two-part program consisting of compulsory hospital insurance (HI) or part A, and supplementary medical insurance (SMI) or part B. HI provides basic hospitalization benefits and limited nursing home care, while SMI includes physician services, some home health visits, office drugs and supplies, emergency-room treatment, and ambulance service. However, as will be discussed later, many essential medical needs are not covered. Individuals sixty-five and over who are covered under Social Security are automatically eligible for HI benefits, and since 1972, others meeting the age requirement can purchase the insurance, which was $89 per month or $1,068 annually in 1981. SMI, on the other hand, is an entirely voluntary program, although most elderly participate in it.

For the elderly, Medicaid is largely supplementary to the Medicare program. In 1981 individuals sixty-five and over comprised 15 percent of Medicaid beneficiaries (2.5 million persons) and received about one-third of its benefits, largely for nursing home care. With restrictive eligibility standards which are set by each participating state, Medicaid serves the indigent, and in thirty-four states the "medically needy" population. Although the range of health services offered, eligibility requirements, limits imposed on such services, and reimbursement policies vary considerably among state programs, the federal government provides from 50 to 83 percent of the costs through a variable matching formula that is related to a state's per capita income.

Allocation of the Medicare and Medicaid Pie: The Health Service Profiteers

Health expenditures are currently a large and growing sector of the American economy. Total outlays for health-related activities have risen dramatically over the last several decades, reaching $247 billion by 1980 (9.4 percent of GNP) as compared to $42 billion in 1965 (6.1 percent of GNP). In the latter year, approximately 25 percent of these costs were publicly funded. By 1980 the government was administering funds for health-related expenses totaling a staggering $104 billion or about 42 percent of total health outlays in the country.[17]

Personal health care costs have grown from $37 billion in 1965 to $169 billion in 1978 to $218 billion in 1980, with older people accounting for one-third of the total. Federal outlays for older people's personal health care costs under Medicare and Medicaid in 1980 were estimated at $30 billion and $4.8 billion, and together with other national, state, and local programs represented nearly 65 percent of their personal health service bill. (These figures, however, do not take into account amounts paid directly by the elderly for cost-sharing provisions under Medicare.) In 1980, total federal, state, and local expenditures for all persons under Medicare and Medicaid were $35.8 billion and $24.8 billion, respectively. Nearly 40 percent of all public spending on personal health care, and 60 percent of federal outlays for health services, are devoted to the aged, primarily through the Medicare and Medicaid programs.[18]

Since the enactment of Medicare and Medicaid, costs have risen rapidly. Expenditures for Medicare's HI program rose 500 percent and for SMI, 633 percent between 1967 and 1979, increasing from $3.4 billion to $20.6 billion, and from $1.2 billion to $8.8 billion, respectively.[19] Although a greater number of older people eligible for and enrolling in the programs and higher utilization rates can account for part of the growing costs, the vast proportion of the rise in this period can be traced to inflation in the price of hospital care and in fees for physicians and other outpatient services.[20] For example, between 1979 and 1980, inflation accounted for 60 percent of the increase in health and medical care expenses in the nation. Outlays for the Medicare and Medicaid programs are expected to increase by $8.7 billion between 1981 and 1982, largely as a result of higher medical care prices.[21]

As shown earlier, even prior to the passage of Medicare and Medicaid the cost of health services was increasing steadily and the medical marketplace was firmly controlled by health service providers. By infusing billions of dollars into new programs for the aged and indigent populations without reforming radically the structure of the medical and health insurance industries, the state assured cost unaccountability, rampant inflation, high salaries, and excessive profits. In fact, the principal beneficiaries of Medicare and Medicaid have been hospitals, physicians, insurance companies, nursing homes, and the medical supply and equipment firms.

Until 1965 a substantial number of hospitals were forced to provide charity care for some patients, particularly in emergencies. When public welfare departments provided vendor payments for the indigent, hospitals had received only from one-third to one-half of their customary charges. Under Medicare, on the other hand, hospitals were guaranteed the full costs of care for older people who had previously accounted for a substantial percentage of charity and public assistance patients.[22] With the influx of medicare beneficiaries hospital revenues increased considerably. Moreover, reimbursement to hospitals for patient care, which continued existing private health insurance practices, was based on "reasonable costs," including liberal equipment depreciation allowances, capital investments, and interest. Assessment of reasonable costs was left in the hands of insurance companies, which in turn were chosen and controlled by the hospitals themselves. The state merely funnels funds to these fiscal intermediaries, of which 90 percent are Blue Cross associations, who are then responsible for negotiating costs, auditing the institutions, and paying the bills.[23]

As noted by Brown, "while private health insurance provided a stable cash flow on which hospitals could depend and expand, Medicare and Medicaid seemed a limitless largess."[24] By 1979 nearly one-fourth ($21.7 billion) of total hospital care payments in the country were derived from Medicare alone.[25] Moreover, Medicare provided greater financial stability for hospitals, thus enabling them to borrow increasingly from banks and other lending institutions. Since 70 percent of hospitals are nonprofit, both growing revenues and access to outside capital provided ever-increasing funds for larger administrative salaries and, even more important, for acquisitions of overly elaborate and expensive technical equipment. In turn, these changes contributed substantially to higher costs for all patients, including those covered under Medicare. Thus a vicious cycle was created—hospital costs and reimbursements under Medicare grew simultaneously, leading to further investment opportunities and even greater inflation in costs. As Brown further observes:

> Capital investment per hospital bed rose three times as fast in the five years after Medicare and Medicaid began as it did in the five years before, reaching $56,000 per bed in 1976. . . . Hospitals felt assured that everything from automated blood-chemistry analysis machines (costing upwards of $100,000) to computerized axial tomography (CAT) scanners (costing $300,000 to $750,000) could be paid for. Expansion has resulted in as many as 100,000 excess hospital beds in the country, averaging about $20,000 per bed in annual operating costs.[26]

Between 1970 and 1979 the nation's hospital bed supply increased from 833,264 to 1,372,000 while the average occupancy rate in the nation remained at about 76 percent.[27]

In the first year of Medicare alone, increases in hospital prices more than doubled that of past annual rates. From 1970 to 1980 hospital costs grew 2½ times as fast as the consumer price index

(CPI).[28] In 1965 the average daily hospital cost per patient was $40; by 1981 it reached $196.

Moreover, the development of costly "high technology" hospital medical care has only limited benefits for patients in some medical areas. In others it has been shown to be not only ineffective but, at times, harmful. As noted by a 1975 HEW report, "technological advances are often introduced into hospital operations as soon as they are available, in some cases before there has been sufficient evidence of their efficiency or effectiveness."[29] Robert Clark also points out that some technical procedures, such as intensive care units for certain types of illnesses, may be unnessary since studies show that similarly situated patients receiving regular hospital care or even home health services have equivalent rates of recovery.[30]

While hospitals are reimbursed for "reasonable costs," physicians receive renumerations based on "reasonable charges," as determined by the physician-controlled carriers, usually Blue Shield associations. That is, doctors receive their "usual and customary" fees as long as these are not above the level prevailing in a given geographic area for the types of service provided. Accordingly, immediately after the passage of Medicare, physicians raised their usual and customary fees by 7.8 percent, an increase which was slightly over two times that of the previous year and more than double the 3.3 percent rise in the CPI.[31] By altering neither the fee-for-service system nor monopoly control by physicians over both the supply of doctors and demand for their services, Medicare encouraged profiteering by physicians. The rampant inflation in services since 1965, although less than hospital cost increases, has enhanced the income of doctors considerably, making them the highest paid professionals in the United States. Physicians' annual net income from private practice grew to $41,800 in 1970 to $78,400 in 1979.[32] In 1979 16 percent of all outlays for physicians' services in the country (or $6.4 billion) was derived from the Medicare program.[33] Medicaid and Medicare have been particularly lucrative for hospital-based physicians such as anesthesiologists, radiologists, and pathologists.

In addition, congressional investigations have revealed considerable corruption by physicians under Medicare and Medicaid. For instance, a 1976 report shows that about 10 percent of all Medicare money accrues to health care providers, particularly doctors, for services not rendered. Other abuses disclosed included unnecessary and inadequate medical care as well as kickbacks between providers.[34]

The hospital supply and equipment industries, as well as pharmaceutical companies, have also reaped enormous profits from health care legislation for the aged. Writing in 1970, Barbara and John Ehenreich reported that the earnings of traditional hospital supply companies grew by 15 to 25 percent annually after Medicare was enacted. The newer supply companies and the medical electronics industry also emerged as major beneficiaries of Medicare dollars.[35] Moreover, by 1974 nearly 10 percent of all drug sales in the nation were purchased with government funds, primarily for use in hospitals and nursing homes.[36] Currently the elderly consume over $2.8 billion worth of prescription drugs each year, which represents one-fourth of total out-of-hospital drug costs in the country. Robert Butler, for one, has suggested that older people have been encouraged to purchase drugs too readily, with serious and even fatal disorders as a result.[37] Aggressive promotional efforts by drug companies, usually aimed at doctors, have added considerably to the heavy drug usage among the elderly.

The nursing home industry, which consists of about 75 percent proprietary old age institutions (OAIs), has capitalized on public programs enacted to meet the long-term care needs of older people. However, as observed by Bruce Vladick, in *Unloving Care: The Nursing Home Tragedy*, "The people who built nursing homes were very different from those who built hospitals and responded very differently to equivalent incentives. Hospitals took the generosity of reimbursement formulas to construct opulent workshops in which physicians could employ the most esoteric scientific technologies; nursing homes took the money and ran."[38]

Until the 1940s most of the institutionalized (and indigent) elderly had been placed in almshouses or other severely inadequate public facilities, including mental institutions. After the passage of the Social Security Act and its Old-Age Assistance Program, which until 1950 prohibited any payment of benefits to older people residing in public facilities, proprietary OAIs began to replace government institutions. During the 1950s and 1960s, the national government provided easily obtainable capital for profit-making OAIs through government loans and guaranteed mortgage insurance programs. The most important one were administered through the Small Business Administration and Federal Housing Administration (FHA), commencing in 1956 and 1959, respectively. Approximately 10 percent of all nursing home beds in the country have been built with FHA loans. According to Vladick, not only did these policies encourage a rapid proliferation of for-profit OAIs but they also led to the entrance of real estate speculators and banking institutions into the nursing home business. Since these interests were concerned primarily with financial gain they contributed to deteriorating conditions within nursing homes. Vendor payment programs, which increased substantially after the passage of the Kerr-Mills legislation in 1960, were also instrumental in encouraging exploitation of institutionalized older people at public expense.[39]

However, prior to 1965, profit-making OAIs still depended primarily on private patient revenues. Furthermore, vendor payments on behalf of public assistance recipients were below actual costs. With the enactment of Medicaid a substantial number of states switched to reimbursing profit-making OAIs on a "reasonable cost" basis, although some states continued the flat rate method prevalent under earlier programs. In order to enhance profits, private patients were often charged higher fees than those allowed under state Medicaid programs and they, in effect, subsidized institutionalized older people receiving public assistance. In 1972 the national government required all states to adopt some form of reasonable cost reimbursement formula, although they were not required to do so until 1978. Despite resistence and delays, all of the states were in compliance by 1980. In that year, new legislation was enacted that gave the states greater control over the methods and standards on which rates of reimbursement are based. However, the national government retained final authority to review such rates.[40] Medicare, which covers only about 4 percent of the institutionalized elderly, and 2 percent of their total nursing home expenses, also provides for cost-plus reimbursement. Allowable charges under these programs have included depreciation, rent or mortgage payments, interest, taxes, and insurance.

The new sources and methods of public funding under Medicare and Medicaid prompted cost inflation and increased profits as well as the growth, expansion and concentration of the nursing home industry. Public funding rose from $1.4 billion in 1966 to approximately $10.1 billion by 1979, with Medicaid and Medicare together contributing 52 percent of the total nursing home bill in the United

States. Nearly all of the funds are from Medicaid alone, which accounted for $8.8 billion. Fully 40 percent of total Medicaid outlays in 1980 flowed into the coffers of the nursing home industry.[41] OAI revenues, which increased by 3,000 percent between 1960 and 1979, grew from $500 million to $15 billion during this period. Nursing home costs, which currently are increasing at an average annual rate of 16 percent, are the fastest growing category of health care expenses.[42]

Between 1963 and 1973 the number of beds grew by over 100 percent and by 1981 over one million older people resided in OAIs. Many nursing homes were even established with Medicaid funds. Old age institutions have also shifted from small entrepreneurial businesses to major corporate enterprises. By 1972 approximately 106 corporations owned one-fifth of all nursing homes and accounted for nearly one-third of the profits.[43] About one-third are owned or controlled by chains and this number is increasing.[44]

Although only 5 percent of the elderly reside in OAIs at any one time, nearly 20 percent will spend some time in an institution. Consisting primarily of poor, widowed women, the percentage of the aged who are institutionalized increases with advanced age. Over 80 percent of the nursing home residents are age seventy-five and over, and more than 40 percent are over age eighty-five. Consequently, OAI residents are a relatively vulnerable group.

Rising public spending for and enrichment of the nursing home industry have not resulted in commensurate gains for the elderly. Spiraling costs have contributed substantially to the impoverishment and dependency of the institutionalized population. Private pay patients, who comprise one-third of OAI residents, account for nearly one-half of total revenues. By 1980 the average fee for private patients reached over $17,000 annually. The Medicaid skilled nursing rate in that year, which averaged $13,231, ranged from $5,840 to $20,075.[45] These costs are substantially greater than retirement income for the vast majority of older people. Moreover, most private patients are forced to exhaust their limited savings on OAI care until they meet qualifications for public assistance.

The care of institutionalized older people for profit, coupled with cost-plus reimbursement formulas to fund the indigent, have encouraged pervasive and acknowledged exploitive practices by nursing home operators ranging from financial to patient abuses.[46] A four-state investigation of nursing homes participating in Medicaid found, for example, that excessive salaries, travel by administrators, high rents from property transfers among related individuals, and other illegal costs unrelated to patient care were incorporated into bills for Medicaid reimbursement.[47] In 1977 the Senate Special Committee on Aging uncovered, among other things, widespread pressure by nursing home owners for kickbacks from their suppliers, particularly pharmaceutical companies. Nearly one-half of the institutions in New York alone required kickbacks as a condition of continued business relationships with suppliers.[48] Subsequent hearings disclosed cost-cutting efforts at the expense of patient care. A four-month probe of the nursing home industry in Illinois prompted one witness to testify: "The instances of abuse and neglect we found in nursing homes are so fundamental and so widespread that one is compelled to question whether nursing homes themselves are capable of providing good care."[49]

Similarly, a 1977 AFL-CIO investigation of 128 nursing homes in 120 communities discovered haphazard and fragmented enforcement of safety codes resulting in serious and life threatening conditions, deaths and injury due to negligence, unsanitary conditions, poor food, and other abuses directly related to the profit motive. The AFL-CIO report also noted that the prevalence of overworked, underpaid, and inadequately trained nonsupervisory personnel, who constitute the bulk of OAI staff, enhance profits while contributing to low quality care of the aged, and exploitation of nursing home employees.[50] Furthermore, "gang visits" by physicians benefit the medical profession at the expense of the institutionalized elderly.

The primary congressional reaction to financial abuses by providers (including those involving nursing home operators, physicians, pharmaceutical firms, supply companies, and the like) was the Medicare-Medicaid Anti-Fraud and Abuses Amendments of 1977. Under the legislation, any state establishing or operating a fraud control office recovers 90 percent of its cost from the federal government. By 1980, thirty states had set up fraud control offices, and it is expected that eleven more states will do so within the next three years.[51]

The Omnibus Reconciliation Act of 1980 further attempted to strengthen controls against provider abuses in the Medicare and Medicaid programs by giving federal auditors full access to the books and records of program subcontractors, and allowing the government to recover overpayments to service providers. However, all of these efforts have been aimed primarily at reducing costs rather than on protecting beneficiaries or improving the quality of their care.

Tranquilizers, which are part of a $100 million industry, are often used to control patients. A report prepared by the Subcommittee on Long-Term Care of the Senate Special Committee on Aging in the 1970s found that 40 percent of all drugs administered to nursing home residents are painkillers, sedatives, and tranquilizers, with the latter alone accounting for 20 percent of the total.[52] The subcommittee noted: "Perhaps most disturbing is the ample evidence that nursing home patients are tranquilized to keep them quiet and to make them easier to take care of."[53] According to Vladick, the most commonly prescribed tranquilizers, Thorazine and Mellaril, "have serious and often irreversible side effects and . . . are medically appropriate for only a small fraction of the nursing home patients receiving them." Older people residing in institutions having inadequate staff, or lacking other basic means for providing minimum levels of care, are particularly likely to be objects of drug abuse. Vladick concludes that "the use of drugs in nursing homes is clearly more responsive to the economic and administrative needs of the facility than to the medical needs of its residents."[54]

The bias of public funding toward nursing home care when supportive community services are often more appropriate has fostered unnecessary institutionalization. Medicaid, for example, funds a number of necessary services only when they are provided within OAIs. In 1979 Medicaid expended only $183 million or .9 percent of total outlays for home health services. Medicare, which provides for a fixed number of post-hospital days in extended care facilities or skilled nursing homes, and some home health services, covers medical services exclusively. Since 1968 the definition of "medical necessity" has become even more restrictive. Custodial care within institutions, and support services outside OAIs that are not prescribed by a doctor, are not reimbursable under the program. Moreover, less than 3 percent of Medicare outlays contributed to home health care in 1979. Yet it was estimated in 1981 that from 2 to 3.8 million older people require some aid in performing daily tasks, including personal care.[55] Although legislation enacted in the 1980s will increase Medicare reimbursements for home health services, with costs expected to rise from $912 million in 1981 to $1.15 billion in 1982,[56] these revisions will not alter the focus on medical services nor will they substantially reduce unnecessary institutionalization.

The emphasis on health maintenance within OAIs, based on a medical model and buttressed through Medicare and Medicaid policies, ignores resident needs for "quality of life" services such as educational opportunities, maintenance of interpersonal relationships, meaningful recreation, aesthetic features of facility design and privacy. Government regulations fail to provide for quality of care guidelines and inspectors evaluate the capacity of facilities to provide care, rather than how well OAIs actually serve residents. In a 1974 study of licensed nursing homes in Detroit, Gottesman and Bourestrom found that the institutionalized aged spent more than 50 percent of their time doing nothing.[57]

Manard, Woehle, and Heilman, in their survey of 258 OAIs in three states, serving 14,000 residents, found that although nearly 50 percent of the patients were physicially independent and mobile, the residents rarely left the facility, were provided with few interesting recreational opportunities, tended to be unoccupied in any activities, and rarely regained independent living once institutionalized. The study also found generally oppressive conditions, including institutionalization without the patient's consent (55 percent of the sample OAIs accepted residents without the applicant's personal consent and only 3 percent required legal validation of a protesting applicant's "incompetency"); arbitrary guidelines for allowing patients to leave the facilities permanently; limited resident input into major decisions affecting their lives, such as rules, food, activities, or staffing; generally drab, hospital-like atmospheres; and lack of privacy, with two or three occupants per bedroom in the majority of OAIs. The researchers concluded than in one-third of the sample OAIs, resident life was nearly as restrictive as that in the earlier poorhouses.[58]

In 1980, proposals to improve basic nursing home resident rights were introduced in Congress but they failed to be enacted. These included private, unlimited visitation privileges, access to medical records, protection against unnecessary drugs or physical restraints, and the freedom to form patient councils. Such rights were to be part of the minimum federal standards necessary for participation by providers in the Medicare and Medicaid programs. New nursing home fire and safety rules, and protection of resident's personal funds, were proposed unsuccessfully as well. As a Senate Special Committee on Aging report notes: "Budget pressures halted the development of Federal rules to expand nursing home resident's rights."[59]

The Manard, Woehle, and Heilman study also disclosed an inverse relationship between the quality of OAIs and the percentage of Medicaid recipients. The investigators argued that there is "no reason for the poorer quality facilities to improve, as they have an assured source of residents and are required only to satisfy their 'institutional clients.'" These clients most often place public welfare recipients and tend to be unconcerned with factors not related to health maintenance. Further, it was noted that while quality of services are superior in smaller institutions, profits are greater in the larger ones.[60]

Nursing home referrals for public assistance recipients, which as suggested above are usually made by service providers such as hospital social workers or welfare workers, often ignore patient needs and result in highly discriminatory living arrangements. Convenience of families or proximity to former places of residence are usually not considered when placing recipients.[61] Overt racial discrimination and referral patterns also promote segregated facilities. Moreover, the number of beds available to minorities are severely limited.[62]

Despite the increase of nursing homes, many areas have a shortage of beds for the low-income elderly population. A large number of institutions refuse residency to Medicaid patients, and even oust paying clients when their personal funds are exhausted. Since it is easier and more lucrative to service a private market, welfare clients tend to be admitted in less desirable homes, and only when the beds cannot be filled with paying customers.[63] Pennsylvania, for example, does not require nursing homes participating in the Medicaid program to set aside a specific number of places for publicly supported residents. Consequently, some accept Medicaid patients only after they have paid privately for a number of years.[64] Moreover, the patients (or their relatives) often must guarantee payments for up to two years or more.

Who Pays?

By the 1960s it had become increasingly apparent that despite Social Security and other income supports for the elderly, dependency was not prevented. Without protection for the high and growing costs of health care, particularly hospitalization, retirees were becoming a growing burden on public resources. Underlying the funding and benefit provisions of Medicare was the basic assumption that individuals should be forced to save for and assume greater responsibility over their own health care costs during old age. The Medicare program was only to supplement individual initiative by helping those older people, who had an earned right through years of payroll deductions during their working lives, to avoid dependency when faced with high medical bills.

Though the program is often viewed as a national health care program for the elderly, in actuality part A (HI) is funded almost entirely by the working class through mandatory and regressive payroll taxes. The employer contributes a share equal to that of the employee under HI; however, the incidence of that tax tends to fall on labor. HI thus represents a disproportionate burden on the working poor who must pay the same tax rate as higher wage earners. Since the separate trust fund for hospital insurance is expected to be self-supporting, the regressive nature of the tax intensifies as the program expands or costs swell. A little over a year after Medicare was enacted, Medicare taxes rose by 25 percent, primarily due to inflation in hospital charges which were spurred largely by the program itself. By 1969 Medicare expenditures were double the amount that had been predicted in 1965. Congress has thus been forced to increase steadily the social security tax rate and wage base in order to meet growing HI costs.

SMI, which is also a self-supporting and separate trust fund, is supported by the aged themselves through a monthly premium as well as federal general revenues, the latter accounting for about 70 percent of SMI outlays. Costing $36.00 in 1967, the premium has been increased in response to growing medical costs and by 1980 reached $115.20 per year. In July 1981 this rose to $11.00 per month or $132.00 on an annual basis. There is also a $75.00 annual deductible, with the beneficiary required to pay 20 percent of approved costs thereafter.[65] Medicare allows physicians to charge higher fees than are reimburseable under the program, an option which was taken on about 53 percent of the claims in 1979 and which has been increasing steadily from 35 percent of the total in 1969. If the provider does not accept assignment (Medicare reimbursement levels as payment in full) the patient must pay the difference between billed and allowable charges. In 1979, these latter patient fees added over $1.1 billion to medical costs paid directly by the elderly.[66]

Under HI, program recipients are required to pay a deductible for each benefit period equal to the average daily cost of hospital care. This fee grew from $40 in 1966 to $260 by 1982. Coinsurance, which cost the elderly $65.00 per day in 1982, begins after the first sixty days of hospitalization and continues for the remaining thirty days of hospital care allowable under the program. After that, except for a lifetime reserve of sixty additional days, for which the elderly are required to pay one-half of the average daily cost ($130 in 1982), all hospital benefits cease. Up to one hundred days in an extended care facility, and unlimited home health visits,[67] are also covered, although coinsurance is required for each day of institutional care in excess of twenty. In 1982 the daily coinsurance charge for nursing home care grew to $32.50. HI benefits begin again (including the deductible and coinsurance provisions) after the individual has been out of the hospital or nursing home for at least sixty days.

Medicare conspicuously fails to cover the full costs of illness, and personal funds are essential for meeting the vast array of cost-sharing provisions and exclusions. Since the shared costs, such as part A premiums and the various deductibles and coinsurance, are designed to rise with increasing costs for and greater utilization of health care services, the elderly have been forced to contribute a high percentage of their income for their medical needs. Although Social Security pensions are indexed for inflation, medical costs have grown at a substantially higher rate than the CPI. These problems are exacerbated by the steady decrease in the number of physicians accepting assignment and the essential services that are not covered under the programs.

Consequently, Medicare covers only about 44 percent of the health costs incurred by the aged, and if SMI premium payments are deducted, this percentage is reduced to 40 percent. Even given Medicaid, which accounts for another 13 percent of outlays, and other public programs, the elderly are still responsible for approximately one-third of their total health bill.[68] In fact, out-of-pocket costs, taking inflation into account, were higher in the 1970s than they had been prior to the passage of Medicare and Medicaid. According to one source, basing their estimates on constant 1966 dollars, the actual average expenditures by the aged grew from $312 in 1966 to $324 by 1975.[69] In 1966 direct payments for health care represented 24 percent of the average retired worker's Social Security check; by 1975 health costs still accounted for 17 percent of the Social Security benefit.[70]

Total annual per capita health costs for older people averaged $2,029 or nearly 3.4 times that of younger people in 1978. During 1977, the latest date for which data is available, the elderly contributed approximately $462 per capita from personal resources as compared with $164 by those under age sixty-five. Moreover, if Medicare and other insurance premiums are included, older people averaged $530 in out-of-pocket expenses.[71] Hospital care is heavily subsidized, with public programs accounting for 88 percent of total expenditures in 1978. Medicare and Medicaid contributed 60 percent of all physician fees, and from 3 to 42 percent of other medical services provided to the aged. Moreover, Medicare payments represented only 31 percent of physician charges to Medicare beneficiaries.[72]

Of course, averages obscure the higher per capita costs of those elderly requiring substantial services, particularly the low-income and oldest age groups. The uniform premium and cost-sharing provisions, regardless of income, also result in a relatively greater impact on the poor. From 1980 to 1981 Medicare part A and part B out-of-pocket expenses increased by 13.3 percent and 14.5 percent, respectively. Even higher cost-sharing amounts, along with more restrictive enrollment rules, were the primary revisions of this program enacted during 1981. These savings initiatives, which are expected to reduce program costs by $1.9 billion in 1982, will not only increase older people's personal medical expenses but also will burden disproportionately persons at the lower end of the income scale. Low-income older people are thus forced to pay a larger and rising percentage of their income for health care than do the better off.

For most individuals receiving SSI and those elderly classified as medically needy, Medicaid programs are allowed to buy into Medicare by paying for part B premiums, deductibles, and coinsurance, as well as to provide funds for additional services not covered under Medicare. Although all states except Arizona participate in Medicaid, only thirty-five states cover all aged recipients of SSI and sixteen states do not exercise the option of including the medically needy.[73] These factors, along with increasingly restrictive eligibility standards for defining "medical indigency" have produced large gaps in coverage for those elderly who are "just poor." In 1976 Medicare coverage was purchased by the states for only 2.3 million older people or 12 percent of the total aged population. Even where states provide for the medically needy the elderly must exhaust their personal resources on health care needs prior to receiving any medical assistance. Moreover, unable to afford SMI premium costs, about 460,000 older people are not even covered for part B services.

About 50 percent of the elderly have purchased costly private supplementary insurance, and nearly 23 percent own two or more policies.[74] These policies vary considerably, often duplicating existing coverage and placing severe restrictions on benefits. Although they pay a portion of those expenses not covered under Medicare, including the cost-sharing amounts in some cases, "medigap" insurance covers only 5 percent of the elderly's total health bill.[75]

Adequacy and Equity: How Well Is the Job Done?

Despite the large sums of money available for the purchase of health services by the elderly, Medicare and Medicaid have not served to enhance the organization and delivery of medical care itself. In its growing focus on dollars rather than on structural reform, Congress has failed to improve the quality of services or to redistribute health care providers and facilities more equitably among the income classes and geographic regions. As forcefully argued by Brown:

> Rather than need determining the allocation and distribution of health services, which equity would require, we find that services become distributed according to their prevailing markets. The "commodification" of health services remains the major cause of the inaccessibility of health services to the poor and a major factor in the distortion of care to the entire society.[76]

Moreover, Medicare's cost-sharing provisions and gaps in covered services, coupled with rising medical prices, leave essential health needs unmet for a large percentage of the aged population.

Many medical services such as optical and dental examinations and preventive health services (e.g., routine checkups) as well as prescription drugs, hearing aids, dentures, eyeglasses, and long-term nursing care are not covered under Medicare. Although many of these benefits are available to some elderly Medicaid recipients there is considerable variation among the states. The federal government mandates certain basic services for public welfare recipients (e.g., home health and skilled nursing care) and allows the states to provide this group, as well as the medically needy, with additional services such as optical and dental care, prescription drugs, dentures, eyeglasses, intermediate care, and prosthetic devices. However, many states fail to cover a significant portion or in some cases all of these optional benefits. Thus, for example, although studies show that nearly one-fourth to one-half of the elderly need dentures and most older people have some type of peridontal disease that requires dental care, only 20 percent of the aged with incomes under $5,000 had visited a dentist in 1975, as compared with 50 percent of those with incomes over $15,000.[77]

Growing Medicaid costs, which rose 15 percent annually from 1975 to 1980, have also led to consistent retrenchment in the program during the 1970s. Since the legislation provides an open-ended budget for covered services and eligible recipients, states have steadily lowered benefit levels, the number of optional services, and eligibility requirements. They have also imposed some cost-sharing expenses on recipients.

Although the administration failed in its effort to impose a cap on Medicaid outlays in 1981, which would have limited increases in 1982 to 5 percent of the previous year's program costs, Congress reduced federal payments to the states below the amounts to which they otherwise would have been entitled. Federal matching funds will be cut by 3 percent in 1982, 4 percent in 1983, and 4.5 percent in 1984. However, these reductions can be offset—or eliminated entirely—in states that engage in specified activities aimed at controlling Medicaid costs.[78] Given the underlying causes of the growth in Medicaid outlays, attempts to lower federal and state funding for the program primarily will engender even more stringent eligibility standards, fewer services offered, greater limitations placed on these services, and more cost-sharing provision during the 1980s and beyond. Legislation enacted in 1981 also allows the states to place greater restrictions on a Medicaid recipient's choice of medical provider, a provision that will differentiate even further the quality of health care facilities and services available to persons at the lower and upper ends of the income scale. Moreover, reduced allowable fees for providers have and will continue to result in fewer dentists and physicians willing to serve Medicaid patients.

Although all older people covered under Medicare are entitled to the same benefits, the better-off elderly tend to receive a larger share of expenditures as well as more comprehensive health services in general. For example, based on a 1970 National Opinion Research Center survey of Medicare outlays, Davis and Schoen have estimated that Medicare provides about 70 percent higher benefits for those elderly with annual incomes over $11,000 than for those receiving less than $6,000. With benefits steadily increasing with income, the latter group averaged $326 per person while the former averaged approximately $553 per person. The differential in hospital expenditures alone ranged from $196 for the lower income group to $242 for the highest income class. They also calculated that in 1968 older people with incomes above $15,000 received about $160 per capita in services from Medicare's SMI as compared with $79 per capita expended on those with incomes under $5,000. In addition, 50 percent of the former and only 43 percent of the latter income groups exceeded the $50 deductible applicable at that time.[79]

The differential benefits received among the income classes are due both to the uniform cost-sharing provisions and the unequal geographic distribution and costs of health care services. Since Medicare did not remove all financial barriers to health care, the legislation has the effect of discouraging utilization of necessary health services, even when they are partially covered. Nearly half of the differences in benefits received among the income classes for SMI services are due to greater frequency of use by the higher income older population. The remainder can be accounted for by their higher physician costs and better access to specialists. Although the average rate in the utilization of physician services by the elderly poor covered under Medicare has increased since 1966, and currently is commensurate with that of middle-income groups having similar health problems, the premiums, deductibles, coinsurance and excluded benefits serve as a major, and increasingly greater deterrent for the low-income aged not on public assistance. For example, the high-income elderly "see physicians 72 percent more often than the poor elderly who are not on welfare but have the same health problems."[80] Moreover, since the incidence and severity of health problems is inversely related to income, even when utilization rates are similar among income groups, the poor tend to be disadvantaged relative to need.

As suggested above, Medicare and Medicaid have not affected the unequal distribution of health care services or the dual class system of medical care that provide more costly and sophisticated treatment for the more affluent urban dwellers. Since under capitalism the medical market is privately controlled and distributed on the basis of profitability rather than need, low-income urban and rural communities ·suffer from shortages of both physicians and adequate health care facilities. On the other hand, in high-income urban areas, as observed by Waitzkin and Waterman, "one finds a multiplicity of technologically advanced facilities, which often compete with each other for patients. . . . Because of duplication and overlap, health costs rise, while appropriate facilities remain poorly distributed outside metropolitan medical centers. Furthermore, within urban areas, duplicated facilities often remain underutilized."[81]

The growth of highly technical medical centers in metropolitan areas, usually affiliated with large universities, and the prestige system of the medical profession, have contributed to the medical neglect of rural communities. In addition to providing more sophisticated and complex equipment, services and programs, these medical centers have encouraged the concentration of interns, residents, and physicians in limited geographic areas. "The 'less-coveted' hospitals, which are most often located in rural areas or urban ghettoes, thus remain understaffed or must turn to graduates of foreign medical colleges to provide internship or residency services."[82]

The pressure among physicians to go into academic research or to specialize has resulted in increasing shortages of primary care doctors. By the early 1970s about 16 percent of all medical graduates selected careers in teaching, research, administration, or industry.[83] Of those graduates actually providing patient services, only 55 percent were involved in primary care, including internists, obstetricians, and pediatricians, and less than 18 percent were general practitioners, as compared to 28 percent in the early 1960s.[84] At least half of all physicians are specialists, with a particularly high concentration of surgeons relative to actual need.[85] According to a recent report issued by the Graduate Medical Education National

Advisory Committee (GMENAC), the percentage of physicians entering surgical specialties is increasing and by 1990 there will be even larger surpluses in these medical fields.[86] These highly trained specialists are reluctant to practice in rural or urban communities far from the better equipped facilities. Moreover, there is a marked tendency for specialists to choose affluent urban areas in order to ensure a sufficient number of patients for their services and consequently to sustain their high incomes.[87] Even primary care doctors prefer to locate in the more lucrative urban communities. Although GMENAC projects that the national supply of and requirements for primary care physicians will be balanced by 1990, the group warns that uneven utilization rates resulting from geographic maldistribution, and other problems faced by underserved populations and underserved areas, will continue unabated.[88]

Consequently, most rural areas and low-income urban and ghetto neighborhoods, where older Americans tend to reside, have only limited medical facilities and physician services. Nearly one-fourth of older people live on farms or in rural communities with populations under 2,500. The poor, black, and rural aged are often forced to utilize inadequate hospital outpatient departments, emergency rooms, or clinics, usually distant from their homes, in lieu of office-based physician care, or to forego medical services entirely. They also tend to wait longer for care, receive summary and superficial treatment, and have less access to specialists. For those elderly with substantial mobility limitations and/or lack of adequate transportation, coupled with the paucity of physicians willing to make home visits, medical care has become even more inaccessable.

In the 1976 national survey on aging, Louis Harris disclosed that approximately 23 percent of older people viewed "not enough medical care" as a serious or somewhat serious problem; the lower income aged were disproportionately medically neglected. Approximately 18 percent of those with incomes under $3,000 responded that not enough medical care was a serious problem as contrasted with only 1 percent of those with incomes over $15,000.[89] Moreover, between 1964 and 1973 the elderly residing in non-metropolitan areas fell even further behind those living in metropolitan areas in the use of physician services.

Medicare, which has intensified the trend toward inpatient hospital care rather than ambulatory or home-based services, further distorts the allocation and types of health services available to the elderly. Between 1965 and 1975 alone, the number of older people admitted into hospitals increased by 36 percent, and the use of surgery by 105 percent. Hospitalization rates among the poor rose by 47 percent and for the nonpoor by 18 percent.[90] However, low-income groups, particularly minorities, tend to be disproportionately placed in overcrowded, understaffed, and underfinanced institutions.[91] Since patients are dependent on private physicians to admit them into hospitals, and racial discrimination compounds the problem of poverty, "blacks even when covered by medicaid or medicare receive more of their hospital care from crowded city or county hospitals than do whites."[92]

The appreciable gains in hospital-based services for the elderly have come under strong attack in recent years. With excess beds and underutilized expensive equipment, hospitals have encouraged greater inpatient care and a wide variety of elaborate and often excessive diagnostic procedures. Physicians, who also benefit from utilization decisions, are able to create limitless demand for their services, a problem that is particularly acute in areas where there is an overabundance of surgeons. According to the GMENAC study discussed earlier, there will be a 35 percent increase in the supply of physicians by 1990, compared with an 8 percent growth in population. The group notes that the "unneeded growth of physician supply has been shown to hold the potential for many adverse consequences; not the least of these are increased expenditures and unnecessary utilization."[93] Older patients, who are more adequately covered for hospital services than for other forms of care, and who, for the most part, trust doctors' diagnostic and therapeutic decisions, have often been victims of costly, unnecessary, risky, and even harmful medical procedures.[94] In her study of hospitals, Judith Feder concluded that Medicare funding practices, coupled with low quality standards for Medicare certification and perfunctory enforcement efforts, also have encouraged the perpetuation of inadequate and even unsafe hospitals.[95]

HEALTH CARE UNDER CAPITALISM: SOME LIMITATIONS OF THE MEDICAL MODEL FOR THE AGED

Although the unequal distribution of, access to, and quality of medical care among the aged, the paucity of general practitioners, provider profiteering, gaps in Medicare and Medicaid coverage, rampant inflation of costs, and other issues discussed in previous sections are critical factors in the failure of national policies and programs to meet the health needs of the aged, they provide only partial explanations. Underlying the approach to illness under capitalism is the misguided assumption that enhanced medical services per se are sufficient for promoting health. This diverts attention from the host of negative social and environmental causes of disease.

In a recent article, Sylvia Tesh explores three current theories of disease causality. She notes that the germ theory confers responsibility on health professionals to develop preventive vaccines, or curative medical techniques and drugs. The life-style hypothesis holds that the most important cause of chronic diseases is unhealthy personal behavior. This approach, which she labels "victim-blaming," assumes that individuals are responsible for their own ill health. Rather than transform social and economic institutions, such a perspective advocates personal behavioral change. Tesh argues that the third hypothesis, the environmental one, is the most valid for understanding disease causality. This theory "places responsibility on the owners and managers of industry." She concludes:

> When we place the environmental causes of disease at the far end of the chain, we condone the very limited disease-prevention practices advocated by industrialists. We buy into the idea that protecting industry takes precedence over protecting health. We opt for the disease-prevention program which least interferes with industrial production. Thus, we sacrifice our health to the health of "the economy" without examining the unequal manner in which economic benefits are distributed.[96]

Medical services are most effective in treating acute diseases that stem from single identifiable causes. However, the aged not only have fewer incidences of acute illness than younger people but also their major health problems tend to be chronic.[97] About 85 percent of older people are afflicted with at least one, and may suffer from multiple chronic conditions.[98] In 1979, 27 percent of the noninstitutionalized elderly reported that they had some form of heart disease; 39 percent, hypertension; 28 percent, diminished hearing; 12 percent, visual impairment; 12 percent, arteriosclerosis; and 44 percent, arthritis.[99] Heart diseases, cancer, and cerebrovascular lesions, particularly strokes, account for approximately 75 percent of deaths among the aged.[100]

Critically, many of the chronic disabling conditions associated with old age are gradual and progressive ones and, as stressed by Rick Carlson, "are among the diseases which medicine has the least impact." He concludes that:

> Environmental factors—polluted air and water, noise, stress— are the most important determinants of ill health. If this is so, and if environmental conditions linked to health worsen over the next 30 years, the future promises more business for physicians but poorer health for everyone.[101]

Similarly, Marc Renaud points out that while medical care may alleviate some suffering and delay death, it is less effective than is generally assumed, particularly when applied against chronic and degenerative conditions. He also argues that the curative approach of current technological and scientific medicine obfuscates the industrial causes of disease and mortality among the population.[102]

Medicare and Medicaid funds, then, flow exclusively into a costly medical system that seeks to control and alter disease processes within individual patients while ignoring the effects of industrial pollution, stressful working environments, poverty, and other external conditions that have contributed substantially to morbidity and mortality among the aged and the rest of the population. What is required is to alter not only the practice but the definition of health care itself.

There is, in fact, impressive evidence that industrial cleanup and adequate income may be more effective than medical treatment for many health problems prevalent among the aged. It is estimated, for example, that from 80 to 90 percent of cancers are environmentally induced, with up to 40 percent attributable to occupational carcinogens alone.[103] As Tesh observes, "a growing list of chemical compounds has been linked to cancers in dozens of occupations," affecting the majority of blue collar workers.[104] Lung cancer, which is more prevalent in industrial regions, is directly related to specific occupational health hazards. A 1981 report by the National Institute of Health (NIH) notes that "the clustering of lung cancer along certain coastal areas has been linked to asbestos exposures in the shipbuilding industry during World War II. Many of the geographic clusters of cancer appear to reflect high-risk environments."[105] Environmental toxins, including air and water pollution from chemical wastes, radiation, industrial plant smoke, pesticides, and other industrial sources, all are significant causes of cancer among the general population.

Despite surgical techniques for removing pathenogenic tissues, and millions of dollars devoted to researching its microbiological causes, diagnosis, and treatment,[106] cancer is responsible for over 20 percent of fatalities among the aged, a percentage that has increased parrallel with industrialization. According to Dr. Samual S. Epstein, author of *The Politics of Cancer*,

> There has been over the last 40 years little overall improvement in our ability to treat and cure most cancers. The modest improvement from the 20 percent overall five-year survival rates in the mid-30s to about 33 percent in the mid-50s reflects advances in surgery, blood transfusion, and antibiotic treatment, rather than specific advances of cancer treatment. Over the last two decades, there has been no further significant improvement in overall cancer survival rates, nor in survival rates for major cancer sites such as lung, stomach, pancreas, and brain, which are still virtual death sentences.[107]

The five-year survival rate for breast cancer has increased from 63 percent in 1960 to 68 percent in 1970 to 73 percent in 1979, an overall improvement of only 10 percent in twenty years. The corresponding figures for cancer of the colon are 43 percent, 49 percent, and 50 percent, or an overall increase of 7 percent since the early 1960s. During the last ten years the five-year survival rate for cervical cancer improved by 8 percent; uterine cancer, by 3 percent; prostate, by 5 percent; and cancer of the bladder, by 9 percent.[108]

In contrast, according to NIH, "over 400,000 persons will die of cancer while almost twice as many new cases will be diagnosed . . . in recent years between 50 and 55 percent of new cancer cases were in persons over 65."[109] The overall incidence of cancer increased by 1 or 2 percent per year in the 1970s. The number of deaths from cancer, especially among persons over age fifty-five, also is growing.[110] Clearly, only through an expensive cleanup of hazardous working conditions and pollution in our environment and food products will society even begin to address this major cause of suffering and death.

It appears that work roles and conditions (e.g., stress), diet, and other social factors are major causes of heart disease, conditions that affect nearly 20 percent of the aged, and from which about 44 percent of older people die. Improved working environments and nutritional intake would probably contribute more to the control of these health problems than increased medical intervention. In fact, an HEW Task Force report, *Work in America*, found that "in an impressive 15-year study of aging, the strongest predictor of longevity was work satisfaction."[111] Moreover, studies show that nearly one-fourth of sickness and death associated with respiratory conditions, such as asthma and chronic bronchitis, could be eradicated by a 50 percent reduction in air pollution alone.[112]

Many of the ailments plaguing older individuals can be traced to poverty throughout their lifetimes and even greater poverty upon attaining age sixty-five. In fact, one's standard of living may be the salient determinant of health and disease.[113] In the 1976 Harris survey on aging discussed earlier, it was reported that although half of the aged respondents considered poor health a serious or somewhat serious problem in their lives, this was directly related to economic conditions. Fully 36 percent of older respondents with incomes under $3,000 reported that poor health was a serious problem, as compared to only 11 percent of those with incomes of $15,000 or more.[114] Other studies show that limitations on activity due to chronic conditions are also inversely related to income.[115]

In its final report, the Post-Conference Board of the 1971 White House Conference on Aging points out that from one-third to one-half of the elderly's health problems stem from inadequate nutrition.[116] Given spiraling costs for food and other necessities, older people who are forced to live on insufficient retirement benefits will probably have increasing difficulty in meeting their basic nutritional needs. Moreover, while doctors can mend broken bones and hips, funded through Medicare and Medicaid, low-income patients are often forced to return to their unhealthy and economically deprived living environments which may include five flights of stairs to climb.

THE CUMULATIVE NATURE OF DISEASE: HEALTH CARE
AND THE UNDER-SIXTY-FIVE AGE GROUPS

Enhanced working conditions, better nutrition, more adequate incomes, environmental controls, and other social and institutional alterations, along with better access to and quality of medical care for the under-sixty-five age groups, would contribute to the improved health status of the future elderly population. If medical intervention is to be most effective where it can lessen the prevalence and/or severity of disease among older people, adequate health care, particularly for preventive services and rehabilitation, is necessary during childhood and younger adult years. Davis and Schoen forcefully argue that:

> Many of the untreated acute conditions of childhood and adolescence show up as dehabilitating and crippling chronic conditions only in middle and old age. The ability of the aged to move about with ease, retain their auditory, visual, and mental facilities, and care for themselves is related, in part, to the adequacy of health care in earlier years.[117]

The poorer health of low-income people at all ages is well documented. Inadequate financial resources and its associated conditions of nutritional deficiencies, dilapidated housing, physical and psychological stresses of deprivation and chronic insecurity, as well as lack of access to adequate medical care, particularly for preventive services, are among the factors linking class status and health. The middle-aged poor suffer from many of the same ailments commonly associated with old age. For those individuals between ages forty-five and sixty-four with family incomes below $5,000, 30 percent reported arthritis; 14 percent, a known heart condition; 17 percent, hypertensive disease; 16 percent, hearing impairment; and 11 percent, visual problems. These figures can be compared to only 16 percent, 7 percent, 11 percent, 9 percent, and 5 percent, respectively, reported by middle-aged individuals with family incomes of $15,000 or more.[118] Yet, for example, arteriosclerosis is both difficult to treat medically or to reverse after a lifetime of poor nutrition, and "no amount of medical care will eliminate chronic conditions for those who already have visual and hearing impairments, arthritis, diabetes, or heart conditions." At best, medical intervention can relieve pain or reduce functional incapacity.[119] Current governmental health programs, which are restricted to older people and public welfare recipients, fail to provide funding for the early prevention, diagnosis, or treatment of diseases.

Although Medicaid provides limited health services for indigent younger adults and their dependents, about 8 to 10 million people with incomes below the poverty line, representing nearly a third of the poor, are not eligible.[120] Widows and other single people under age sixty-five are among those frequently excluded. Moreover, low participation rates among physicians and dentists, cutbacks and gaps in services covered, and a wide variety of other problems, all of which are increasing because of severe cost-cutting measures in the 1980s, will further restrict access to medical care for both younger and older Medicaid beneficiaries.

In addition, low-income workers who are forced to contribute to Medicare throughout their working lives tend to incur higher insurance costs than their better-off cohorts, or to forego protection entirely. Competitive sector workers frequently are unable to purchase the less expensive and more comprehensive group policies. It has been noted that although 70 percent of full-time workers were covered under group health insurance plans in 1972, the highest coverage rates were in large-scale, high-wage, unionized firms. Eighty percent of uncovered workers were employed in agriculture, construction, retail trade, and service occupations. Public sector employees had the most extensive coverage, with from 87 to 90 percent participating in a group health plan.[121] Significantly, nearly half of every dollar spent on individual insurance policies accrues to insurance companies as profits, administrative costs, and other nonhealth-related expenses.[122]

Moreover, nearly 60 percent of the full-time working poor and 30 percent of the near poor are not even covered by any private health insurance and over 90 percent and 80 percent, respectively, lack protection for physician services.[123] Approximately 22 million people are excluded from both private and public health care programs.[124] Regardless of whether they are covered by private health insurance, however, all workers indirectly support those who are. Exclusions of employer contributions to health insurance plans represented an estimated $14.2 billion in lost tax revenues during 1981 alone. Total federal health-related tax expenditure items, including exclusions of contributions for medical insurance and personal deductions for medical care costs, amounted to $17.7 billion in that year.[125]

Even workers who have access to insurance through the work place may find that their policies have low ceilings on total benefits, and exclude many nonhospital related health services. At least 20 million persons have private health insurance policies with inadequate coverage.[126] With nearly 31 percent of rising health costs paid out of pocket, health care has become financially prohibitive for a large percentage of the under-sixty-five population. Consequently, an anomalous situation arises, where many workers who are contributing to a compulsory health insurance program for the aged are unable to meet current health service costs for themselves and their families. As E. Harvey Estes, Jr. concludes: "Some few illnesses seem directly attributable to aging and its effects. The problems that have led to poor delivery of health care to the population at large have a more profound effect on the elderly."[127]

SUMMARY

The Medicare and Medicaid programs have spurred mounting health costs in the United States without commensurate benefits for the elderly or the general population. Medicare, which is supported primarily by the working class and the aged themselves, fails to cover a significant portion of the elderly's health bill or health care needs. Medicaid does not cover essential services for indigent older and younger people, and rising medical costs threaten to curtail the scope of benefits even further. The quality of and access to care also have not improved considerably, particularly for the low-income aged population and those living in rural areas. The program operates within the context of a medical system that has been designed, developed, and run by a medical-industrial complex to serve its own interests.

Medicaid has encouraged the institutionalization of the elderly, has enriched the nursing home industry, and has allowed exploitive and injurious practices. The growth and expansion of high technology medicine, supported largely through Medicare and Medicaid, have enhanced the prestige, power, and revenues of hospitals, resulting in increased medical costs and only limited gains for older people. Doctors, the hospital supply and equipment industries, pharmaceutical companies, and other partners in the privately controlled medical market also have engaged in Medicare/Medicaid profiteering, often at the expense of the elderly's health needs.

Moreover, the emphasis on medical services and the medical model of health care have served capital by diverting attention from the fundamental causes of chronic ailments, many of which stem from unhealthy working and living environments, poor nutrition, inadequate housing, and low income in general. Medicare's exclusive focus on the 65-and-over population ignores the fact that most chronic diseases have their roots in childhood or younger adult years, at which time prevention, diagnosis, and treatment are most effective. Yet a large percentage of the working class cannot afford to obtain adequate health care services. Clearly, Medicare and Medicaid have not served the interests of the aged or the general population.

Chapter 6

The Housing Crisis: Private Power and Public Resources

Housing deprivation, prevalent among a substantial number of older Americans, is manifested in several, often interrelated forms. Physically inadequate homes and rental units, which are dangerous and unhealthy, as well as lacking in essential facilities, have contributed substantially to pressing shelter needs in the United States. For many families residing in relatively decent dwellings, high and rising housing costs relative to income have caused severe financial hardship. Limited shopping, lack of easily accessible medical care and social services, inadequate transportation and other public amenities, and deteriorating, high crime neighborhoods impose additional problems. Underlying these issues, however, are the high cost of housing, generated by the private housing and credit markets, inadequate and unequal distribution of income in society, and racial and ethnic discrimination. The major determinant of adequate housing is income and minority status, rather than age per se. Consequently, the well-documented acute shelter needs of most older people stem predominantly from their disproportionately low income levels.

While about 10 percent of the general population reside in physically inadequate or flawed homes and apartments, as defined by the Department of Housing and Urban Development (HUD), this does not differ materially from the situation of households headed by an elderly person.[1] In a study based on HUD's 1976 Annual Housing Survey and the 1976 Current Population Reports, Anthony Yezer argues that, in terms of physical adequacy alone, the housing situation of "comparable groups of the elderly and the total population are in most respects remarkably alike. Indeed, the elderly differ more among themselves than they do from the general population against which they are compared." While 9.7 percent of all housing in the United States had one or more flaws, 9 percent or about 1.3 million dwelling units occupied by elderly households were similarly defined as substandard.[2] Older households, however, are more likely to live in older structures (60 percent reside in housing built before 1950 and 47 percent in units constructed prior to World War II) requiring costly maintenance and heating, to own their own homes, and to live in central cities or isolated rural areas. Consequently, the Housing and Urban Development data, which relies exclusively on the physical characteristics of dwellings, seriously underestimates housing deprivation among the elderly. Given their poor neighborhood conditions, inaccessibility of essential supportive services, high maintenance and rental costs relative to income, and other housing-related problems, the vast majority of older people lack adequate housing.

The most economically deprived elderly are housed in inner cities and rural areas where isolation from essential services is often a severe problem. Approximately 30 percent of all older households occupy housing in central cities and are concentrated within slums or slowly deteriorating communities; one third live on the fringes of central cities—often in older working-class neighborhoods; and 40 percent reside in nonmetropolitan areas, mostly in small rural towns or on farms.[3]

About 28 percent of the older population live in apartments, boarding homes, or hotels, and 61 percent of these renters consist of single people with extremely low incomes. Rental units are often more deficient than owner-occupied homes. In 1976, 17 percent of all rental units and 16 percent of those occupied by the elderly had one or more major flaws as compared to 4 percent of all owner-occupied homes and 6 percent of those owned by older people.[4] The housing of older rural residents is the most substandard, and in 1970 nearly one-fourth of these structures lacked complete plumbing. In fact, 31 percent of older white and 86 percent of older black rural renters lived in units without plumbing, as contrasted with 6 percent and 8 percent, respectively, of older urban renters. However, 16 percent of white and 78 percent of black younger rural renters similarly lacked plumbing facilities.[5] Older urban dwellers, on the other hand, regardless of the condition of their individual housing, are more likely to be surrounded by deteriorating and unsafe neighborhoods.

The most important determinant of "adequate" housing appears to be income level. Yezer shows that households with an adjusted annual income of less than $2,499 in 1976, which approximated the poverty level, had about a 20 percent chance of living in substandard housing while family units with adjusted incomes ranging from $3,000 to $3,999 had about a 10 percent chance. On the other hand, those with adjusted incomes of $10,000 or more had less than a 5 percent chance of living in substandard housing. The situation is also compounded by discrimination. Poor black or Hispanic families headed by a person sixty-five years or older had about a 21 to 33 percent chance of living in flawed dwellings as compared to a chance of from 13 to 16 percent for whites. The probability of single, older people being inadequately housed was 43 percent for black males; 27 percent for black females; 56 percent for Hispanic males; 18 percent for Hispanic females; 27 percent for white males; and 13 percent for white females.[6]

It is generally assumed that family outlays for housing should represent approximately 25 percent of income. Low-income older people, who are confronted with rising housing costs and fixed retirement benefits, tend to pay a larger (and growing) share of their income for housing than do the rest of the population. For most, housing is their major financial burden. Approximately 41 percent of older households were unable to find adequate housing for 25 percent, and one-third of family units, for even 30 percent of their income in 1976. About 15 percent of older households (and 7 percent of all U.S. households) were unable to secure decent shelter for under 50 percent of their income.[7]

While the cost of housing relative to income has been growing for all people, it has increased even more dramatically for the aged. Rent or household maintenance averages over 30 percent of an older family unit's total resources, up from 22 percent in 1950.[8] In 1976, 35 percent of older households (65 percent of renters and 23 percent of owners) were forced to spend over 25 percent of their income on housing, and a large percentage paid 35 percent or more.[9] Even the 25 percent standard, however, is excessive for those with extremely low financial resources, given the high and rising costs of other essential commodities.

ELDERLY HOMEOWNERS: AN ELUSIVE DREAM

Home ownership has symbolized the fulfillment of the American dream for a large percentage of working class families, although the costs have accounted for a substantial and growing share of personal income. After twenty or thirty years of mortgage payments, consisting primarily of interest to lending institutions, the accrued equity often represents the only significant (although nonliquid) financial asset held by middle-aged and older people. Approximately 70 percent of the elderly (including 71 percent of the white and 57 percent of the black aged population) currently reside in their own homes. Of these homes, 84 percent are mortgage free. In 1977 the median value of homes owned by older people ranged from $32,500 for families to $24,000 and $25,700 for single older men and single older women, respectively.[10]

Nearly two-thirds of elderly homeowners consist of families, generally couples. Even though most of their incomes are low, they tend to be, on average, slightly higher than those of elderly renters. In 1977 the median income of older couples living in owner-occupied dwellings was $9,200 as compared to $7,100 for renters. The median income of single, aged women and men residing in their own homes was $4,300 and $5,100, respectively, as against $3,700 and $4,100 for renters.[11] The rural elderly are more likely to own their homes (79 percent in 1973) than urban dwellers (55 percent), although the owner-occupied units of the former tend to be more physically inadequate.[12]

Despite the prevalence of fully paid mortgages among elderly homeowners, their dwellings tend to be old, low-cost and, for many, substandard units, often requiring costly utility, repair, and other maintenance expenses that have absorbed an increasing share of retirement income. While the CPI increased by 197 percent between 1969 and 1979, the cost of home maintenance and repair increased by 231 percent.[13] Unable to afford repairs, or to provide even simple maintenance tasks, large numbers of older people find their homes deteriorating even further. Where proper maintenance is provided, the household may be trapped in blighted neighborhoods or isolated in rural communities with inadequate supportive services. Rising costs have forced many older people to sell their homes and rapidly deplete the assets on nursing home care or high-priced rental appartments.

High and growing utility and property taxes have contributed substantially to the pressing financial problems of elderly home-owners, as well as renters. Between 1971 and 1976 alone, average property taxes in the nation increased by 47 percent. Inadequate housing stock and real estate speculation have driven up property taxes in some areas even further.[14] While the elderly pay an average of 8 percent of their income on property taxes, as compared to 3.4 percent for all households, the lowest income groups are forced to spend even higher percentages.[15] Moreover, the property tax heavily burdens older people, particularly those at the lowest income levels, since it is based not only on their major and often only form of asset but also on one that does not provide any investment returns for current living expenses. In addition, studies have shown that deteriorating and blighted neighborhoods, where large numbers of older Americans reside, have higher median effective tax rates than do newer neighborhoods.[16]

Although nearly all states have passed some property tax relief measures for the aged, such as circuit breakers and homestead exemption programs, these tend to be both insufficient and inequitable. As the Federal Council on Aging notes, "the average *level* of benefits ($143 for circuit breakers and $173 for homestead exemption programs) is unable to significantly upgrade any household's standard of living." In 1974 circuit-breakers cost state and local governments nearly $.5 billion and homestead exemption programs over $1 billion.[17]

Rapidly increasing energy costs also have a regressive impact on low-income households. Between 1972 and 1979 the price of fuel grew by 293 percent, natural gas by 155 percent, and electricity by 75 percent, far outdistancing the rise in the CPI. According to the Department of Health and Human Services, the poor will spend $2 billion in higher energy costs between 1978 and 1981 as a result of decontrolling domestic oil prices alone.[18] It has been estimated that the 1979 increases in heating costs have caused older households to spend an average of 25 percent, and in the Northeast nearly a third, of their income on energy.[19] Between 1980 and 1981 energy costs rose 31 percent, as compared to a 13.5 increase in the CPI.[20] According to a Department of Energy Advisory Committee, "during 1980, the low-income household was spending, on average, at least 35 percent of its income on energy." In some areas heating and electricity costs represented 50 percent of income.[21] Moreover, unit rates for electricity and natural gas are highest for low volume consumers such as the elderly poor. The Energy Policy Project of the Ford Foundation's study on energy and growth in the United States argues that:

> The lower income groups use most of the energy they purchase for functions closely associated with their well-being. To cut back from current levels of energy use would be difficult for the lower income groups; similarly, retaining current levels or moving to higher consumption in the face of escalating prices could also cause difficulty.[22]

The Department of Energy Advisory Committee "reported that low-income households will continue to pay four times more the percentage of their income on energy than the average American household, but will use less than 50 percent of the total energy consumed by that average household."[23] For some very low income older households the growing heating costs have reduced consumption levels to life-threatening levels, and have forced some people into nursing homes.

Since 1976 the national government has provided only limited relief for high energy expenses. Restrictive income-eligibility levels and insufficient outlays ($400 million from 1976 to 1978) have prevented the programs from alleviating substantially the growing energy burden. In 1980, $1.6 billion, and in 1981, $1.85 billion was available for energy assistance purposes for all needy groups, with $400 million allocated exclusively for SSI recipients. However, the $250 maximum amount per household served during 1980 did not offset the growing home heating costs which were estimated to average $700 in 1979 for an elderly homeowner using fuel oil.[24] An additional $400 million was available in 1980 for energy crisis situations affecting poor and near-poor households, including the aged, which states were allowed to pay directly to providers.[25] Under the Low-Income Home Energy Act of 1981, only $1.9 billion was authorized for 1982 and 1983.[26] The meager amounts allocated each year, which reach only a fraction of older people in need of aid, contrasts sharply with energy industry profits, the latter reaching 163 percent for some companies in 1979.[27] Although the state has enacted ad hoc measures to reduce energy burdens it has failed to address fundamental structural issues and to meet needs sufficiently.

THE STATE, FINANCE CAPITAL, AND THE HOUSING MARKETS

Subsidizing the Credit Market: The Rise (and Decline) of Suburban Expansion

The federal government has been a major participant in and subsidizer of housing since the collapse of the housing and mortgage markets during the depression of the 1930s. Stone argues that in the early part of the twentieth century the housing market provided new profitable investment outlets for the vastly growing funds held by financial institutions.[28] By 1929 the construction industry and developers as well as homeowners had become dependent on lending institutions for credit and mortgages, while the interests of financial institutions were inextricably tied to continuous economic expansion in order to protect their growing mortgage lending. However, during the depression, widespread destitution, particularly among the unemployed population (some 13 to 15 million people were out of work in 1933), a growing inability to pay mortgages or rents (nearly 50 percent of all home mortgages were in default by 1932), and a paucity of personal savings and other sources of capital accruing to financial institutions led to massive foreclosures on homes and farms, eviction of renters, and the collapse of the mortgage system and construction industry. In turn, the stagnation of the housing and credit markets contributed substantially to the worsening economic situation.

In response to the problems of high unemployment and inadequate incomes, a depressed housing market, and faltering financial institutions, the state focused on stimulating construction, profits, and private capital formation rather than on meeting the need for quality housing among various sectors of the population, particularly the poor and elderly. Housing policies emerging during the 1930s and continuing through the 1980s have been designed primarily to buttress financial institutions and other private housing interests by underwriting the credit structure of the housing industry.

Federal Housing Administration (FHA) mortgage insurance in 1934 and the Veterans Administration (VA) housing program in 1944 encouraged renewed construction and purchase of single-family homes, particularly in the suburbs, by guaranteeing lenders against the risks of nonpayment and foreclosure. With an emphasis on low downpayments and long repayment periods, these publicly supported housing programs fostered the growth of home ownership among middle- and upper middle-income families. Rising interest payments accruing to financial institutions, however, remained at market rates.

The tendency of lending institutions to utilize a policy of "economic soundness" in dispersing loans (which until 1967 was mandated through the enabling legislation) generally restricted the availability of FHA mortgages, as well as uninsured loans, for low-income households. High interest costs further reduced the ability of low-income classes, particularly the elderly, to participate in the program.[29] Many older people were excluded from multifamily apartments built with FHA guaranteed loans as well, since rents were typically higher than they could afford. For example, in 1964 only .3 percent of FHA supported units rented for less than $100 per month, a cost that was equal to the entire median income of older individuals and 35 percent that of older families at the time.[30]

Other national measures such as the Federal Home Loan Bank System (1932), the Federal National Mortgage Association (1938), and later the Government National Mortgage Association (1968) and the Federal Home Loan Mortgage Corporation (1970) similarly supported capital accumulation and profits of financial institutions, reduced the risks of mortgage lending, and promoted real estate investment opportunities, assuring a stable risk-free market for finance capital. National tax measures allowing liberal mortgage interest and property tax deductions for homeowners and landlords have also enhanced the housing markets while disproportionately benefiting better-off households. In 1979 alone, these tax deductions amounted to nearly $17 billion in lost revenues. About $4.7 billion and $10.8 billion represented reduced housing costs for households with annual incomes of $50,000 and over, and $30,000 and over, respectively. It is estimated that deductions for mortgage interest and property taxes on owner-occupied homes will rise to $36.2 billion in 1982.[31]

Consequently, since the end of World War II, construction has been the country's second largest industry, accounting for about 10 percent of the GNP. Over 20 million families have purchased homes with federally insured mortgages alone.[32] From 1959 to 1978, slightly over 32 million units of new housing have been built in the nation. By 1976, 65 percent of all housing units were owner occupied, as compared to 44 percent in 1940.[33]

Growing construction and mortgage debt spurred the economy during the 1950s and 1960s, enriched substantially the private housing market, and increased dependence on credit. In addition to contributing to the rise in home ownership among the middle and upper strata of the working class, state programs supporting finance capital fueled the growing migration to the suburbs over the last several decades. Well-funded highway programs have also made it relatively easy to commute from cities to suburban communities.

Since the late 1960s, and especially after 1979, there has been an overall tightening of the housing market,[34] resulting in curtailed suburban expansion and construction of moderate-income homes in these areas. Family incomes have stagnated, limiting the ability of large sectors of the working class to support the growing costs of home ownership or to afford the spiraling prices of new homes. Moreover, financial institutions have become increasingly unwilling to provide mortgages for the less profitable residential constructions. As will be discussed in the next section, staggering and mounting interest rates, real estate speculation (resulting in escalating land costs), and the growth of more lucrative industrial and commercial investment and construction opportunities in lieu of housing have also contributed to the decreased construction and higher costs of low and moderate-income multifamily rental units in metropolitan areas, generating inflationary pressures on rents.

In 1949, 69 percent of new housing construction costs were labor and materials; 11 percent, land; 5 percent, finance; and 15 percent, the builder's overhead and profit. By 1977 labor and materials plummeted to 47 percent of total costs while land increased to 25 percent; finance to 11 percent; and the builder's overhead and profit to 18 percent.[35] Thus growing land costs and finance charges, both fostered by and benefiting financial institutions, have been the major causes of rising housing costs in the United States.

As Stone concludes, "Mortgage-lending institutions are the dominant force in the housing sector and contribute directly to the existence and maintenance of the housing problem."[36] The primary response of the state in the 1980s has been to expand policies aimed at private accumulation and profits. The federal government introduced the six-month "money market" certificates, and expanded federally sponsored secondary market facilities, interest subsidies, and other programs to buttress even further the operation of private mortgage credit markets. These activities have increased the revenues of financial institutions and have guaranteed them against losses; they also have enhanced the profits of developers and other private housing interests. However, in its continuing effort to support financial institutions, and thus the housing industry and the lagging economy, the state has enacted housing policies that are unrelated to the need for or availability of decent and affordable shelter. Although the heaviest burdens have fallen on low-income groups such as the elderly, the housing crisis is affecting increasingly the vast majority of middle-income, working-class families as well.

Housing the Urban Low-Income Elderly: Failure of the Private Market

The provision of housing for poor and low-income households has been provided primarily through the filtering down process. As more affluent families have taken advantage of public programs and private policies encouraging single-family suburban developments over the past several decades, the poor and elderly have either acquired or remained in the older homes and apartments within central cities and surrounding fringe areas. Housing units that are filtered down, of course, have decreased considerably in value, whether measured in terms of the physical condition of the building or dwelling itself, the desirability of the community, or the accessibility of services and amenities.

Private developers and lending institutions, who have concentrated their activities on the more profitable high-rise multifamily apartments and suburban homes, and increasingly on condominiums and commercial or industrial properties, have not provided sufficient numbers of new or rehabilitated housing units for low- and moderate-income households at affordable costs. In fact, demolition of low-income structures, supported by state income tax and other housing policies, has proven more profitable than either renovation or maintenance in many blighted communities, reducing further the housing stock available to the poor. As will be discussed later, government urban renewal and revitalization programs, as well as highway constructions, have encouraged the destruction of homes and rental units occupied by low-income households without providing for sufficient replacements. The growing housing shortages, and the deterioration of neighborhoods have been exacerbated by lending policies of financial institutions which "redline" declining districts, particularly in central cities and surrounding areas where older people reside, support high-income residential, industrial, and commercial ventures, and finance real estate speculation in reviving neighborhoods.

Where substantial renovation has taken place, a growing trend in most major cities, the cost of housing rises beyond the means of the poor and elderly, thus displacing them from existing units. The conversion of low-income housing units, and single-room occupancy hotels into more profitable luxury apartments, supported through local tax incentives, has also been accompanied by harrassment tactics intended to force out poor and often elderly tenants. According to New York City Councilwoman Ruth Messinger, since 1956 New York City has foregone nearly half a billion dollars through tax exemptions under its J-51 program, which from 1976 to 1980 alone had cut available single-room occupancy housing in half for elderly persons.[37]

The conversion of rental apartments to condominiums, which are more profitable for landlords who relinquish obligations for maintenance costs and avoid battles over rent increases, also have added to the housing problems of less affluent income classes, such as the aged. The Senate Special Committee on Aging has noted that 50,000 apartments in 1977, and 130,000 in 1979, have been converted into condominiums—conversions that are growing steadily.[38]

Increasing housing shortages in low-income neighborhoods, and real estate speculation in reviving ones, have generated rising rents. Unable to afford housing outside of declining areas, the poor, including a significant percentage of the elderly, have been forced to bid for a limited and decreasing supply of housing stock, thus pushing up prices to the highest possible level, often reaching over 35 percent of the tenant's total income. However, as Stephen Barton notes, when landlords are unable to maintain or increase rents sufficiently to sustain high profits or when faced with rising fuel bills, property taxes, and interest rates, they curtail maintenance and other services. Moreover, if the landlord's or lender's *rates* of profit are not competitive with those in other sectors of the economy, they will have little incentive to make (or in the case of financial institutions to lend funds for) repairs or renovations of the structures, and will use their capital for other investment purposes instead.[39] The buildings, however, usually are retained by the owners until the lucrative tax shelter provisions have decreased in value, at which time the properties are sold, converted, or increasingly, abandoned.

These pressures have not only led to inadequate and weak enforcement of building codes but have discouraged the enactment or retention of strong rent control laws. Where housing regulations and controls lower the rate of return on investment they merely accelerate the ongoing process of disinvestment by owners and lenders. The withdrawal of funding for services and repairs results in physical deterioration of the buildings, as well as fires, vandalism, and other unsanitary and dangerous conditions.[40] Older people residing in deteriorating rental units or neighborhoods are often unable to afford the cost of alternative housing. Moreover, to the extent that the elderly benefit from rent control provisions (e.g., special laws for older people) landlords tend to use various techniques to force them out.

Low levels of affordable new and rehabilitated rental units available to the elderly poor and the inadequate maintenance of their current structures have been accompanied by a massive withdrawal of funds for municipal services in many urban areas. The movement of more affluent families, jobs, and retail enterprises to the suburbs has eroded the tax base of major cities. Rapidly rising costs for services and interest rates on debts incurred, increasing unemployment, underemployment, and poverty among the urban population, and growing expenditures to serve the needs of central business districts and more affluent residential neighborhoods have resulted in fewer locally financed amenities such as garbage collection, public transportation, police, fire protection, and the like, particularly in depressed inner-city communities.[41] The movement of stores, medical facilities, and other private services to the more lucrative urban and suburban areas also has added to the problems of older people residing in inner-city ghettos. Moreover, many of the shops remaining have deteriorated, and provide goods and services at relatively higher costs than those in better neighborhoods.

SUBSIDIZED HOUSING PROGRAMS

Despite growing housing shortages among low and moderate income households, rising housing costs relative to income, and the

1949 Housing Act's goal of "a decent home and a suitable living environment for every American family," the state has responded primarily by supporting urban renewal and redevelopment projects that have reduced the supply of low-income housing even further. Moreover, since the 1930s, the primary vehicle for aiding economically disadvantaged households, including the elderly, has been subsidies and guarantees for developers, landlords, and financial institutions. These have increased the production of housing and enhanced profits without threatening existing interest rates and high rents. Only a few inadequately funded programs have been aimed at increasing the purchasing power of the economically disadvantaged population directly.[42] This contrasts sharply with federal tax and interest payment deductions for homeowners that provide substantial and direct relief, particularly at the highest income levels.

Subsidized low-income housing also has aided only a fraction of needy households. Between 1935 and 1967 slightly over 1 million units were made available to low-income households under all government programs. In 1968, as a result of lobbying efforts by the National Association of Home Builders (NAHB) numerical goals were established to maintain the overall housing market at high production levels.[43] The ten-year construction objective, which was set at 26 million homes and apartments, included 6 million federally assisted units, or 600,000 annually, for the poor. By 1978 21.4 million units, or 80 percent of the production target was reached for middle- and upper-class families, and only about 1.6 million, or 27 percent of the goal was met for low-income households.[44]

From the mid-1950s until 1973, when a moratorium was placed on the principal subsidized housing programs, the Department of Housing and Urban Development (HUD) had rehoused only about 750,000 older households. Of these, 600,000 resided in special facilities for the aged, consisting mostly of high-rise apartments.[45] Despite the enactment of revised federal programs since the suspension was lifted, decreased funding for assisted housing, and industry profiteering have continued to prevent publicly supported efforts from providing decent and affordable housing to the indigent older population. Scarce revenues for publicly assisted housing also has pitted the elderly poor against disadvantaged younger households; any gains by older people have been at the expense of other needy groups.

Moreover, only limited supportive services have been provided in conjunction with these projects. It has been estimated that over 3 million noninstitutionalized elderly need assistance in their daily tasks, with at least 2.4 million requiring congregate living arrangements. Without adequate programs, the entire 3 million may be forced into nursing homes unnecessarily.[46] Yet despite authorizations for congregate facilities under the 1978 congregate housing services program (CHSP), there have been insufficient efforts in this direction. Only $6 million of the $10 million authorized for demonstration grants in 1978 was appropriated—and not until 1980.[47] During 1981 the budget for congregate housing services was rescinded, and Congress did not provide any budget authority for the program effective in 1982. In addition, under current public housing regulations a maximum of 10 percent of annual contract costs can be used for special supportive facilities. In contrast, privately developed retirement communities, with social, medical, commercial, recreational, and transportation services, have grown to serve the relatively better-off elderly population, often with government-backed mortgages.

Public Housing

Until 1973 one of the primary though small-scale national efforts to aid economically disadvantaged households in their pressing housing needs was the public housing program enacted as part of the Housing Acts of 1937 and 1949. Its central foci were to stimulate employment in the construction industry and to improve central cities through slum clearance. The provision of housing for low-income families has been only a peripheral goal of the legislation.[48]

The acts authorized local housing authorities (LHA) to develop and operate rental units for low-income families. However, financial commitments have never matched even the modest housing goals of the programs. The active opposition of landlords, mortgage lenders, and other representatives of the private housing industry, who feared that an oversupply would adversely affect their interests, has been instrumental in restricting the number of dwellings constructed. These groups have been formidable contestants against public housing programs. In fact, due to restrictive eligibility standards, which were established to exclude all households who could purchase rental units on the private market, a substantial number of older people with inadequate income levels are ineligible for assistance.

At the end of 1969, only 670,000 public housing units had been constructed, substantially fewer than the 810,000 authorized under the 1949 legislation for completion by the mid-1950s. Moreover, the population served had changed dramatically, further limiting appropriations for new projects. Initially, public housing legislation had been designed to aid an upwardly mobile, younger, white clientele who would require subsidized apartments only as a temporary expedient; after a few years these families purchased their own homes, usually in the expanding suburban developments. By the late 1940s and early 1950s, however, public housing was occupied increasingly by permanently poor and predominantly black families, adding to the growing public hostility toward the program.[49]

In order to curtail popular discontent with the projects, the latter evidenced by the number of successful local referenda opposing new developments, greater emphasis was placed on the elderly beginning in 1956. Legislative amendments eased qualification requirements (e.g., single older people were made eligible), authorized housing designed specifically for the aged, and provided for an increase in allowable construction costs per room when built for people age sixty-two and over. In 1961, LHAs received an additional annual subsidy of up to $120 for each unit occupied by an older household. As Meehan observes: "since the only special features required for 'elderly' housing seemed to have been a few feet of handrail in halls and bathrooms and a warning device to be pulled (if time permitted) should cardiac arrest set in, the increased construction allowance was a windfall for the builder."[50] By 1966 nearly 50 percent of public housing units constructed annually were designed for occupancy by older (and white) people.[51]

Consequently, the percentage of elderly tenants in publicly supported developments rose steadily in the 1960s and 1970s, growing from 20 percent in 1961 to 32 percent in 1966. By 1980 older people accounted for approximately 44 percent of all occupants.[52] Although the elderly benefited disproportionately from the program, due to the low level of construction overall only a small percentage of older people residing in substandard or high rental units relative to income has been affected. A 1977 study showed that about 1.3 percent of all aged households were receiving aid through the public housing program.[53] Of the total units constructed for people age sixty-two and over, only 3 percent has been available for older black households and two-thirds of these units are located in predominantly black facilities.[54] Yet about 70 percent of the black elderly, comprising 8 percent of older people, live in poverty.

Increasing commitments to the elderly have been "made by substitution and not by addition, by diverting resources from one target population to another and not by increasing the total enough to handle the additional burden."[55] Thus any gains achieved by the elderly have been at the expense of other needy households. By 1981 the public housing programs had produced only 1.2 million operating rental units, representing about 1 percent of the nation's total housing stock. Although 155,000 units are scheduled for production, the number of new units funded by Congress has been decreasing steadily; only 24,000 additional ones have been authorized for 1982.

Public housing has been beset with a host of well-known problems, including conflicts over and poor selection of sites, insufficient design and construction standards, inadequate operating and maintenance funds, and low levels of supportive services. The major solution for these problems, urged by private housing interests, has been to increase privatization of public housing activities. The Housing and Urban Development Act of 1965 introduced the Turnkey Program, where private developers became responsible for all aspects of construction, including siting and financial arrangements. Completed projects were then sold to LHA. Rental units produced through this method were used largely to house the elderly. However, as noted by Meehan, privatization did not result in improved siting, enhanced tenant access to services, or better design or construction standards. Instead, it simply increased public outlays by introducing new costs such as profits for developers.[56] The 1965 act also provided for the leasing of privately owned existing rental units under section 23, which was soon expanded to include new construction as well. New construction for lease by LHAs included higher interest rates and private profits, as well as local taxes, all adding to the cost of the facilities without commensurate benefits for the poor and elderly tenants. In 1974, as will be discussed later, privatization was completed as national efforts shifted to other programs, particularly section 8 of the Housing and Community Development Act. By the 1970s the government had, to a large extent, "Abandoned public ownership, inaugurated a holding operation in existing developments, and turned back to the same private sector whose failures had been responsible for the program in the first instance."[57]

Whether developed by public housing authorities or private firms, the design and construction of the buildings tended to be poor. Without quality controls, the construction industry and private developers were able to meet their contract costs and sustain high profits by reducing the quality of the projects. LHAs, which relied on rent receipts for the high and rapidly growing maintenance and operating costs (the latter due, in part, to facilities "designed to maximize profit and not durability")[58] were forced to defer improvements, repairs, and capital investments. Moreover, as costs rose rapidly, particularly during the 1960s, rents increased steadily. Thus tenants incurred growing rental payments relative to income, particularly those on fixed pensions.

When the latter problem was addressed in 1969 through the Brooke amendment, which fixed the maximum rent at 25 percent of the tenant's adjusted income, public housing authorities were even more financially limited in their ability to provide proper care of the facilities. Although annual operating subsidies were made available by the national government for units occupied by the elderly in 1961, and for all projects in 1971, these have not been adequate to alleviate the economic problems faced by public housing authorities. Moreover, growing utility costs and inflation in general have eroded substantially the purchasing value of the subsidies which reached about $1 billion per year in fiscal 1981. In that year Congress enacted the comprehensive improvement assistance program, which authorized $2 billion for capital improvements—an amount that will meet only a fraction of the cost necessary to rehabilitate these rapidly deteriorating public housing facilities. In addition, beginning in 1982, the maximum rent paid by tenants will increase gradually to 30 percent of adjusted income.

Physical deterioration of the buildings themselves, particularly in central cities, has been compounded by their location in deteriorating or high crime neighborhoods. Siting decisions also have failed to include such criteria as the availability of transportation, shops, medical care, social services, and other amenities. As suggested earlier, efforts to provide supportive services within the projects themselves have been vastly insufficient.

Souring maintenance subsidies required by the public housing

authorities contributed substantially to the moratorium on new construction imposed by the Nixon administration in 1973. Although
conventional public housing was revived in 1976, the program has
been curtailed sharply and aid for the elderly has been promoted
primarily through alternative activities. During 1980, 34 percent of
the 15,000 new public housing units available for occupancy were
filled by older people.[59]

Just as important as the low volume of public housing and the
inadequacies of the projects has been the urban renewal and redevelopment emphasis concomitant with the programs. In order to
gain business support for the legislation, the 1937 act specified that
units would be destroyed at a rate equivalent to that of new constructions. The Housing Act of 1949 and subsequent legislation,
which provided growing funds for the clearance of slums and
blighted areas, "enabled private developers to obtain land from
cities at a very substantial write-down of its actual cost with the
difference being subsidized by the U.S. government."[60] Over the
years, particularly since the 1960s, urban renewal and rehabilitation
efforts have expanded considerably to include a growing number
of inner-city localities and projects.

With developers and financial institutions focusing on profit maximization and public officials attempting to generate dollars for city
budgets, most of the redevelopment projects have consisted of high-
rise apartment buildings for middle or upper-income households
as well as industrial or commercial constructions. Low-income
dwellings within deteriorating neighborhoods where a large proportion of older people live have been destroyed at a faster rate
than the provision of new or rehabilitated units at affordable costs
for the poor and elderly.[61] Between 1949 and 1968 alone, the General Accounting Office noted that the government spent $7 billion
on urban renewal with a net loss of 315,000 homes or apartments.
For every new unit constructed, 3.5 were demolished.[62] From 1973
to 1978, a total of 9.2 million new housing units were constructed
in the nation, of which 144,619 were low-income public housing.
During this same period, 1.3 million units were demolished, and
another 2.5 million were lost because of conversions to nonresi-
dential use, condemnation, and the like.[63] In 1979 alone, 11,937
households were displaced under the Uniform Relocation and Real
Property Act of 1970. Half of these families were black, and another
10 percent were Hispanic.[64]

Although older people are less likely to move than younger households, as noted by one observor, the poorest elderly move most frequently "not because they want to, but often as a consequence of condemnation proceedings or urban renewal, which forces them out of the deteriorated sections of town where they can afford the rent."[65] Renewal neighborhoods generally have consisted of from one-half to one-third elderly residents.[66] A large percentage of older people currently reside in center-city neighborhoods which have been newly targeted for destruction or rehabilitation.

The displaced poor, who usually are unable to obtain public housing, have been forced to move into substandard high rental units in other blighted areas of the city. Many older people, particularly older men, often drift to old hotels and rooming houses. Still others find that nursing homes are the only available option. Financial reimbursements for relocation and related expenses have been vastly insufficient to meet the costs incurred by people having to move.

Other Housing Programs

In addition to public housing, the major vehicles for serving the elderly have been through the section 202, section 236, rent supplements, and new section 8 programs. By 1974 the primary thrust of these activities had been redirected to support even more amply the profit-making housing and credit markets.

Enacted in 1965 to aid low-income households (particularly older people) displaced by public action, and who were unable to obtain or afford housing under other subsidized programs, rent supplements provided additional funding to support the privately controlled low-income housing market. Rent subsidies were made available for low income persons residing in privately constructed housing financed through the Federal Housing Authority (FHA), or in units leased by the government under section 23. Households eligible for and accepted into the needs-tested program were required to pay participating landlords the larger of 25 percent of their income or 30 percent of the "market rate." The national government, which assumed the difference in cost between the tenant's obligation and "prevailing rentals" in a specified area, paid the participating landlords directly. While rent relief was provided for some needy households, amounting to only $3.3 million for older people by 1972, major benefits accrued to the private owners who were able to maintain high rents in low quality housing at public expense. It has been estimated that rental costs of these units have been about 10 percent higher than those of comparable private sector housing not receiving assistance.[67] The program, which was eventually phased out, has been revived in altered form as section 8 under the Housing and Community Development Act of 1974.

Section 8 is currently the largest program serving the elderly. It is the only major subsidized housing legislation aiding low-income households that is not tied exclusively to increasing the supply of rental units. Similar to the rent supplement program, the government pays the landlord the difference between an upper limit for rent (the fair market rate established by HUD) and the tenant's share of costs, the latter ranging from 15 to 25 percent of adjusted income. Legislation enacted in 1981, however, has increased the maximum amount to 30 percent of adjusted income. This revision, which is to be phased in over a five-year period, will burden considerably older people and other residents supported through section 8 housing subsidies.

The act authorizes HUD to subsidize rents of eligible tenants in approved existing units, new construction, or substantially rehabilitated units, as well as to guarantee landlords financial support for vacancies. HUD is allowed to enter into contracts with public housing authorities or private developers. The latter generally obtain capital for construction through the private money market at prevailing rates. Sponsors, however, can utilize FHA insured mortgages. In 1977 section 8 rental assistance funds also were designated for use in conjunction with 202 projects.

The act established income eligibility ceilings for families at less than 80 percent and for single people at 56 percent of the community's median income. However, at least 30 percent of households served must have gross incomes that do not exceed 50 percent of the area's median. The mean income of elderly households benefiting from the program in 1979 was $3,155.

Despite the vast number of households potentially eligible for the supplements, a number of factors have restricted the scope and advantages of the program considerably. Since the level of fair market rents set by HUD tends to be low in many areas, the existing and new housing available for section 8 tenants is often of lesser quality than generally available in the community, thus discouraging participation by all but the poorest households. Moreover, as Straszheim observes, "to the extent that Fair Market Rents are below market rents of units in neighborhoods with better public services or amenities, or neighborhoods with higher income households, or predominantly white neighborhoods, entry is discouraged in these areas." The unwillingness of landlords to accept section 8 tenants in more affluent communities further restricts the poor to low-income, sometimes deteriorating inner-city locations.[68]

The low number of units available for assistance has also precluded the program from serving more than a fraction of households with pressing needs for decent and affordable shelter. Though older people have benefited disproportionately from the program, representing over 40 percent of all tenants, by 1981 a total of only about 1.4 million households were being supported through section 8 housing. Over three-quarters of these subsidized housing units have been standard existing apartments. Twenty percent of the total were newly constructed, and 2 percent were substantially rehabilitated units.[69] Furthermore, in 1981 the program was cut substantially; Congress provided funds for 126,500 new units, down from 177,000 in 1980.

Under section 202, enacted as part of the National Housing Act of 1959, direct government loans were made available exclusively to nonprofit sponsors for the full costs of housing constructed for the aged and disabled at a reduced interest rate of 3 percent annually. Despite the act's potential benefits for older people, a substantial construction effort was prevented by major private housing interests. These groups objected to the provision of capital outside of the private money market, particularly at interest below prevailing rates, and to the potential infusion of low-cost housing that would compete with their own activities, thus depressing rents and profits. At the end of 1968, after providing support for the production of only 45,000 units, section 202 was phased out and substituted with the more business-oriented section 236 enacted under the 1968 Housing Act.

In 1974, a revised section 202 was instituted, which utilizes a higher interest rate (in 1980, 9 percent for construction and 8.5 percent thereafter) and allows section 8 rental assistance payments for units constructed or substantially rehabilitated under the program. At the end of 1980, 26,200 section 202 housing units were completed and occupied since the program's renewal in 1974. Although there are long waiting lists for 202 housing, Congress authorized only 18,400 and 17,200 new units for 1981 and 1982, respectively.[70] Not only is the program limited in scope but it serves primarily a white middle-class clientele.[71]

The 236 program provided for direct subsidies to profit-making housing interests as well as nonprofit sponsors in order to encourage the construction of rental units for low- and moderate-income households, particularly the elderly. Until its suspension in 1973, sponsors paid as low as 1 percent interest on mortgages, which were secured through the private money market at existing rates, with the national government providing subsidies for the difference. The program has served essentially to enrich the private interests involved. The mortgage banking industry has benefited substantially while builders and investors obtained quick profits. In fact, section 236, along with section 235, were the main supports of home-building activity, accounting for about 12 percent of all housing starts in 1970.[72] The program also provided a lucrative tax shelter for affluent individuals investing in the projects.[73] On the other hand, the program was unable to meet the housing needs of older people, particularly the lowest income groups. In addition to high government costs and large private sector profits, developers took advantage of the program by keeping rents relatively high and structural quality low, continued existing patterns of housing low-income households in deteriorating neighborhoods, and failed to provide adequate supportive services. High default rates, mismanagement, and other problems also have been common. HUD has estimated that 20 percent of 236 projects would be foreclosed by 1983.[74] In 1979, Congress was forced to appropriate additional subsidies in order to maintain the financial solvency of some of these projects; during 1982, $65 million will be available for repairs and short-term operating costs. At the end of 1978, 18 percent of the 463,000 units constructed under the program, or 82,000 apartments, were occupied by older households.[75]

Other publicly supported programs for the elderly have also focused on lowering provider costs and increasing profitability, including section 231 (Housing Act of 1959) and Sections 504 and 515, supported by the Farmers' Home Administration (FmHA).

Section 231 provides mortgage insurance for private and nonprofit sponsors producing new or rehabilitated rental units for the elderly and disabled whose income is higher than the low or moderate income level. By the end of 1979 the program had insured 63,447 units occupied by older households. The FmHA-supported section 515 offers direct and guaranteed loans for the construction, improvement, or repair of rental or cooperative housing for low-income rural households. By 1980, there were a total of 224,000 section 515 housing units—50 percent of these were occupied by older persons.[76] The 504 program provides direct grants or low interest loans for home rehabilitation. Given the poor housing situation of the rural elderly and the urban focus of other legislation, the FmHA programs are obviously insufficient to meet needs. In addition, a recent congressional investigation of New Mexico's 504 program found, among other things, nepotism in the awarding of grants, distribution of funds, and selection of contractors; incomplete and shoddy work; and low quality materials. The investigators concluded that such abuses are probably nationwide in similar home rehabilitation programs administered by FmHA and HUD.[77]

SUMMARY

The availability, quality, and cost of housing is firmly controlled by private interests, particularly financial institutions, despite massive infusions of public money. Growing rents and maintenance costs relative to income have contributed substantially to the pressing housing problem in the United States, with the burdens falling primarily on those at the lowest income levels, including the vast majority of older people. These rising costs, in turn, have been fueled by financial institutions, developers, landlords, land speculators, oil companies and other representatives of the privately controlled market as well as by public housing policies supporting private capital accumulation and profits. However, activities promoting these goals have proven to be unrelated to the provision of decent and affordable housing for the poor and elderly, and increasingly for middle-income people as well.

In addition to high housing costs, large numbers of older urban households currently live in rapidly deteriorating homes and multifamily dwellings, and many are trapped in blighted neighborhoods where supportive services have become scarce and expensive. As Barton argues, these problems are a necessary by-product of the capitalist system where decent multifamily housing is provided only for those groups that can support, through their rents, rising mortgage interest payments, private profits, and taxes, as well as ensure a competitive return on private investments. Unless the capital required for repairs and services enhance the economic value (e.g., profitability) of the structures sufficiently, lenders and landlords will divert funds to more lucrative investments, resulting in the deterioration of the buildings and eventually entire communities.[78] Moreover, urban renewal and revitalization efforts have further enriched developers, lenders, and landlords while reducing affordable housing stock available to the poor and elderly.

The primary form of housing assistance provided for the aged and economically disadvantaged younger households has been in the form of subsidies to providers, aimed at increasing the profitability of low- and middle-income housing construction, maintenance, and rehabilitation. The emphasis has been on new developments. In addition to providing aid for only a fraction of those in need, these programs have failed to address the root causes of their housing problems, the most important being vastly insufficient incomes as well as structural constraints imposed by the privately controlled credit and housing markets. The most fundamental issues related to housing deprivation are inextricably linked to the problems of poverty and the unequal distribution of power and income in society. These cannot be solved through housing policies alone.

Chapter 7
Human Services

Limitations of the Older Americans Act and Related Programs

D espite the expanding volume of goods and services in the United States there is a widely recognized catalogue of unmet needs for human services, many of which are by-products of capitalist development itself. Only demands that are coupled with "dollar votes" prompt a market response, and these tend to be biased toward the private wants of relatively affluent groups. Because so many of the elderly have low incomes, vital services that would enhance their well-being have not emerged in the marketplace. Where benefits are supplied by proprietary firms, particularly those that appeal to wider and wealthier sectors of society as well as to the aged, they have not been affordable for most of the elderly population. Moreover, services that are created in response to market rather than human criteria enhance profits, and only incidentally do they improve the quality of life. As a result, the primary service problems of older people have included the availability, affordability, and quality of benefits and facilities.

The production and allocation of goods and services for the needy that cannot be marketed profitably by private firms are generally left to voluntary groups and increasingly to public entities. The government usually designs its limited programs ostensibly aimed at the poor in such a way as to serve larger structural interests, usually to socialize the costs of private production and growth. However, as documented by Piven and Cloward, when mass protest erupts among the welfare-dependent population the national gov-

ernment responds with new and expanded public programs to pla-
cate and absorb the agitating groups into the existing order, and
then contracts them after these goals are achieved. For example,
the Great Society poverty programs instituted through the Office
of Economic Opportunity (OEO) during the 1960s were attempts
to integrate the uprooted turbulent minority population into the
system as well as to channel their energies into political support
for the Democratic administration.[1] By the 1970s most of these
OEO programs were either sharply curtailed or abolished entirely.
Entitlement and other programs serving low-income persons also
were reduced considerably through provisions aimed at lowering
eligibility standards and benefit levels, cost-cutting strategies that
were accelerated in the early 1980s.

Community based social services focusing exclusively on the
aged were developed under the Older Americans Act (OAA) of
1965, the latter emanating from a few congressional activists.[2] Instead of providing opportunities for the elderly to exercise power,
or developing a direct funding relationship between the national
government and beneficiary groups, as had been the case with the
Great Society presidential initiatives, the Older Americans Act was
a limited and poorly funded service strategy that avoided challenges
to existing political structures or allocations of social benefits in
society. Its national administrative agency, the Administration on
Aging (AoA) was located within the Department of Health, Education, and Welfare, as contrasted with the initial placement of
OEO in the executive office of the President. OAA was used by the
executive branch as a political tool for strengthening its position
with Congress and state political leaders, and until the early 1970s
AoA actually bypassed age-based organizations.[3] Prior to 1973, federal grants-in-aid for community services under OAA's title III were
channeled through the newly created state units on aging (SUAs).
Title IV research and training programs were under the direct jurisdiction of AoA. Although expenditures for the "war on poverty"
were relatively small, totaling $15.5 billion from 1966 to 1973, as
compared to $120 billion for the Vietnam War during the same
period,[4] funding for OAA was even more restricted. In the seven
years prior to the 1973 Comprehensive Service Amendments, less
than $250 million was appropriated, reaching only about 1.1 million
people or 3 percent of the older population.[5]

THE OLDER AMERICANS ACT

The alleged goals of the Older Americans Act are to enable people to obtain and/or maintain independence in their homes and communities as well as to improve the quality of their lives. The act states that the national and state governments have the responsibility to enable the elderly "to secure equal opportunity to the full and free enjoyment of the following objectives:

(1) an adequate income in retirement in accordance with the American standard of living.

(2) the best possible physical and mental health which science can make available and without regard to economic status.

(3) suitable housing, independently selected, designed and located with reference to special needs and available at costs which older citizens can afford.

(4) Full restorative services for those who require institutional care.

(5) Opportunity for employment with no discriminatory personnel practices because of age.

(6) Retirement in health, honor, dignity—after years of contribution to the economy.

(7) Pursuit of meaningful activity within the widest range of civic, cultural, and recreational opportunities.

(8) Efficient community services, including access to low-cost transportation, which provide social assistance in a coordinated manner and which are readily available when needed.

(9) Immediate benefit from proven research knowledge which can sustain and improve health and happiness.

(10) Freedom, independence, and the free exercise of individual initiative in planning and managing their own lives.[6]

As Estes has observed, despite these grandiose and sweeping goals "The Older Americans Act has restricted the means of achieving its larger objectives of independent living for the elderly to planning, coordination, and service strategies."[7] To meet the real needs of the vast majority of older people and the objectives set forth in the act, including the provision of an adequate income, sufficient employment opportunities, enhanced living environ- ments, and quality medical care, would entail a massive redistri- bution of income and power in society, and fundamental institu- tional change. The service intervention strategy, on the other hand, relegates the problems of the aged to safe issues and projects that do not challenge the status quo. It funds only limited programs and activities that attempt, at best, to treat and mitigate some of the symptoms of poverty and deprivation. The programs are efforts to accommodate the elderly to the system rather than promote needed structural reform.

The OAA implementation strategy defines the problems of the aged and the alternatives for meeting them in ways that fail to alter the trend toward institutionalization or improve substantially the conditions or quality of most older people's lives. Even the limited potential benefits of a service strategy have been undermined by insufficient resources, the range and types of services offered, and the failure to focus on those aged with the highest priority needs.

In order to promote a comprehensive and effective service de- livery system for the sixty and over population, amendments in 1973 authorized the creation of area agencies on aging (AAAs) which were to be new levels of planning organizations in desig- nated service districts under the purview of the state units on aging.[8] The latter were given responsibility for developing state- wide service plans, and allocating funds to and monitoring contracts executed with the new local agencies. This elaborate bureaucratic structure was to be established and supported, however, without sufficient increases in funding, thus further limiting money available for services. By the end of 1980 there were 610 private nonprofit and governmental area agencies on aging operating throughout the United States.[9] Beginning in 1973, separate title VII nutrition pro- jects, established to serve hot meals to the elderly at designated community sites, also were operating within each of the planning and service areas.

By 1981, funding for OAA activities under the auspices of the Administration on Aging had increased to $673 million.[10] Fifty-two percent of the total outlay (or $350 million) was utilized to support hot meal projects, and only a part of the $251.5 million in title III B community service funds was devoted to the actual delivery of services administered by the state and area agencies on aging. The primary thrust of title IIIB activities, particularly since the 1978 amendments, has been on planning, as well as coordinating already established agencies and programs so as to render them more "efficient."[11] Such an emphasis reflects the national government's overall approach, since the 1970s, to meeting the needs of economically disadvantaged persons. Instead of mobilizing additional revenues for establishing, expanding, or improving concrete and quality services, the state had focused on restructuring social service delivery systems. AAAs also are expected to increase community resources available to the elderly by diverting funds from limited national, state, and local programs serving other needy groups. This approach, euphemistically labeled "pooling," attempts to meet the service deficiencies of the aged at the expense of disadvantaged younger people.

Except for information and referral systems (I&R) and other access and coordinating strategies, the local area agencies are allowed to develop and operate actual programs only when they would otherwise be unavailable or insufficient to meet needs. Therefore, planners have produced an endless number of "needs assessment" surveys as well as state and local plans which simply underscore the extent of poverty and deprivation within service areas, and the wide range of problems that the state and local units on aging do not have the power or financial resources to meet. Only about half of the already limited $252 million in title IIIB community service funds in 1981 were used for operating or funding consumable services, with the remainder devoted to administrative costs, subcontract management, planning, coordination, and pooling. In fact, the key roles of the state and area agencies on aging mandated under the 1978 amendments are planning and coordination, and since these are considered to be actual services rendered to the aged they are not included under administrative costs. In 1980, state and area agency administrative expenses alone amounted to $23 million and $51 million respectively, or 12 percent of title III funds.

ILLUSORY BENEFITS: THE PLANNING AND COORDINATION STRATEGIES

During the 1960s and early 1970s there had been an unsystematic growth and development of services at all levels of government to meet demands by various groups having limited purchasing power. Area agencies are expected to promote and encourage cooperation among public and private organizations as well as to identify unnecessary areas of duplication and fragmentation. As noted by Marmor and Kutza, the focus on coordination under OAA assumes that the major service problem facing older people is fragmentation and that "what is needed is not any dramatically different approach but rather the more efficient linking of existing services with each other." The planning and coordination strategies also are attempts to eliminate duplication and encourage greater efficiency. However, Marmor and Kutza convincingly argue that "citing duplication as a service delivery problem presumes an excess of services. Yet evidence suggests that resources are scarce in the social service field. Even if ten local agencies provided an identical service, waiting lists would likely be found in each. If demands for a service are not being met, duplication may not be a problem."[12]

Coordination involves establishing and strengthening linkages between and among diverse, and mostly autonomous organizations as well as rendering them more accessible to elderly clients. These are formidable tasks and area agencies are ill equipped to accomplish them. Tobin, Davidson, and Sack aptly note that providers of services "all pay lip service to the importance of coordination but in realty coordination involves giving up autonomy. Autonomy, however, is not ceded without compensation . . . without additional resources for providing services."[13] Rivalry and competition among agencies for the relatively scarce public and private funds, and the tendency for each organization to advance its own organizational interests, especially those of survival and growth, make it highly unlikely that integration efforts will succeed. Agencies may also have goals that differ substantially from those of the state and area agencies on aging: "Each agency has its own priorities, guards its own turf, and views the clients' needs in its own way."[14] Since title IIIB discretionary funds are vastly insufficient to enable AAAs to expand social services substantially in their respective communities, these agencies have limited "clout" with which to bargain or provide incentives for cooperation.

In order to use title IIIB funds, participating subcontractors must adhere to a variety of rules and guidelines promulgated by AoA, state units, and area agencies, thus adding another set of regulations on their endeavors. This tends to alienate potential partner organizations unless adequate political and economic incentives are available. Alternatively, providers of OAA-funded services and entitlement programs often disassociate themselves from needs-tested programs such as title XX of the Social Security Act, food stamps, and Medicaid, since the latter have a welfare stigma. One study, for example, found resistance among social security staff to providing special efforts for linking SSI clients with supportive services since it was presumed that the welfare focus of the programs would undermine social security's insurance orientation.[15]

Steinberg and others have pointed out that "it is difficult for the AoA, SUAs and AAAs to promote the idea of program planning and coordination through AAAs when, within the Older American's Act programs, policy and programs are not integrated."[16] Nutrition projects and multipurpose senior centers, for example, were not under the jurisdiction of area agencies until 1978. It has been difficult to integrate nutrition projects and senior centers with the area agencies on aging since their respective organizational structures have developed separately. The title V Community Employment Program is administered by the Department of Labor, the volunteer public employment programs by ACTION, and research dissemination by the national clearinghouse.

Area Agencies, which have been superimposed on existing community and state political and administrative units, often are forced to struggle for their own legitimacy, particularly when they are not affiliated with politically powerful groups in their localities. They are also relatively new agencies and, as Marmor and Kutza observe, "often have a difficult time gaining acceptance from other agencies."[17] Their precarious existence, coupled with the insecurity of future funding levels under OAA, which requires periodic renewal, have diverted energies into struggles for their own survival as well as for increased resources to sustain even current levels of activities, a situation that has worsened in the 1980s.

Similarly, AoA, which was supposed to be the focal point for coordination of all national programs, activities, and facilities related to aging, has been unable to promote integration successfully. The agency's low-level position in HUDs office of human development services (OHDS), its limited authority, and inadequate funding levels prevent it from having any significant input into decisions affecting the most pressing needs of the aged: income, health care, and housing. AoA activities have been devoted primarily to its own survival, programmatic tasks, and administrative responsibilities over the sprawling and costly aging network.[18] Faced with innumerable obstacles against integration of services, AoA, SUAs, and AAAs have promoted, at best, increased communication among organizations and a number of interagency agreements. It is highly problematic that these efforts have improved considerably actual services delivered to individual clients.[19]

THE POOLING/ADVOCACY STRATEGY IN A REDUCED RESOURCE SETTING

The 1978 amendments provided an impetus for increased state and area agency advocacy or pooling activities. The underlying concern of the government was (and is) that the aging network would require a massive outlay of capital if it were to meet the growing needs of older people. Rather than appropriate sufficient funds with which to expand community services, the legislation encouraged the state and local units on aging to garner other agencies' resources on behalf of the elderly. Title IIIB money was intended as a catalyst for mobilizing untapped resources from other sources, particularly title XX of the 1972 Social Security Act amendments, revenue sharing funds, and state and local budgets. The advocacy focus, then, is an attempt to persuade other organizations to channel larger shares of their current resources to older people.

The pooling intervention strategy is based, however, on the misguided assumption that there are sufficient and expanding social service revenues available that could be diverted to the aged. At the national level, the problem of inflation, and the overall fiscal crisis, increasingly have been defined by political leaders as excessive government spending for human services, resulting in cutbacks in these areas. Fewer resources relative to need are available to the states and localities through federal grants-in-aid, general revenue sharing, and block grants, thus exacerbating the monetary crisis at these levels of government.

The major social service program serving the poor is title XX of the Social Security Act. Since title XX's enactment in 1972, it has operated under a permanent $2.5 billion annual ceiling, although actual federal expenditures for the program have fluctuated between $2.7 billion and $2.9 billion from 1977 to 1981.[20] Due to inflation, the purchasing power of federal allotments had declined to about $1.3 billion in 1980, rendering it difficult for the states and localities to maintain even existing levels of services.[21] Consequently, many states began to lower eligibility requirements, and charge fees for services; the latter revisions primarily affected childcare, homemaker, and chore services. Between 1979 and 1980 alone, twelve states decreased the allowable income levels at which persons were eligible for specified services.[22]

Total funding under title XX, including state, local, and private contributions, amounted to $3.5 billion in 1979.[23] According to the 1981 Department of Health and Human Services' annual report to Congress, 15 percent of these funds, or $519 million, was spent on aged SSI recipients. This group represented only 6 percent of all persons served under the act, down from 7.5 percent in 1976.[24]

Since its conversion to a Block Grant, legislated by the Omnibus Reconciliation Act of 1981, title XX funds have been sharply reduced. Effective in 1982, federal contributions will amount to only $2.4 billion, representing a 20 percent cut from the program's 1981 expenditure level. Moreover, the requirement that states must spend at least 50 percent of federal title XX money for public assistance recipients was rescinded, as were all other national income eligibility guidelines aimed at targeting programs to needy persons.

These revisions, along with rising inflation, will not only further reduce the number, types, and range of services available to the poor but also will accelerate the trend toward fee-for-service provisions. In addition, since persons at all income levels will now be eligible for program benefits, there will be even greater competition for the reduced amount of funds. These changes come at a time when there are growing numbers of older people in need of community support programs.

The curtailment of the federal Food Stamp Program, stabilized funding levels for low-income energy assistance despite rising energy costs, and the decline in governmental resources for antipoverty programs in general,[25] all attest to the limited prospects for meeting current and future social service needs of older people. The decentralization of such efforts begun under the Nixon Administration, and pressed forward in the 1980s, has given greater financial responsibility to state governments, which have fewer resources for supporting community services, and the poorest records of serving the most deprived groups.

Growing poverty, and high unemployment among younger persons, coupled with stagnating wages (particularly in the competitive labor market) and rising inflation, have produced greater needs for expanded state-supported programs overall, thus pitting the poor (and their allied service providers) against each other. Rather than mobilize jointly for the redistribution of power and resources in the United States, each of the needy population groups struggles to press its claim for larger shares of scarce funds. Consequently, in the context of a fixed, or reduced resource setting, successful advocacy on behalf of the elderly entails channeling money from other disadvantaged sectors of society. In addition, the aging network itself will find it increasingly necessary to devote its energies "to defending past gains rather than marshalling new benefits."[26]

Although another component of advocacy is to increase power by mobilizing the elderly in their own behalf, and encouraging client input into decisions affecting them, AoA, SUAs, and AAAs have not placed a high priority on involving the elderly in their activities. On the contrary, Estes has observed that the National Association of State Units on Aging, National Association of Area Agencies on Aging, National Association of Nutrition Directors, National Institute of Senior Centers, other organized service providers, and national membership organizations, many of which have been spawned by OAA itself, are the dominant actors influencing debate at the national level over OAA reauthorization decisions. Similarly, at the state and local levels information about and definitions of problems and needs, service priorities, and the formulation of strategies to meet these have become the province of professional staff, service contractors, and local affiliates of national groups. One consequence has been to achieve greater control over elderly Americans, rather than to provide them opportunities for increasing control over their own lives. Estes further argues that the aging network tends to frame the issues and implementation processes in ways that meet the interests and needs of its respective organizations, often at the expense of the elderly.[27]

The primary means available for older people to influence state and area agencies on aging, and nutrition projects, are advisory councils. However, studies of these councils consistently show that they are not effective mechanisms for providing adequate participation by those people affected by decisions made. In addition to having limited authority over agency activities, the participating members are, for the most part, unrepresentative of the elderly population or of those who are served by the programs. For example, a recent study by Malakoff and McQuaide of forty-six advisory councils to area agencies in Pennsylvania showed that the median family income of its members was from $12,000 to $16,000 annually; over 61 percent of participants held professional or managerial positions in their current or previous employment; and the vast majority did not have any personal contact with the services provided.[28]

SUPPORTIVE SERVICES: DISTRIBUTING
SCARCE RESOURCES

Despite the unresolved problems inherent in the current foci under title III, which appears to have only limited benefits for the elderly, Estes concludes that: "to challenge the planning, pooling and coordination paradigm would be to attack the official definition of the problem as one of fragmented services. Such a challenge would also raise the awkward question of what other government policy could be substituted at a time when there will almost certainly be no additional federal appropriations to make possible new definitions of the problem."[29]

Many of the supportive services required by older people and other disadvantaged groups have been and continue to be engendered by the market system itself, and public policies supporting private accumulation. By ignoring the social consequences of production for profit, political and economic institutions actually have created growing unmet needs for a wide range of collective benefits and facilities. The major service problems of the elderly, then, "are explicable in their current as in their historical conditions as 'by-products' of a process of development in which profit and power—not natural balance, not human needs and possibilities, not social balance—were the guiding criteria."[30] OAA services can be viewed as a limited attempt by the state to cover some of the social costs of growth and "development" under advanced capitalism and to conform older people to system deficiencies.

At the 1971 White House Conference, participants cited transportation as the third major problem faced by older people. Only income and health needs were considered to be higher priorities.

Transportation, in fact, is one of the four priority services mandated under the OAA amendments, and constitutes one of the largest expenditure items under OAA's title IIIB.

The limited expansion of specialized transportation for older people under OAA, however, does not affect the power and influence of the automobile, oil, rubber, and construction industries. By encouraging an emphasis on highways and automobiles, hindering development and maintenance of public transportation systems, and playing a decisive role in the dismantling of the national railroad system, these private interests have created and continue to generate what has been labeled as the "transportation problem" of the elderly.[31]

In many parts of the country, especially rural areas, there is no public transportation system at all. In other localities facilities are inadequate to meet the needs of the general population for safe, convenient, and reliable services. The limited outlays for transportation programs under OAA does not even begin to address the transportation problems of older people, let alone the rest of the population. In 1977, 2.5 million elderly or about 8 percent of those eligible, participated in transportation services funded through title IIIB at a total cost of $16 million. This would represent an average expenditure of about $6.50 for each person served. Moreover, in that year only $1.6 million was spent on escort services which reached slightly under 290,000 people, according to official estimates.[32] The funding available to each of the small number of participating clients is obviously an insufficient amount to seriously affect anyone's mobility or to promote independent living. Even combined with funding available to the elderly and handicapped under the Urban Mass Transportation Act of 1974, which will amount to about $0.7 million in 1982 (down from $0.9 million in 1981), OAA expenditures on public transportation are sorely inadequate relative to need.

The emphasis on the automobile for meeting transportation needs has made car ownership and the ability to drive a major determinant of mobility in American society. The Motor Vehicle Manufacturers Association found that in 1974 39 percent of households headed by a person sixty-five and over did not own an automobile, as compared to 15 percent of younger family units.[33] However, the 1976 Harris survey on aging in the United States shows that "income affects mobility even more dramatically than does age." Not having a car or being able to drive was viewed as a serious problem by 17 percent of the older and 22 percent of the younger respondents with annual incomes under $7,000 as against only 3 percent and 4 percent, respectively, of those with incomes of $15,000 or more.[34] High and growing costs of energy, insurance, and automobile repair and maintenance prevent many of the poor, including the elderly poor, from owning cars.

Moreover, inadequate access to medical care by needy older people, as shown in chapter 5, has been fostered by the medical market, which concentrates its services in more affluent urban neighborhoods. Distances from other vital community and commercial services and facilities, as suggested in chapter 6, are often attributable to the reluctance of private providers to locate in the less profitable, deteriorating neighborhoods where the poor and low-income elderly have been forced to reside. Publicly supported amenities have also become scarce in these areas. The transportation intervention strategy, then, is a limited attempt to accommodate older people to systemic deficiencies (e.g., poorly located services) rather than to reform the underlying structural causes of the problems. Transportation programs bring some elderly, at best, to distant services rather than provide public and private facilities in convenient locations.

Another priority "service" emanating from the assumption that the major problems of the elderly stem from inadequate access to and linkages with currently operating programs is information and referral (I&R) systems. Confronted with a bewildering array of agencies and organizations, older people are often uncertain where to turn for help. Even those elderly who are aware that a service exists may be unclear about eligibility requirements, where to apply, or costs. Rather than become involved in the bureaucratic maze, many in critical need of services merely do without them at the risk of deteriorating health and home environments. Consequently, under this definition of the problem—inadequate knowledge about programs and the complexity of the service network itself—the "remedy" has been enhancement of I&R. Funding for information and referral systems under OAA represent a significant percentage of all title IIIB expenditures.

The rapid proliferation of diverse, often specialized, I&R programs since the mid-1960s has engendered competing, fragmented, and overlapping I&R systems within the states and individual communities. At least three different federal agencies have a mandate to institute I&R facilities for the aged alone: the Community Services Agency (CSA); the Social Security Administration (SSA); and the Administration on Aging (AoA). In many cases these systems operate independently of each other. Lack of coordination among these efforts has limited any potential benefits for the elderly.[35] One study observes that despite the rapid growth of I&R programs, "the social service structure is no less complex now, and it is as difficult to find services as it was in 1966."[36]

Moreover, as aptly noted by Schmandt, Bach, and Radin "the best I&R service amounts to little if it does not lead to services beyond I&R itself." Since communities have developed limited social services and facilities, particularly in rural areas, and do not have the fiscal capacity to initiate and expand sorely needed new ones, I&R is usually not the most critical requirement. The benefits of I&R are further undermined by the fact that many agencies are not financially capable of accommodating additional clients.[37] Just as important, I&R activities usually do not include attempts to assess whether the aged who are provided with information actually receive services, the appropriateness of referrals, the quality or effectiveness of services rendered, or whether clients are satisfied with them.

Although I&R activities can be linked with outreach, the latter has received only limited attention; these types of services account for only a fraction of title IIIB outlays and reach only a small percentage of the elderly population. Outreach activities are focused on disseminating information through the mass media (television, radio, and newspaper advertisements), special newsletters or flyers aimed at age-based groups and organizations, and appearances before senior clubs. Such efforts tend to inform primarily the better educated or more affluent older people about available programs. An adequate outreach program, one that would seek out those who are the most needy, would entail large expenditures of staff time and agency resources. With an emphasis on serving large numbers of older people at low unit costs, area agency outreach efforts have not aided substantially the disadvantaged elderly.

In addition to access and linkage services such as transportation, I&R, and outreach, the 1978 OAA amendments established priorities for legal counseling and in-home services. The largest expenditure for concrete services provided under title IIIB is devoted to in-home services, such as homemaking, friendly visiting, home health aide tasks, and chore maintenance. In 1977, these programs totaled $16.9 million, and served 486,529 persons. This would have amounted to an average cost of less than $35 per elderly client. These outlays are clearly insufficient for facilitating independent living or reducing institutionalization.

Demand for in-home supportive services also tends to exceed supply in most areas, thus further limiting the potential for fulfilling these needs.[38] The growing tendency for area agencies to contract with proprietary firms to supply homemaker services presents opportunities for abuses similar to those encountered within nursing homes. As one source notes: "in addition to the red-tape surrounding programs, which limit availability and use, there are not adequate standards to ensure quality care for those who receive it. The workers are typically underpaid, expected to work long hours, under difficult conditions, and often without any training."[39] Such problems are likely to worsen; legislation in 1981 eliminated the requirement that for-profit organizations must demonstrate clear superiority to nonprofit agencies in order to be funded through the area agencies on aging.

Legal counseling services under OAA are provided through Legal Service Corporation (LSC) projects or other providers coordinating services with them. Older people also are served by the Legal Service Corporation through its own federal funding which amounted to $321 million in 1981. Twelve percent of its program recipients in that year, or 150,000 persons, were elderly. Not only are OAA and LSC legal service expenditures insufficient to meet need but, in addition, the Reagan administration has proposed that LSC be abolished, an action that would limit even further the availability of legal aid to the elderly poor and other low-income persons.

The OAA outlay for residential repair and renovation are also vastly inadequate, particularly given the large percentage of elderly living in deteriorated housing who are unable to afford the high costs of repairing leaking roofs, poor electrical wiring, and faulty plumbing or heating units. Funding levels for housing repair and renovation do not even begin to remedy the situation. Nor can OAA address the fundamental housing problems of older people (outlined in chapter 6) that have been created by financial institutions, developers, and other powerful private housing interests.

Although OAA requires area agencies to spend 50 percent of their budgets on the priority services (i.e., access services, in-home services, legal aid, and residential repair) it does not designate how the money is to be allocated among these areas or specify a minimum funding level for each. In addition, the remaining funds are distributed according to state and local priorities. These other services include telephone reassurance, health screening, education, and recreational, cultural, and exercise programs.

In attempting to develop or expand all of these programs, as well as to accommodate diverse service providers and other powerful interests in their communities, the state and area agencies on aging have spread out their limited title IIIB service funds on scattered projects that do not meet vital needs or increase substantially the availability of any particular service. In Pennsylvania, for example, despite OAA, title XX, and other publicly supported social service programs, it was estimated that 81 percent of all older people requiring homemaker care in 1976 were not receiving this service. The percentage of elderly with unmet needs for other essential supportive services included the following: transportation/escort, 62 percent; legal services, 72 percent; protective services, 81 percent; shopping assistance, 80 percent; chore services, 86 percent; and day care, 97 percent.[40]

Title V grants for the acquisition or renovation of multipurpose senior centers were enacted in 1973, although funding was not available until 1977. By 1980, there were about 4,200 of these centers supported by OAA funds. Since the consolidation of title V with title III in 1978, outlays have been available for the limited construction of these facilities as well as for personnel and operating costs.[41] The 1978 amendments mandated area agencies to divide their planning and service districts into "community service" areas and designate a focal point for aging programs in each. Emphasis has been placed on the growth of multipurpose senior centers to serve as these central age-based facilities.

Several studies of these centers have shown that they "serve a rather elite group of older people . . . (who tend to be of) . . . higher socioeconomic status, healthier, and more sociable than nonparticipants."[42] With a current emphasis on recreational and other social activities that cater to the nonpoor older population, it is highly unlikely that senior centers will meet the pressing needs of indigent older people. Because of scarce resources available under title III,

any successful attempt to increase funding for multipurpose facilities would result in less money available for other programs.

The Older Americans Act is premised on what Estes astutely has
described as a classless view of aging. This has allowed the relatively better-off elderly substantial access to scarce resources.[43] The
1978 amendments, which maintained universal eligibility standards, merely state that "preference" is to be given to older persons
having the greatest social or economic needs, categories that include advanced age (seventy-five and over); physical impairment;
social isolation; minority status; and low income. Local agencies,
however, have considerable latitude in deciding which older people will receive support in their respective communities. There is
no effort to compel AAAs to target resources to specified groups.
Nor does the OAA distribute funds to AAAs on the basis of need;
funding is allocated according to the number of older persons in
each state, rather than on the number of elderly poor.

The effect of avoiding issues of class, and not targeting resources
to the neediest has been to neglect a large percentage of the economically deprived older population. In addition, the bias toward
countable accomplishments, which accommodate agency rather
than client interests, has skewed funding in favor of projects having
low unit costs and those affecting large numbers of people, regardless of the quality of service or whether they meet the most urgent
needs. Programs and facilities that have relatively low per capita
costs such as special buses, mass health screening, and recreational,
cultural, and other social activities have been preferred by area
agencies over adult day care, outreach, homemaker, and escort services. Many of the former programs are utilized primarily by the
middle class. Moreover, where large numbers of people are served
with low levels of funding, the impact on individual lives tends to
be negligible. Serving 9.3 million persons in 1980, funding under
title IIIB would have amounted to an average of less than $30 per
person.

The haphazard and piecemeal implementation of programs, coupled with the unwarranted expectation that services developed
with title IIIB funds would be seed-grant programs to tap other
sources, particularly local governments, have prevented long-term
structural commitments to the elderly. Until 1978, title IIIB projects
were supported by area agencies for a maximum of only three years.

However, with inadequate resources currently available for human services overall, area agencies have had to extend their financial commitments for selected projects. Other programs initially established with title IIIB revenues have been terminated after a few years.

In segregating service programs by age, the government has defined the needs of older people as different from those of the under-65 disadvantaged population. This strategy, which will be discussed later, has excluded the elderly from job-related programs that would provide those interested and capable of working with the resources necessary to enhance their purchasing power and to reduce their dependency. On the other hand, although many of the needs of older Americans are the same as those experienced by poor younger people, age-segregated programs tend to prevent the latter from participating in special services developed exclusively for the aged. Transportation provided for older people residing in isolated rural areas, for example, ignores the plight of similarly situated indigent younger families.

The tendency of AAAs to fund only traditional social services has impeded the development of new, flexible, and varied intervention strategies that would not only meet the diverse needs of the elderly more effectively but also would allow them sufficient service options from which to choose. Instead of having programs adapted to their particular circumstances, individuals and their families must adjust to the types of support services available. This limits the control of clients over decisions affecting their lives.

FEEDING OLDER PEOPLE

The largest, single program under OAA, instituted in 1972, is the title VII congregate dining facilities. In 1978, when the nutrition projects were incorporated under title III, area agencies were given administrative authority over them. However, separate funding for the nutrition programs has been maintained. In 1981, $295 million was allocated to establish or operate nutrition projects which served about 3 million people at 12,475 local sites.[44] The outlay for the hot meal program, including an additional $55 million for home delivered meals, represented over 50 percent of total OAA expenditures under the purview of AoA.

The primary impetus for title VII was the identification of malnutrition and nutritional deficiencies as key problems faced by many older people. The underlying thrust of congregate meals is to "remedy" these conditions by altering the nutritional practices and social environments of participants. Thus along with the provision of a daily meal, project directors provide lectures and information on proper nutrition, health, budgeting, and home management. The provision of opportunities for socialization is also a major component of the food program; its purpose is to surmount the presumed poor motivation of single older people to cook for themselves. By defining the nutritional problems of the elderly as personal inadequacies, often attributed to loneliness or advanced age, the program deflects attention from larger structural issues. It underemphasizes the fact that low income prevents adequate nutrition. Similarly, the problem of disproportionately high food prices in the deteriorated urban neighborhoods or isolated rural communities where most of the elderly reside is not addressed. Nutritional projects are short-range expedients to meet long-term, systemic problems.

Cost limitations per meal and an emphasis on efficiency often restrict the ability of providers to offer a variety of daily meals or to meet ethnic preferences. The low level of client input into decisions at most meal sites also adds to the powerlessness of recipients and the control of professionals over their well-being. Activities stressing nutritional education through such approaches as "food bingo," and lectures entitled "Let's Talk About Milk," or "Everything You Always Wanted to Know about Cereal,"[45] treat those who are financially incapable of purchasing adequate meals as (using Maggie Kuhn's terminology) wrinkled babies.[46]

Although the nutrition projects attract large numbers of elderly, they serve only about 9 percent of those eligible, and due to insufficient funding they cannot accommodate all people expressing an interest in the program. The number of people on waiting lists for the hot meals has been growing steadily. Recent increases in funding have been utilized to offset the impact of inflation on food costs, and not to increase substantially the number of people served.

Despite requirements for outreach activities, there is little evidence that the most impoverished have been brought into the program. In a 1975 Research Opinion Corporation study undertaken for AoA, it was disclosed that most nutrition projects "filled their budgeted numbers of meals within a short time subsequent to funding without significant outreach efforts to locate needy elderly. Outreach efforts often became attempts to follow-up on dropouts from the program and not to recruit those elderly who were seriously malnourished or isolated."[47] Project sponsors, which tend to be groups with an already established (and usually middle-income) clientele, primarily serve older people who are members of their respective organizations. They do not attempt to locate hot meal sites in areas with high concentrations of low-income elderly. Consequently, those individuals suffering from poor nutrition have not been the primary beneficiaries of the program.

Another program aimed at nutritional sustenance, which is outside the jurisdiction of AoA (and the Older Americans Act) is the food stamp program. Initially developed as a pilot project in 1961, "it was sold partly on the idea of helping not only low-income people, but also agriculture and those who sell food."[48] Rather than provide cash, which would enable people to purchase food commodities without being stigmatized, the Department of Agriculture (USDA) distributes stamps to the eligible poor. Restrictive eligibility standards have prevented the program from reaching a substantial percentage of people having poor diets. The welfare stigma associated with the program, inadequate outreach efforts, and the purchase requirement (the latter eliminated in 1977) have encouraged low participation rates among income eligible older people. In 1980 only 1.7 million elderly persons aged sixty or over, representing less than 5 percent of the aged, were served by the program. Insufficient benefits accruing to recipients also have contributed to the failure of the program to meet the nutritional needs of the elderly and other deprived groups.

The open-ended commitment by the national government to pay the full costs of the program has generated growing federal outlays. USDA allocated under $1 billion in 1970, and slightly over $5 billion in stamps by 1976, thus prompting drastic revisions by Congress.[49] Although the 1977 food stamp reform law was ostensibly aimed at targeting benefits to those most in need, it also instituted a number of cost control provisions that curtailed the program sharply. In addition to removing the purchase requirement, a revision that was to increase the participation of the elderly in the program, the amendments substituted a standard deduction for previously allowed exclusions; older people, however, were eligible for a special medical deduction. Congress also imposed a cap on annual funding. Maximum outlays were set at $5.9 billion in 1978 and $6.2 billion in 1979 and 1980.

In 1980, Congress was forced to increase the spending cap and appropriate additional funds to meet rising program costs that reached $11.4 billion, or $5.2 billion over the original cap set for that year. Consequently, Congress enacted new amendments that reduced asset limits for program eligibility (except for older households with two or more persons), froze the amount of the standard deduction, and eliminated the twice-a-year cost of living increases in benefit levels. Although the medical deduction for persons aged sixty and over was expanded, this provision was deleted the following year.

The Omnibus Reconcilation Act of 1981 provided for even lower eligibility standards and benefit amounts. It has been estimated that 1.1 million people will become ineligible for the program as a result of the 1981 amendments alone. Even though older people were exempt from some of these revisions they, along with other beneficiaries, will receive fewer stamps because of changes in benefit inflation adjustments.[50]

The Reagan administration has proposed additional cost-saving measures, including one that would allow the states to set eligibility guidelines. Such a change would result in wide variations in eligibility and benefits among the states, as had existed prior to 1971. Since that year the food stamp program has been governed by national standards set by Congress and the Department of Agriculture. The Reagan administration also has attempted to reduce or eliminate the standard deduction, minimum benefit (now set at $10 per month for a household with one or two persons), and the separate, higher test of eligibility for older persons, as well as to increase the benefit reduction rate.[51]

Given the steady rise in the number of impoverished households in the United States, including the elderly, and the imposition of congressional spending limits below what the program is expected to cost, Congress will be forced to appropriate additional funds, legislate new cutbacks, or temporarily suspend the program when it exhausts its annual appropriations.[52] Furthermore, in a reduced resource setting, exemptions for older people, no matter how beneficial, only foster fewer benefits for all needy persons.

Clearly both OAA and USDA food programs are inadequate attempts to meet the problem of nutritional deficiencies prevalent among low-income people. Growing medical, energy, and housing costs will force the elderly to choose increasingly between satisfying health, heating, shelter, and nutritional needs.

EMPLOYMENT SERVICES

Most supportive services required by the elderly do not directly or even indirectly enhance capital accumulation, profits, or economic growth, and this factor has contributed to the minimal support for them. In fact, the primary social services provided in this country have focused on job training. The vast array of manpower training programs emerging in the early 1960s, which were consolidated under the Comprehensive Employment and Training Act (CETA) in 1973, the Work Incentive Program (WIN), vocational rehabilitation for economically deprived and handicapped people, and similar measures, have been strategies to "rehabilitate" potentially employable people so as to remove them and their families from public welfare rolls. They also have become subsidies for large corporations. According to the General Accounting Office, such programs serve "to reimburse employers for OJT (on-the-job-training) which they would have conducted even without the government's financial assistance."[53] Under the 1978 amendments to CETA, Congress has enlarged the role of the private sector in the program. Outlays for job training and other employment-related programs have grown steadily since 1962, reaching about $10 billion annually by 1981.[54] However, in 1981 Congress eliminated the CETA public service program, which amounted to $3.1 billion, and imposed a cap on expenditures for general job training and youth employment and training programs. As a result, CETA will support approximately 900,000 fewer jobs in 1982.

Employment activities directed specifically at the aged have been implemented through the Senior Community Service Employment Program (SCSEP). Established as Operation Mainstream and funded under EOA from 1965 until 1974, the program was incorporated into OAA as title IX in 1975, and reauthorized as title V in 1978. Funds are administered by the Department of Labor which, in turn, contracts with the state units on aging and nine national organizations. These include: Green Thumb, Inc.; the

National Council on the Aging; National Council of Senior Citizens; the National Retired Teachers' Association; the American Association of Retired Persons; the U.S. Department of Agriculture's Forest Service; the National Center on Black Aged; the National Association of Pro-Spanish Speaking Elderly; and the National Urban League. The program provides part-time, low-paid community service employment for people aged fifty-five and over whose incomes do not exceed 125 percent of the poverty level. It is an extremely limited program which has had to struggle against repeated attempts at termination by the Executive Branch. Only 9,000 job slots were available in 1973 and 1974, and 12,400 in 1975 and 1976.[55] By 1981 the program was expanded to a mere 54,200 part-time positions at a cost of $277 million. Although funding will be increased to $294 million in 1983 to meet the costs of inflation, the number of job openings will remain at the 1981 level. Consequently, fewer than 1 percent of eligible older people will be aided.

Other federal employment initiatives aimed at older people are administered under ACTION. These include the foster grandparent program (FGP), senior companion program (SCP), the retired senior volunteer program (RSVP), and the newly created fixed income counseling (FIC) and helping hand (HH). RSVP, HH, and FIC provide opportunities for unpaid volunteer work; FGP and SCP supply older workers with low-paid community service employment at a wage level of $2 per hour. In 1981, there were approximately 22,000 paid, and 28,000 volunteer jobs funded at a cost of $89 million. Despite some community benefits that are provided by the elderly participants, these volunteer and part-time, low-wage programs do not redress the economic deprivation suffered by the vast number of indigent unemployed older people.

Viewed primarily as a permanently dependent population, the aged poor have typically been excluded from the larger employment and training programs. It was estimated in 1976 that only 40,000 persons or 1 percent of the 4 million low-income people aged fifty-five and over defined by the Department of Labor as employable were served through federal job-related services.[56] Under the Vocational Rehabilitation Act "individuals are denied services if a rehabilitation center feels that a person's age will limit his or her employability. Americans over sixty-five make up only 1.8 percent of the total number accepted for rehabilitation."[57] Pierce A. Quinlin, who had responsibility for administering both the OAA title IX (now title V) and CETA programs, "admitted that CETA, as the principal Federally supported manpower program, has served the needy older worker far less adequately, but stated that the very existence of the specialized title IX effort is a disincentive to do more for that group on the part of those who devise and operate CETA programs at the state and local levels."[58]

Despite mandates under the 1978 CETA amendments which called for greater emphasis on obtaining job training and employment opportunities for persons aged fifty-five and over, and enactment of the Older Workers Initiatives, program sponsors have not been responsive. According to one source, "the data indicate that a substantial portion of the prime sponsors do not intend to operate programs designed for older workers."[59] In a recent government report it was disclosed that in 1980 only 3.2 percent of CETA funds were spent on older persons, and that the percentage of elderly participants actually had declined since 1979.[60]

FEEDING GERONTOLOGISTS: RESEARCHING THE ELDERLY

Under title IV, OAA provides funding for the training of professionals and other persons serving older people, age-based research, multidisciplinary centers of gerontology, and model projects. In 1980 these activities accounted for $17 million, $8.5 million, $3.8 million, and $25 million, respectively, although funding for title IV was cut significantly effective for 1982; total program costs cannot exceed $23.2 million in 1982, and $24.7 in 1983. The purpose of title IV is to enhance the capabilities of individuals working with the elderly, generate knowledge about and potential solutions to problems affecting the aged, and encourage people to choose careers in gerontology. The underlying assumption is that the absence of trained manpower and insufficient empirical research are important barriers to proper service delivery.

Serious questions, however, have been raised as to whether the proliferation of data, knowledge, and information generated under AoA sponsorship actually furthers the interests of older people. Maggie Kuhn, for one, has observed that these endeavors "often benefit gerontologists and the institutions they serve: not the victims of the system." While enriching universities and other host institutions, and meeting the needs of "prolific professionals in search of publication, a grant or professional identity," many research projects fail to contribute substantially to the improvement of public policy, service delivery systems, or the well-being of the elderly population in general.[61]

In their relentless pursuit of data, social scientists generally confine the focus of their research to narrow issues and questions that are quantifiable, while ignoring urgent problems that are less easily measured. The current thrust of gerontological research and demonstration projects, funded through AoA, promotes the idea of specific remedies to cure specific problems faced by the elderly. This reductionist approach ignores political and economic causes of social problems, and their linkages to broader structural issues. Similarly, questions of class, race, and sex tend to be underemphasized. Current research is often premised on the view that the critical problems of older people are technical ones that are amenable to scientific solutions.

Where important research findings are made, inadequate dissemination and limited funds for implementation prevent utilization of the data by policy makers and practitioners. Typically, even model projects are discontinued after their initial funding is exhausted. Moreover, it has been argued that practitioners often "see research projects as ending with a final report to the funder which gathers dust in the Archives, or one or two journal articles (a year or more later), but with little or no usable feedback to the people who might benefit from the findings."[62] Research is rarely translated into workable programs. The use of age-related research has also been hampered by the sheer volume of information, which is estimated at about 34,000 publications between 1960 and 1978 alone.[63]

Title IV grants also have contributed to the burgeoning of college and university multidisciplinary centers of gerontology and other programs aimed at gerontological career training. These endeavors have promoted the growth of a cadre of professional practitioners, administrators, college teachers, and researchers, coupled with a commensurate increase in research data, articles, journals, agencies, and technical approaches to social problems—activities that meet professional rather than client needs. On the other hand, the dearth of trained homemakers, home health aides, and nursing home assistants, and the low wages, low status, and poor working conditions faced by these workers who perform important main-

tenance tasks for the elderly, have not been addressed through title
IV grants.

SUMMARY

The Older Americans Act has not been effective in reducing
institutionalization or enhancing the well-being of most older people. The limited scope of the programs, strategies pursued, and the
types of services and projects developed have prevented any significant amelioration of the pressing problems experienced by older
people, particularly the elderly poor. Rather than providing opportunities for the aged to control their own lives, which would
entail radical structural reform, the act has promoted the growth of
an elaborate and costly labyrinth of national, state, and local agencies, as well as a cadre of professional administrators, planners,
researchers, and practitioners. This aging network has pursued activities that enhance its own interests and needs.

Only a small proportion of the limited resources available for
community services is devoted to developing, improving, or expanding consumable benefits. Instead, the funds have been utilized
unsuccessfully to increase the efficiency of social service delivery
systems and to render them more accessible to the elderly through
better planning and coordination. Moreover, professionals have
been encouraged to garner larger shares of already scanty funds
available for human services overall on behalf of the elderly. The
effect of this pooling/advocacy strategy has been to promote greater
competition over scarce resources, thus diverting attention from the
inadequate provision of collective community resources in general.

Private and public activities under capitalism have generated
many of the well-documented problems experienced by older people and other indigent groups. The services provided through OAA
merely represent a limited attempt to socialize the human costs of
private accumulation and production for profit and to adapt the
elderly to current systemic deficiencies. Moreover, even where
beneficial services have been more readily available, they have not
aided sufficiently those people with the greatest needs.

The most significant activities in terms of total outlays under OAA
have been the congregate dining and employment programs. In
addition to serving only a small percentage of poorly nourished

older people, the food projects are merely attempts to treat one major symptom of inadequate income, thus avoiding the root causes of nutritional deficiencies prevalent among indigent elderly people. Similarly, the senior Community Service Employment Program, which provides only part-time, low-wage work for the aged poor, has not seriously enhanced older people's employment opportunities. Nor has it addressed their urgent income needs.

OAA has funded a wide range of haphazardly developed programs, services, and facilities that have not improved materially the quality of older people's lives. While providing a few desperately needed services for a fraction of the elderly poor, recreational, social and other activities for the relatively better-off elderly, and other benefits for service providers, administrators, professionals, and researchers, OAA avoids fundamental issues such as inadequate income, high unemployment, poor housing conditions, and inaccessible and costly medical care. It focuses only on safe problems that can be addressed without requiring a rearrangement of current institutional practices or a reordering of priorities in society.

Chapter 8
Epilogue: Perspectives on Reform

The United States has entered the 1980s plagued with economic turbulence, high and rising unemployment and inflation, low levels of economic growth, and a host of other structural problems that are proving increasingly difficult to resolve. The myriad social ills associated with aging, documented throughout this volume, have their roots in the same forces that generated the general U.S. economic crisis. The political economy of old age has contributed substantially to the fiscal crisis, growing state intervention in the economy and expansion of the public sector on behalf of capital, concentration of industrial and financial power, reinforcement of inter- and intraclass as well as intergenerational inequalities, and other adverse social, political, and economic conditions.

CAPITAL, THE STATE, AND AGING

The ascent of monopoly capitalism, supported through state policies, was accompanied by the steady proletarianization and deskilling of the work force, increasing mechanization, and an intensified pace in the work process. These changes, which fostered greater structural unemployment, superannuation, and informal and forced retirement, resulted in growing poverty for vast numbers of older people who had become dependent on a wage for subsistence. The rise of the privately controlled medical market, which served the needs of health care providers and corporate interests, led to exploitation of illness for profit. Escalating health care costs contributed to indigency among older people, who were generally unable to obtain, or afford, private insurance. Growing housing costs relative to incomes, deteriorating urban neighborhoods, a paucity of private and public services, the decreasing availability of low- and moderate-income dwellings, and other adverse conditions, fueled by the privately controlled and publicly supported housing markets, led to growing shelter problems, particularly for the elderly poor. Unfettered industrial growth and development created rising unmet needs for a wide variety of community facilities and services.

Public and private programs affecting the elderly are part of the more general state-business partnership which has strengthened during the last several decades. Sustained economic growth in the past was possible only because of the myriad functions provided by the national state for the maintenance of capitalist production and private accumulation, and for insuring profitability. Similarly, the goals of age-based policies were broader than merely providing benefits for older people. The various programs were designed and implemented in ways that directly, or indirectly, benefited capital and monopoly professional interests. The funding and taxing systems of the more important and costly programs, such as Social Security, Medicare, and private retirement systems, also tended to be structured so as to avoid any substantial deductions from profits accruing to the capitalist class.

The underlying objectives of policy initiatives on behalf of the elderly have had the effect of enhancing the private accumulation of capital and profits, of adapting workers and older people to fit the requirements of capitalist society, of aiding in the discipline of labor, of lowering employer costs of production, of reinforcing existing inequalities of income, wealth, and power, and of mediating in the intergenerational transfer of income *within* social and economic classes. To contain potential and actual political discontent and to socialize some of the human costs of production for profit, the state also expanded efforts to aid the welfare-dependent populations, including the aged. However, these programs, which often do not enhance business-oriented growth, have been limited at best.

Increasing state expenditures has led to a corresponding growth in public sector employment at all levels of government. In an effort to hold down immediate labor costs, public employers promised their workers retirement benefits through inadequately funded pension systems. Escalating pension costs and mounting future obligations threaten to outpace available revenues, and have added considerably to the fiscal crisis. At the same time public and private retirement trusts have amassed enormous assets since the 1960s. Under current administrative arrangements, this capital has served to buttress the power of financial institutions and to support corporate practices antithetical to working-class interests and community needs.

Despite massive infusions of public money into age-based programs, the state has failed to lift substantial numbers of older people from poverty or near-poverty conditions. Some gains have accrued to higher paid, long-term corporate and public sector workers through the private and public pension systems. Competitive sector employees, and nonworking wives or surviving spouses, on the other hand, are forced to rely exclusively on Social Security income, often at the lowest benefit levels, and on supplementary security income (SSI) welfare payments.

By 1981, over 26 percent of the total annual national budget was devoted entirely to cash and income in-kind programs for the 65-and-over population. Yet most older people are unable to obtain a decent standard of living and one in six has an income below the "official" poverty line. And as pointed out by Hudson, older widows and black couples continue to have only a 50 percent chance of overcoming their poverty status through current public programs.[1] Inequality of income between age groups has increased steadily despite the expansion and liberalization of Social Security and other retirement systems. Middle-aged and older people are still more prevalent among the long-term unemployed, notwithstanding the Age Discrimination in Employment Act and title V of the Older Americans Act. Total public costs for Medicare and Medicaid reached $60.6 billion in 1980. Yet the 65-and-over population continues to have burdensome personal health care costs. Many still suffer from insufficient and low-quality health services. Furthermore, the enormous resources flowing into medical services for the elderly have had, at best, only a limited impact on their life expectancies. Although more people currently reach age sixty-five than at the turn of the century, the average life expectancy for those who do has increased only 4.1 years. Greater life expectancy at birth can be attributed primarily to advances in combating infectious diseases through improved sanitation, and other environmental measures, in addition to the use of antibiotics. In focusing on technological and scientific medical care practices, the medical-industrial complex has diverted attention from industrial and environmental causes of disease and ill health in society. Within this context, medical intervention strategies have provided only limited gains for those, such as the aged, suffering from chronic diseases.

The practice of forcing unnecessarily large numbers of older people into oppressive nursing institutions continues unabated, despite the goals of the Older Americans Act to enable the aged to maintain independence and to improve the quality of their lives. Growth of funding under OAA has not seriously improved nutritional deficiencies, inadequate transportation facilities, or access to other sorely needed benefits and community services. Low-income housing projects, and other publicly supported programs, have not ameliorated the well-documented shelter problems of the elderly poor. The list of unresolved social ills faced by older people is endless. The most fundamental issues underlying pressing problems experienced by older people are linked to the maldistribution of power, income, and wealth in society, as well as to class, racial, and sexual stratifications that are perpetuated and legitimized through work roles and market relations. These are not only reinforced, but also exacerbated, during old age. Programs aimed at improving the situation of the aged have served primarily to enhance the accumulation of private capital and profits, control workers and the elderly, and legitimate, perpetuate, and deepen inequalities in society.

It would appear that the prospects for improving the position of the elderly are severely restricted under prevailing institutional arrangements. Proposals for change offered by free-market conservatives and liberal accommodationists are unlikely to solve the myriad structural problems documented throughout this work. I will briefly outline below some of the limitations of free-market conservative and liberal accommodationist reforms. In the concluding section, I contend that the specific problems experienced by the aged, and the larger societal crises to which these are linked, can be resolved only through a progressive transformation of the American political economy. Given the basic structural contradictions of advanced capitalist society, and their negative impacts on older people, it is my view that arguments for radical reforms are compelling.

FREE-MARKET REFORMS: THE PROBLEMS WORSEN

Since the late 1970s, current debate on solving the U.S. crisis has been dominated increasingly by strategies advanced by free-market conservative reformers. However, as David Plotke has noted, these imply a return to the market, and renewed economic growth "through intensified exploitation within the framework of the traditional industrial structure."[2] The aim is even greater concentration of economic and political power to foster stable conditions and profits, more reliance on the private sector for mitigating public problems (along with "sufficient" economic incentives, such as direct business subsidies and tax reductions), a slowdown in or reversal of the political and economic gains of labor, and a retrenchment in state expenditures and programs for welfare-dependent populations. Free-market reformers argue that measures which improve the accumulation process will stimulate economic growth and the ability to provide for needy groups, including the elderly.

Free-market reformers assume that reindustrialization and renewed economic expansion, supported by the state, are vital for meeting the needs of older people. However, even if it were possible to duplicate high growth rates characteristic of the American economy prior to the 1970s, a doubtful prospect for the 1980s and beyond, rewards would accrue primarily to those who receive their income from the ownership and control of capital. Low-income employees in the competitive sector, and other marginal members of the labor force, the hard-core unemployed, and other state-dependent groups are unlikely to gain considerably from economic growth under existing institutional arrangements. There is no evidence that the relative income position of these latter groups, which comprise a large proportion of the older population, has improved materially during periods of sustained economic expansion. Periods of prosperity did not, and do not, prevent growing dependency and poverty among the aged. In fact, by 1976 approximately 60 percent of all elderly households would have had incomes below the "official" poverty level without Social Security and other public programs.[3]

Free-market conservatives have advanced several proposals under Social Security aimed at "discouraging" early retirement and "motivating" a longer employment span. Accordingly, the Reagan administration has suggested measures such as reducing benefit levels for "early" retirees and their dependents, raising the age of entitlement for full annuities from 65 to 68, expanding the delayed retirement credit,[4] and eliminating the retirement test. Yet one of the by-products of economic growth and technological improvement under a system of monopoly capitalism is an increase in structural unemployment, which adversely affects particular groups such as middle-aged and older workers. Furthermore, partly due to job terminations, layoffs, plant closings (especially in the Northeast), and other systemic forces, the percentage of early "retirees" has increased steadily. In addition, employers, who can replace older workers with less highly paid younger ones, have imposed an informal or mandatory retirement age—rules established by about half of all private sector firms. Unions tend to support such policies since they view them as lessening competition over jobs.

Displaced older employees, who have difficulty finding new employment opportunities at decent wages, are forced into dependency on already inadequate private and public income support systems; a substantial number are reliant on Social Security alone. Even those who continue to work past age sixty-five, most of whom have part-time or low-wage employment, supplement their earnings with Social Security benefits. Consequently, any attempt to increase either the normal retirement age or actuarial reductions for workers "retiring" prior to age sixty-five will tend to foster greater economic deprivation rather than longer labor force participation rates. Such changes also would have negative effects on women who have been economically dependent on their spouse's wage and whose husband dies or divorces them prior to age sixty-five. And nearly all of the increased benefits from eliminating the earnings test, or expanding the delayed retirement credit, would accrue to upper-income persons.

Since the Social Security System indexes benefit increases to prices rather than to wages, it produces growing income gaps between employed and retired workers during periods of sustained economic growth. As Kreps observes:

Retiree's incomes (which are lower than earnings at the beginning of the retirement span) gradually deteriorate relative to those in the active population. If the retirement span is long and the rate of economic growth high, the ratio of the aged's retirement benefits to average earnings will be altered drastically during retirement. . . . This curious condition can thus be drawn: the faster the pace of technology and the higher the rate of economic growth, the greater is the disparity between earnings and retirement benefits, under present income-allocation arrangements.[5]

Thus increased capital accumulation and real economic growth adversely affect those no longer able to sell their labor power for a wage, relative to the overall gains realized by the working population. Only during recessions does price indexing improve Social Security benefit increases relative to those of wages.[6]

Free-market conservatives have offered changes to the Social Security System that inevitably would enlarge income inequalities between the generations, regardless of overall economic conditions. One such initiative would link initial retirement benefits and subsequent increases either to wages or prices, whichever was lower during the year. Other suggestions include imposing a cap on or delaying post-retirement increments, and revising the CPI formula in order to reduce the rise in benefit levels.[7]

The primary programs focusing on the elderly are horizontal transfers of resources from the working class to the aged. The Social Security system has been sustained in the past by a growing population, and an expansion of newly covered occupations, as well as by increases in productivity. These factors broadened the resource base which supports the program. Given declining birth rates, and rising numbers of beneficiaries relative to workers, nearly universal coverage of job categories, and high levels of structural unemployment, it is unlikely that the system will be able to sustain the future older population even at current benefit levels without more burdensome taxes than it already requires. Higher payroll taxes, which fall predominantly on labor, exacerbate the regressivity of the funding structure. They also fuel inflation and generate unemployment, reducing the total amount of payroll taxes. Just as important, free-market reformers, currently in power, have successfully slowed down the economic gains of labor (e.g., their increases in real wages), generating an even greater inability of workers to support the program. Free-market conservatives reject any attempt to draw upon corporate wealth and profits for financing either the old age or medical insurance schemes. They have offered, instead, new financing proposals such as the value-added tax (VAT), which is less visible than payroll deductions. While this revision potentially could improve the fiscal soundness of Social Security, it would not eliminate the regressivity of the taxation structure, and the social and economic problems this fosters.

To alleviate strains on the Social Security system, free-market conservatives also have proposed measures for cutting overall benefit levels. These include altering the PIA formula so as to lower replacement rates even further than had been achieved by Congress under the 1977 amendments; revising the weighted benefit, thus strengthening the system's insurance features; and reducing the percentage of the worker's PIA received by spouses. All such initiatives would burden considerably those persons who rely on Social Security for a major share—and in some cases all—of their retirement income, fostering even greater economic deprivation among the aged. Their relative position also would worsen. The greatest burdens would fall on women and minorities, who are disproportionately represented among persons relying on Social Security as their only means of economic support.

Market reformers also would expand private retirement systems in order to stimulate capital accumulation and to provide supplementary income support. However, although they already have amassed enormous assets, these systems fail conspicuously to meet the economic needs of older people. As shown in chapter 3, limited coverage and vesting, no portability, low and inequitable benefit levels, and insufficient inflation adjustments are among the problems inherent in private retirement programs. In addition, integration rules allow firms to lower the amount of—or exclude entirely—private pension annuities paid to low-income workers. Given the constraints within the competitive sector, it is also unlikely that a large number of new private retirement programs will be established.

Free-market reformers urge greater reliance on individual initiatives for supplementing retirement incomes. Major proposals include higher deductible amounts for encouraging the growth of individual retirement accounts (IRAs), keogh plans, and employee stock-ownership plans (ESOPs). The evidence indicates, however, that most workers, particularly those in the competitive sector, are financially incapable of utilizing these programs. As Fischer notes: "During the past one-hundred and thirty years, the net savings of the lower two-thirds of the population has commonly approached zero."[8] The amount of savings tends to be inextricably linked to the ability to save. Low-income employees are unlikely to benefit materially from these tax-sheltered programs, which provide economic rewards to the more affluent. Moreover, economic fluctuations, endemic to the capitalist order, increase economic insecurity even for those who manage to save something for their retirement years. In the case of ESOPs, the worker's economic security is tied to both fluctuations in the economy, and to the prosperity of a particular firm.[9] Greater roles for private pension systems, IRAs, keogh plans, and ESOPs, in lieu of improvements in Social Security benefits, would increase capital accumulation at the expense of providing for the income needs of the elderly poor.

Free-market reformers advocate increased privatization of the welfare state. However, the private sector, which produces and distributes goods and services for profit, will not provide for the needs of disadvantaged sectors of society, without substantial state subsidies. In fact, the establishment of Social Security, Medicare, Medicaid, the Older Americans Act, low-income public housing, and other programs for older people were a response, in part, to the inability of the private sector to supply basic commodities to "nonproductive," and economically deprived, older people.

As shown in chapter 6, greater reliance on the private sector did not lead to improved housing conditions for the elderly or other needy groups. Instead, it simply increased public expenditures by introducing new costs, in the form of profits to developers, builders, landlords, and financial institutions. Similarly, physicians, nursing home operators, hospital officials, and other partners in the medical-industrial complex have been adept at exploiting public resources for private gain, rather than improving the delivery, allocation, and quality of health care services. In sum, market reformers would place greater responsibility for meeting the needs of the elderly in the hands of the same groups that have not only created many of the social and economic problems of old age, but who have also proven incapable of mitigating them.

Reductions in public costs for social programs, achieved by restricting eligibility, lowering benefit levels and inflation adjustments, or enlarging cost-sharing provisions, generate greater economic deprivation among a significant percentage of older people as well as other disadvantaged groups. Budget cuts under the Reagan administration aimed at Medicaid, low-income energy assistance programs, title XX social services, low-income housing, legal services, and the like, already have worsened the social and economic problems of the elderly poor.

Finally, free-market reformers advocate rational planning, greater efficiency, and better coordination of service delivery systems in order to maximize the use of what they view as limited public resources available for social needs. In the case of the Older Americans Act, this has implied an accommodation of the elderly to the system; the funding of projects serving large numbers of people, at low unit costs, regardless of quality or of whether they alleviate the most pressing problems; the use of resources to meet professional needs, rather than those of clients; loss of control of beneficiaries over their own lives; the transformation of social and political questions into technical issues; and only moderate improvements in actual services. These efforts have not, and will not, reduce institutionalization or improve materially the well-being of older people.

SOME PROBLEMS WITH LIBERAL ACCOMMODATIONIST REFORMS

Liberal accommodationist reformers focus on remedying deficiencies of the established order without addressing the roots of the problems they identify. They demand not major structural changes, but instead, limited improvements to mitigate and treat symptoms of social ills. Their proposals, which do not question the basic logic, or resolve the inherent contradictions of monopoly capitalism, are shaped to conform to the requisites of capitalist production and values. Liberal reforms represent "reproductive" demands that subordinate the needs of the elderly to the requirements of capital. Liberal accommodationists share with free-market reformers a basic commitment to the private production and allocation of goods and services. Liberal accommodationists argue that publicly supported benefits should be more extensive and better funded than they are at present. However, as astutely observed by Wolfe: "Rather than trying to alter the private sector by using the public sector, liberals came to rely on the private sector (business confidence) to expand the public sector so that they could offer benefits (the fiscal dividend)."[10]

Furthermore, in advocating greater political controls over private economic activities, liberal accommodationists do not sufficiently take into account systemic barriers to change. For example, given the fundamental structural constraints underlying housing issues, a regulatory system alone cannot resolve the antagonistic goals of decent housing, reasonable rents for low-income groups, such as the elderly, and "adequate" profits for suppliers. Housing controls serve essentially to expedite the ongoing process of disinvestment in low- and middle-income housing construction and maintenance.

Similarly, cost controls over physician fees, nursing homes, and hospitals participating in Medicare and Medicaid lead to fewer services and facilities for needy groups, lower quality services, or both, under established health care arrangements. The unequal access to medical care among income classes, growing inflation in costs, provider profiteering, and other issues discussed in chapter 5 are inextricably linked to a system of services where profit, and not need, determine decisions. As argued by Waitzkin and Waterman: "Despite widespread concern about the costliness, maldistribution, and poor quality of services, the medical profession and large American corporations continue to exploit illness for profit. In this sociopolitical context, it is probably naive to presume that a responsive and effective health system can emerge through incremental reforms—without basic (and perhaps revolutionary) transformation of the social order."[11]

The private sector cannot meet expectations by liberal accommodationists for improved community and supportive services, and the capitalist state cannot afford the costs of meeting pressing needs of an expanding older population. Moreover, under conditions of monopoly capitalism, any attempts by accommodationists to improve the private retirement systems would inevitably increase employer costs, fostering plan dissolutions, lower wage increases for workers, higher commodity prices, unemployment, and other negative societal consequences.

Liberal accommodationists are also committed to the concept of wage-related Social Security benefits calculated on the basis of work histories. However, they encourage upward revisions in annuity levels, particularly for those at the lower ends of the income scale. Liberal accommodationists assume that more adequate minimum benefits should be accompanied with increases at the higher income levels, although at a lower percentage rate. These changes would require a greater transfer of income from a working class already overburdened by, and unwilling to support, increasingly regressive taxes. Even if funding for the system were to be shifted to general revenues—a revision which liberal accommodationists support—increased benefits would entail the following alternatives: increased deficit spending and thus heightened inflation, the latter triggering a rise in costs; higher federal taxes which exacerbate unemployment (and probably more people requiring public support); or fewer social programs for other state-dependent population groups. Liberal proposals for revising the Social Security system do not address fundamental issues, such as social class stratifications within the labor market, and the general inability of the program to meet the real needs of the aged, within the context of capitalist market relations. Further, any attempts by accommodationists to eliminate inequities for women and minorities, by tinkering with the funding and benefit structures, leave basic systemic problems intact.

It has become increasingly clear that the contradictions inherent in advanced capitalist society cannot be resolved through liberal accommodationist reforms. By working within established structures and relationships, liberal reforms tailored to the specific needs of the elderly may ameliorate some problems temporarily. Ultimately they would undermine the ability of the system to respond adequately, worsen other problems as the structural contradictions are exacerbated, leave the larger questions of inequality unresolved, and inevitably provide resources for older people at the expense of other needy groups in society. As Estes argues, policies limited to a particular age group "do not advance society or the cause of social justice but rather they perpetuate acceptance of the status quo and the inevitability of scarcity, inequity, and intergroup rivalries."[12] In sum, the failure of liberal accommodationists to view the problems associated with old age as rooted in the larger issues of social relations of production, structural inequalities and class privilege, and dominance of profits over human needs, makes their reforms at best inadequate and at worst damaging.

Most revealing is the fact that liberal reforms, which tend to neutralize serious challenges to the established order, simply have not worked in the past, despite growing public expenditures and vastly expanding programs. Liberal reforms have fostered, among other things, escalating costs and a larger public sector, while failing to solve the pressing problems experienced by large numbers of older people. They have also reinforced inequalities in wealth, income, and power.

Importantly, since the mid-1970s, liberal accommodationists have been forced to defend past gains rather than press for new or expanded programs. For the first time in its history, the Social Security system is being scrutinized by national political leaders for ways to control costs rather than to improve benefits, or eliminate inequities. A number of state and local governments are attempting to revise their retirement systems by lowering annuity levels, or raising mandatory contribution rates. Under its own retirement systems, the federal government has eliminated the twice-yearly cost-of-living adjustments, and is offering proposals to reduce pensions for workers who retire prior to age sixty-five, increase employee contributions, and impose a cap on benefits. Overall, national leaders are addressing questions of "overpensioning" instead of issues related to inadequate provision of retirement income. Discussion on gaps in coverage, burdensome recipient expenses, and maldistribution of services under Medicare have been superseded by debates exclusively over reducing overall program costs.

Since political and economic authorities have defined the general U.S. economic crisis as overly high government spending for programs serving welfare-dependent populations, liberal accommodationists have been forced to struggle to keep even current national commitments for low-income housing, food stamps, social services, Medicaid, and other programs. It is highly unlikely that the federal government will expand public programs serving the poor. The state, then, will become the focus of intensified conflict over scarce resources for meeting social needs. Any gains for older people will probably mean less for other needy groups in society.

RADICAL POLITICS AND PROGRESSIVE CHANGE

André Gorz provides some useful guidelines for distinguishing between a "reformist reform" (liberal accommodationist approach) and a "nonreformist reform" (radical approach). He argues: "A reformist reform is one which subordinates its objectives to the criteria of rationality and practicality of a given system and policy. Reformism rejects those objectives and demands—however deep the need for them—which are incompatible with the preservation of the system."[13] Radicals, on the other hand, advance "unreproductive demands"—policies, programs, and activities which, according to Esping-Anderson, Friedland, and Wright, "tend to weaken, destabilize and undermine the basic social relations of capitalism and challenge the underlying premises on which the system is based."[14] Gorz notes: "A not necessarily reformist reform is one which is conceived not in terms of what is possible within the framework of a given system and administration, but in view of what should be made possible in terms of human needs and demands."[15]

Radical reforms are not based on the systemic requisites of capitalism, but rather on working-class and community needs. They entail radical systemic changes, including the abolition of production for profit. Radical reforms involve, among other things, the mobilization of society's surplus to satisfy real human requirements; a more equal distribution of income, wealth, and power in society; fundamental alterations in the social relations of production; the creation of satisfying work and working environments; the elimination of racist and sexist social structures and of economic classes; and the establishment of community based organizations and facilities, which would allow individuals to engage in and control decisions affecting their lives. Whereas many liberals argue that the aged should have access to a decent income, adequate housing, better medical care, and sufficient community services, radicals presume that these are basic social rights of all people. Whereas both liberal and free-market reformers "reduce all social questions to expertise, policy analysis and bureaucratic management," radical reformers such as Burton and Murphy argue that:

> democracy requires a conception of action in which the people constitute their own needs. . . . citizenship is rooted in the recognition of reciprocal need and the necessity of collective action. . . . it is the expression of a substantive understanding of everyone's fragile dependency on the community which everyone actively creates. . . . It is simultaneously a culture of conviction, a sociology of equality and reciprocity, and a politics of participation and creativity.[16]

Radical reforms, then, are progressive changes that move society in the direction of democratic socialism. Reforms which stretch the limits of the capitalist system, and reveal its contradictions to the populace, serve as a means for advancing this goal. Radicals seek to use public power, institutions, and resources for the direct production and allocation of social benefits to satisfy community-defined needs. Progressive programs do not, even indirectly, aid in the private accumulation of capital and profits. Instead of focusing on the requirements of specific social groups, such as the elderly, radical proposals crystallize issues around class. Publicly funded and community-controlled health services, which would function outside the private medical marketplace, a guaranteed, adequate income for all people, and massive community services and housing, produced and distributed by public entities to serve entire communities, are only some potential demands that would challenge the basic premises underlying the capitalist order.

Finally, Gorz persuasively argues that radical reforms should be aimed at worker control of "those powers which will prepare [the working class] to assume the leadership of society and which will permit it in the meantime to control and to plan the development of the society, and to establish certain limiting mechanisms which will restrict or dislocate the power of capital." He suggests that the progressive struggle for autonomous (which he differentiates from subordinate) centers of power by the working class would be a first, and a significant, advancement toward democratic socialism. He further contends that the struggle for and exercise of even partial autonomous power by labor: "prepares the way for a dialectical progression of the struggle to a higher and higher level. . . . what must be done is to make power tangible *now* by means of actions which demonstrate to the workers their positive strength, their ability to measure themselves against the power of capital and to impose their will on it."[17]

In chapter 4, I have argued that private and public pension systems, with their enormous and growing assets, have the potential to serve as autonomous centers of power for the working class. Worker control over these retirement trusts, which are expected to reach $1 trillion in assets by 1985, and provide nearly 50 percent of external capital raised by U.S. firms,[18] could result in the mobilization of vast resources to meet socially defined needs and to promote progressive institutional change.

There are a number of complex issues, however, that should be raised regarding the potential for advancing radical goals through social investing of pension funds. I will address a few of these briefly. One particular thorny issue is that of investing state and local retirement funds to attain maximum benefits for the community, or even region, from which the assets are derived. Political leaders and union officials have become particularly interested in this aspect of social investing. However, community or worker control over locally derived retirement assets would not lead automatically to a redistribution of resources to areas and groups most in need. As Michael Kieschnick points out: "in the absence of a thorough political transformation of local politics . . . poor areas [would] keep control of small underfunded pension funds while rich areas [would] keep control of large funded pension funds."[19]

Second, while it may be possible to invest trust assets in firms and projects adhering to worker and community-defined goals, or use them as a means for influencing the direction of corporate activities through stock-voting rights, the retirement systems currently are, nevertheless, inextricably tied to the capitalist system of production. For example, since pension plans are dependent, in part, on the pursuit of profits for providing benefits, this factor may restrict the achievement of desired social and economic objectives to those ventures that provide "sufficient" investment income.

Third, even if labor wrests pension power from employers and financial institutions, workers may very well become further integrated into the existing system. At best, they may moderate some undesirable corporate practices. One cannot presume that unions would use pension funds as a means for achieving radical change.

On the other hand, attempts by workers to gain control over retirement assets are likely to activate the strong opposition of the financial and business community, a movement that is stirring already. A progressive consciousness can develop among workers, and the general public, as a result of long and hard struggles over pension capital. If employees and communities succeed in wresting control over pension funds, despite some inevitable and fundamental systemic constraints, they can serve potentially as one step toward a fundamental transformation of society.

Notes

1. The Aging Population Today and Tomorrow

1. Robert R. Alford, *Health Care Politics* (Chicago: University of Chicago Press, 1975), pp. 8–9.

2. These figures were compiled from the following sources: U.S. Bureau of the Census, *Historical Statistics of the United States, Colonial Times to 1970* (September 1975); Bureau of the Census, "Projections of the Population of the United States: 1977-2000," *Current Population Reports*, Series P-25 (July 1977), no. 704; and the President's Commission on Pension Policy, staff report, "Overview of the U.S. Retirement Systems," *Background Papers* (Washington, D.C., February 21, 1979).

3. U.S. Bureau of the Census, "Demographic Aspects of Aging and the Older Population in the United States," *Current Population Reports*, Special Studies, Series P-23, (May 1976), no. 59, p. 51.

4. U.S. House, Select Committee on Aging (HCA), *Retirement: The Broken Promise*, 96th Cong., 2d sess., December 1980, p. 90.

5. Sandra Timmerman, "Inequalities of Mandatory Retirement: An Overview," *Journal of the Institute for Socioeconomic Studies* (Winter 1977), p. 37.

6. President's Commission on Pension Policy, "Fact Sheet," (Washington, D.C., 1979). Mimeo.

7. Carroll L. Estes, *The Aging Enterprise* (San Francisco: Jossey-Bass, 1979), p. 77.

8. Federal Council on the Aging, *The Impact of the Tax Structure on the Elderly* (Washington, D.C.: GPO, December 29, 1975), p. 44.

9. U.S. Senate, Special Committee on Aging, *Emerging Options for Work and Retirement*, prepared by James Storey, 96th Cong., 2d sess., June 1980, pp. 67–68.

10. Statement by Chairman Senator Domenici, U.S. Senate, Committee on the Budget, Hearing on the Markup of the Second Concurrent Budget Resolution, September 15, 1981.

11. *Ibid.*

12. U.S. Executive Office of the President, Office of Management and Budget, *Special Analysis of the Budget of the U.S. Government, Fiscal Year 1980*, Special Analysis G (Washington, D.C.: GPO, 1979), p. 183.

13. For more details see Federal Council on the Aging, *Impact of the Tax Structure.*

14. *Ibid.*, pp. 6, 39, 51.

15. Robert M. Ball, *Social Security: Today and Tomorrow* (New York: Columbia University Press, 1978), p. 94.

16. Charles R. Sligh, Jr., "Aging and National Policy," in Harold L. Orbach and Clark Tibbitts, eds., *Aging and the Economy* (Ann Arbor: University of Michigan Press, 1963), p. 193.

17. Arthur N. Schwartz and James A. Peterson, *Introduction to Gerontology* (New York: Holt, Rinehart, and Winston, 1979), p. 83.

18. Peter F. Drucker, *The Unseen Revolution: How Pension Fund Socialism Came to America* (New York: Harper and Row, 1976), p. 168.

19. Milton Friedman, "Payroll Taxes, No; General Revenues, Yes," in Michael J. Boskin, ed., *The Crisis in Social Security* (San Francisco: Institute for Contemporary Studies, 1977), p. 28.

20. See for example, Martin Feldstein, "Social Security, Induced Retirement, and Aggregate Capital Accumulation," *Journal of Political Economy* (September-October 1974), 82:905–926; Martin Feldstein, "Social Security and Savings: The Extended Life-Cycle Theory," *American Economic Review, Proceedings* (May 1976); Alice H. Munnell, *The Future of Social Security* (Washington, D.C.: Brookings Institution, 1977), pp. 113–133; Sherwin Rosen, "Social Security and the Economy," in Boskin, *Crisis in Social Security*, pp. 87–106; and William G. Bowen and T. A. Fenegan, *The Economics of Labor Force Participation* (Princeton, N.J.: Princeton University Press, 1969).

21. Martin Feldstein, "Social Security," in Boskin, *Crisis in Social Security*, pp. 21–24.

22. For an insightful critique of the market reformist view on improving health services in the United States see Alford, *Health Care Politics*, particularly, pp. 1–21 and 190–266.

23. See for example, Edward C. Banfield, *The Unheavenly City* (Boston: Little, Brown, 1970).

24. H. L. Wilensky and C. N. Lebeaux, *Industrial Society and Social Welfare* (New York: Free Press, 1966).

25. Fred Cottrell, "Issues," in Mildred M. Seltzer, Sherry L. Corbett, and Robert C. Atchley, eds., *Social Problems of the Aging: Readings* (Belmont, Calif: Wadsworth, 1978), p. 322.

26. For a discussion of these theories see Jon Hendricks and C. Davis Hendricks, *Aging in Mass Society: Myths and Realities* (Cambridge, Mass.: Winthrop, 1977), pp. 106–125.

27. Louis Lowy, "Social Welfare and the Aging," in Seltzer, Corbett, and Atchley, *Social Problems of the Aging*, p. 301.

28. Harold L. Sheppard, "On Age Discrimination," in Seltzer, Corbett, and Atchley, p. 36.

29. Zeckhauser and Viscusi, "The Role of Social Security in Income Maintenance," in Boskin, p. 52.

30. Robert N. Butler, *Why Survive? Being Old in America* (New York: Harper and Row, 1975), p. 38.

31. Alford, *Health Care Politics*, p. 1.

32. Howard M. Wachtel, "Looking at Poverty from a Radical Perspective," in James H. Weaver, ed., *Modern Political Economy: Radical and Orthodox Views on Crucial Issues* (Boston: Allyn and Bacon, 1973), p. 214.

33. Ira Katznelson and Mark Kesselman, *The Politics of Power* (New York: Harcourt Brace Jovanovitch, 1975), p. 388.

34. Robert Binstock, "Interest Group Liberalism and the Politics of Aging," *Gerontologist* (Autumn 1972), 12(3):268.

35. Frances Fox Piven and Richard A. Cloward, *Regulating the Poor: The Functions of Public Welfare* (New York: Vintage, 1971), pp. 3–4.

36. The following discussion on the tripartite division of labor and the role of the state under American capitalism relies heavily on James O'Connor, *The Fiscal Crisis of the State* (New York: St. Martin's Press, 1973). This will be elaborated further in chapter 3.

37. For a more complete analysis see Wachtel, "Looking at Poverty," pp. 207–224.

38. Dr. Theodore Cooper, quoted in John K. Iglehart, "Health Report: Explosive Rise in Medical Costs Puts Government in Quandry," *National Journal* (September 20, 1975), p. 1327.

39. William Ryan, who labels this approach as "Blaming the Victim," notes that it involves designating particular needy groups to be "helped," defining them as different from the rest of the population, and attributing their problems to personal or group deficiencies that can be "remedied" through either changes in the individuals themselves, or amelioration of particular defects in the community and environment. He further argues that this approach diverts attention from the root causes of pressing needs among disadvantaged people—that is, the inequitable distribution of income and power in society. See William Ryan, *Blaming the Victim* (New York: Vintage, 1971).

2. A Brief History of the Economic Problems of Aging

1. From the 1600s until the early 1800s less than 2 percent of the total population was sixty-five and over. In 1830 the median age was only 17.2 years. *Historical Statistics of the United States*, Series A 86–94, *Statistical*

Abstract of the U.S., Chart 26, p. 26, cited in David Hackett Fischer, *Growing Old in America*, expanded ed. (Oxford, England: Oxford University Press, 1978), pp. 27, 274.

2. W. C. Greenough and F. P. King, *Pension Plans and Public Policy* (New York: Columbia University Press, 1976), pp. 28–29.

3. See Fischer, pp. 52–58.

4. Fischer, p. 60.

5. Joseph G. Rayback, *A History of American Labor* (expanded ed.; New York: Free Press, 1966), pp. 49–50.

6. See Jeremy Brecher and Tim Costello, *Common Sense for Hard Times* (Washington, D.C.: Institute for Policy Studies, Two Continents Publishing Group, 1976), p. 28.

7. See Wilbert Achenbaum, "Old Age in the U.S., 1790 to the Present," (Ph.D. dissertation, University of Michigan, 1976).

8. Rayback, *History of American Labor*, p. 52.

9. Achenbaum, "Old Age in the U.S.," p. 132. This trend continued and by 1940 only 18 percent of the working population were farmers. Rayback, pp. 192–193.

10. Douglas F. Dowd, *The Twisted Dream: Capitalist Development in the United States Since 1776* (Cambridge, Mass.: Winthrop, 1976), pp. 57–58.

11. Gabriel Kolko, *Main Currents in American History* (New York: Harper and Row, 1976), p. 7. This section relies heavily on Kolko's work.

12. Rayback, *History of American Labor*, p. 160.

13. Alan Wolfe, *The Limits of Legitimacy: Political Contradictions of Contemporary Capitalism* (New York: Free Press, 1977), p. 39.

14. Kolko, *Main Currents*, pp. 12, 117–120.

15. Ira Katznelson and Mark Kesselman, *The Politics of Power* (New York: Harcourt Brace Jovanovich, 1975), p. 114.

16. Rayback, *History of American Labor*, pp. 191–192.

17. Rayback, pp. 192–193.

18. Brecher and Costello, *Common Sense for Hard Times*, p. 47.

19. Richard C. Edwards, Michael Reich, and David M. Gordon, "Labor Market Segmentation," in *idem*, eds., *The Capitalist System: A Radical Analysis of American Society*, (2d ed.; Englewood Cliffs, N.J.: Prentice-Hall, 1978), p. 202.

20. Fischer, *Growing Old in America*, p. 143.

21. W. Andrew Achenbaum, "The Obsolescence of Old Age in America, 1865–1914," in Mildred M. Seltzer, Sherry L. Corbett, and Robert C. Atchley, eds., *The Social Problems of the Aging: Readings* (Belmont, Calif.: Wadsworth, 1978), p. 33.

22. W. Andrew Achenbaum, "The Obsolescence of Old Age," in Jon Hendricks and C. Davis Hendricks, eds., *Dimensions of Aging: Readings* (Cambridge, Mass.: Winthrop, 1979), p. 28.

23. Abraham Epstein, *Facing Old Age* (New York: Knopf, 1922), p. 154.

24. Roy Lubove, *The Struggle for Social Security* (Cambridge, Mass.: Harvard University Press, 1968), p. 129.

25. E. A. Vanderlip, "Insurance from the Employers' Standpoint," *National Conference of Charities and Corrections, Proceedings* (1906), pp. 457–458, cited by Lubove, p. 11.

26. Louis Brandeis, quoted by Lubove, p. 119.

27. Epstein, p. 149.

28. Greenough and King, *Pension Plans and Public Policy*, p. 30.

29. Greenough and King, p. 31.

30. Epstein, p. 154.

31. In McNevin v. Solvay Process Company (1898) and a few years later in Dodge v. Dodge (1902) the courts ruled that pension plans were "gifts" to employees and at the total discretion of employers.

32. Epstein, *Facing Old Age*, p. 161.

33. Epstein, p. 3.

34. Achenbaum, "The Obsolescence of Old Age," p. 29.

35. Epstein, p. 68.

36. For an extensive economic analysis of old age between 1840 and 1970 see Achenbaum, "Old Age in the U.S.," pp. 222–258.

37. U.S. Bureau of Economic Analysis, *Long Term Economic Growth* (Washington, D.C., 1973), pp. 212–214, cited in Fischer, *Growing Old in America*, p. 142.

38. Epstein, p. 11.

39. Lubove, *Struggle for Social Security*, p. 134.

40. Cited in Epstein, *Facing Old Age*, pp. 85–86.

41. Epstein, p. 73.

42. Lubove, p. 4.

43. Lubove, p. 133.

44. In 1900 there were 3 million people sixty-five and over. Their number grew to 4 million, 5 million, and 7 million by 1910, 1920, and 1930, respectively. Older people accounted for 4.4 percent of the population in 1900 and 5.6 percent by 1930. However, the drastic increases in the percentage of the elderly ensued primarily after the 1940s. In 1950 there were 12 million aged, representing 8.2 percent of the population. Rising steadily throughout the next several decades, by 1980 the approximately 25 million people sixty-five and over made up about 11 percent of the total. See U.S. Bureau of the Census, *Current Population Reports, Special Studies*, Series P-23, No. 59, cited in the National Council on the Aging, *Fact Book on Aging: A Profile of America's Older Population* (Washington, D.C.: The Council, 1979), pp. 4–5; and Fischer, *Growing Old in America*, p. 272.

45. Achenbaum, "Old Age in the U.S.," p. 370.

46. Joseph F. Drake, *The Aged in American Society* (New York: Ronald Press, 1958), p. 166.

47. Samuel Gompers, quoted in Lubove, *Struggle for Social Security*, pp. 15–16.

48. Lubove, p. 116.

49. Eligibility initially was based solely on disability but soon was expanded to include old-age benefits.

50. For a full discussion of the history of federal military pensions see William H. Glasson, *Federal Military Pensions in the United States* (New York: Oxford University Press, 1918).

51. Fischer, *Growing Old in America*, pp. 169–170; and Lubove, p. 125.

52. Glasson, pp. 270–273.

53. Isaac M. Rubinow quoted in Lubove, p. 125.

54. Glasson, pp. 238–239.

55. Lubove, p. 125.

56. Cited in Epstein, p. 163.

57. Epstein, p. 162.

58. See Drake, *Aged in American Society*.

59. The number of state and local plans and the percentage of new employee groups covered under them grew rapidly in the 1940s and 1950s. By 1962 nearly 75 percent of all state and local workers were covered. At the end of 1979 over 90 percent of federal, state, and local employees participated in a public retirement system. From 1931 to the mid-1950s over one-half of the largest state and local plans were established. Since that time over one-third of the larger plans and two-thirds of the smaller ones have been newly instituted, expanded, or restructured. See Greenough and King, *Pension Plans and Public Policy*, p. 50; and U.S. House, Committee on Education and Labor, *Pension Task Force Report on Public Employee Retirement Systems*, 95th Cong., 2d sess., March 15, 1978, p. 62.

60. Abraham Holzman, *The Townsend Movement* (New York: Bookman, 1963), p. 22.

61. Drake, p. 167.

62. Douglas has argued that this could be attributed to the heavy concentration of indigent blacks, Mexicans, and Indians in these areas and the unwillingness of the states and counties to support them. See Paul H. Douglas, *Social Security in the United States: An Analysis and Appraisal of the Federal Social Security Act* (New York: McGraw Hill, 1936), p. 9.

63. See Drake, p. 167; and Holtzman.

64. See, for example, Francis Fox Piven and Richard A. Cloward, *Regulating the Poor: The Functions of Public Welfare* (New York: Pantheon Books, 1971), pp. 45–117.

65. Nearly 47 percent of all workers were not covered under old age insurance provisions of the Social Security Act in 1935. See Edwin E. Witte, *Social Security Perspectives* (Madison: University of Wisconsin Press, 1962), p. 33.

66. Witte, p. 115.

67. See Holtzman, *Townsend Movement.*

68. Daniel Sanders, *The Impact of Reform Movements on Social Policy Change: The Case of Social Insurance* (Fair Lawn, N.J.: R. E. Burdick, 1973).

69. The following discussion is based on an analysis of the Lundeen bill provided by Paul H. Douglas. See *Social Security in the United States.*

70. Douglas, p. 81.

71. Douglas, p. 82.

72. Robert Stevens and Rosemary Stevens, *Welfare Medicine in America: A Case Study of Medicaid* (New York: Free Press, 1974), p. 8.

73. See Drake, *Aged in American Society.*

74. Douglas, p. 236.

75. J. Douglas Brown, "Philosophical Basis of the National Old Age Insurance Program," in Dan McGill, ed., *Social Security and Private Pension Plans: Competitive or Complementary* (Homewood, Ill.: Irwin-Dorsey, 1976), p. 5.

76. Henry J. Pratt, *The Gray Lobby* (Chicago: University of Chicago Press, 1976), p. 29.

77. Sanders, *Impact of Reform Movements,* p. 105.

78. Cited in Charles Dearing, *Industrial Pensions* (Washington, D.C.: Brookings Institution, 1954), p. 47.

79. Robert M. Ball, *Social Security: Today and Tomorrow* (New York: Columbia University Press, 1978), p. 86.

80. Lloyd Saville, "Flexible Retirement," in Juanita M. Kreps, ed., *Employment, Income and Retirement Problems of the Aged* (Dishan, N.C.: Drake University Press, 1963), p. 141.

81. Conference Board, *Financial Management of Company Pension Plans,* report no. 611 (New York: Conference Board, 1973), pp. 5–6.

82. Greenough and King, *Pension Plans and Public Policy,* p. 65.

83. Dearing, *Industrial Pensions,* p. 48.

84. Katznelson and Kesselman, *Politics of Power,* p. 123.

85. Witte, *Social Security Perspectives,* p. 33.

86. Kolko, *Main Currents,* p. 155.

87. The rapid growth of informal and forced retirement policies, along with increasing mechanization and structural unemployment, were instrumental in reducing the percentage of older people who were working. Participation rates fell from 45.8 percent in 1950 and 33.1 percent in 1960 to 26.8 percent by 1970. At the end of 1980 only about 20 percent of the 65-and-over population was employed, and these workers were heavily concentrated in low-wage sectors of the economy, often in part-time positions.

88. See Kolko, pp. 310–348.

89. Kolko, p. 312.

3. Income Maintenance and the Pension Games: Winners and Losers Under Capitalism

1. Louis Harris and Associates, *The Myth and Reality of Aging in America* (Washington, D.C.: National Council on the Aging, July 1976), p. 130.

2. In 1975 the Department of Agriculture shifted to a slightly higher "thrifty" food plan. The latter is used for setting coupon allotments under the food stamp program.

3. Harrell R. Rodgers, Jr., *Poverty Amid Plenty: A Political and Economic Analysis* (Reading, Mass.: Addison-Wesley, 1979), p. 25.

4. National Council on the Aging, *Fact Book on Aging: A Profile of America's Older Population* (Washington, D.C.: Council on the Aging, 1978), p. 64.

5. See for example, Michael Harrington, *The Other America* (Baltimore: Penguin Books, 1962), p. xii.

6. Cited in Michael Harrington, "Hiding the Other America," *New Republic* (February 26, 1977), p. 16.

7. U.S. Bureau of Labor Statistics, Consumer Expenditure Surveys, 1972–1973.

8. The estimated low-cost food budgets for couples and individuals have been calculated as 20 percent higher than the economy plans. The latter were assumed to be one-third of the older couple and older individual poverty thresholds, respectively, in 1979. These are only rough estimates.

9. U.S. Senate, Special Committee on Aging (SSCA), *Developments in Aging: 1980*, part 1, 97th Cong., 1st sess., May 13, 1981, pp. xv–xvii.

10. U.S. Senate, Committee on Labor and Public Welfare, Subcommittee on Aging, and the Special Committee on Aging, *Post-White House Conference on Aging Reports*, 93d Cong., 1st sess., 1973, pp. 21, 370.

11. Harrington, *The Other America*; and Robert N. Butler, *Why Survive? Being Old in America* (New York: Harper and Row, 1975).

12. In 1974, 14.6 percent of all older people, or 3.08 million persons, were living at or below the poverty line; in 1979, the figure rose to 15.1 percent, or 3.6 million persons. U.S. House, Select Committee on Aging (HCA), *Retirement: The Broken Promise*, 96th Cong., 2d sess., December 1980, p. 7.

13. U.S. Congressional Budget Office, *Poverty Status of Families Under Alternative Definitions of Income*, Background Paper no. 17, 95th Cong., 2d sess., February 1977.

14. Michael Harrington, "Hiding the Other America," p. 17.

15. Arthur N. Schwartz and James A. Peterson, *Introduction to Gerontology* (New York: Holt, Rinehart and Winston, 1979), p. 81.

16. U.S. Bureau of the Census, "Money Income in 1974 of Families and Persons in the U.S.," *Current Population Reports*, Series P-60, no. 99.

17. Rodgers, *Poverty Amid Plenty*, p. 37.

18. Stephen J. Rose, *Social Stratification in the U.S.: An Analytic Guidebook* (Baltimore: Social Graphics, 1979), p. 28.

19. James Schulz, Guy Carrion, and Hans Krupp et al., *Providing Adequate Retirement Income: Pension Reform in the U.S. and Abroad* (Waltham, Mass.: Brandeis University Press, 1974), p. 41.

20. U.S. President's Commission on Pension Policy, "Retirement Income Goals," Working Papers, prepared by Elizabeth L. Meier, Cynthia C. Dittman, and Barbara Boyle Torrey, Washington, D.C., March 1980, p. 8.

21. U.S. Senate, Special Committee on Aging, *Developments in Aging: 1977*, part 1, 95th Cong., 2d sess., 1978, p. 31.

22. Gabriel Kolko, *Wealth and Power in America: An Analysis of Social Class and Income Distribution* (New York: Praeger, 1962), p. 87.

23. James O'Connor, *The Fiscal Crisis of the State* (New York: St. Martin's Press, 1973), p. 139.

24. O'Connor, p. 138.

25. Martha Derthick, *Policymaking for Social Security* (Washington, D.C.: Brookings Institution, 1979), p. 404; and Robert J. Myers, "Concepts of Balance between OASDI and Private Pension Benefits: A Partnership or, Instead, the Lion's Share," in Richard Irwin, ed., *Social Security and Private Pension Plans: Competitive or Complementary* (Homewood, Ill.: Irwin-Dorsey, 1976), pp. 94–109.

26. The Primary Insurance Amount (PIA) is the basic monthly benefit that would accrue to a retired worker, based on his or her average monthly earnings (AME), and since 1977 on his or her average indexed monthly earnings (AMIE), if the worker received the initial Social Security benefit at age sixty-five. It is also used as the base for computing other benefits payable on the basis of the worker's earnings record. For a worker retiring at age sixty-five in 1981, the benefit formula provides 90 percent of the first $211 of the AIME, plus 32 percent of the next $1,063, plus 15 percent of all AIME over $1,274.

27. U.S. President's Commission on Pension Policy (PCCP), "Overview of U.S. Retirement Systems, Background Papers," Staff Report, February 21, 1979. Mimeo.

28. U.S. Department of Health and Human Services, Social Security Administration (SSA), Office of Research and Statistics.

29. Patience Lauriat and William Robin, "Men Who Claim Benefits Before Age 65: Findings from the Survey of New Beneficiaries, 1968," *Social Security Bulletin* (November 1970), 33:3–4, 22.

30. U.S. Department of Health, Education, and Welfare (HEW), *Social Security and the Changing Roles of Men and Women*, February 1979, p. 171.

31. Department of Health and Human Services, Social Security Admin-

istration (SSA), Office of Research and Statistics. Set retirement ages, un-employment, and incentives from the various benefit programs force most older workers to retire prior to attaining age sixty-five. The new protection until age seventy under the 1978ʹ Age Discrimination in Employment Act will have only a negligible impact. For example, the average retirement age at General Motors is fifty-nine. Between 1974 and 1976 only 8 percent of Ford Motor Company's employees worked until age sixty-five. *Pensions and Investments*, August 13, 1979, p. 26.

32. Sherwin Rosen, "Social Security and the Economy," in Michael J. Boskin, ed., *The Crisis in Social Security: Problems and Prospects* (San Francisco: Institute for Contemporary Studies, 1977), p. 105.

33. HCA, *Retirement: The Broken Promise*, p. 58.

34. SSA, Office of Research and Statistics.

35. U.S. Department of Health and Human Services, Social Security Administration, "Annual Statistical Supplement," *Social Security Bulletin* (1977–1979), p. 161.

36. SSCA, *Developments in Aging: 1980*, part 1, p. xxxiv.

37. *Ibid.*

38. SSA, Office of Research and Statistics.

39. Susan Grad, "Income of the Population 55 and Older, 1978," Social Security Administration, Office of Policy, Office of Research and Statistics, Staff Paper, forthcoming.

40. Although Congress eliminated the minimum benefit, both houses subsequently voted to restore it, but only for current beneficiaries and those eligible persons who came on the rolls prior to December 31, 1981. According to official estimates, elimination of the minimum benefit would have affected significantly at least 1.3 million older persons currently receiving it.

41. Donald O. Parsons and Douglas R. Munro, "Intergenerational Transfers in Social Security," in Boskin, *Crisis in Social Security*, p. 71.

42. Robert M. Ball, *Social Security: Today and Tomorrow* (New York: Columbia University Press, 1978), p. 422.

43. This point will be discussed further under the section on Savings and Other Assets.

44. See, for example, George F. Break, "Social Security as a Tax," in Boskin, *Crisis in Social Security*, p. 113.

45. Milton Friedman, "Payroll Taxes, No; General Revenues, Yes," in Boskin, p. 26.

46. Joseph A. Pechman and Benjamin A. Okner, *Who Bears the Tax Burden?* (Washington, D.C.: Brookings Institution, 1974), cited in Federal Council on the Aging, *The Impact of the Tax Structure on the Elderly* (Washington, D.C.: GPO, December 29, 1975), pp. 28–29. According to the Federal Council on the Aging: "With a progressive tax, the ratio of taxes to income rises as income rises. 'Most progressive' and 'least pro-

gressive' refer to the degree of progressivity or regressivity in the overall collection of taxes being discussed."

47. Joseph A. Pechman, "The Social Security System: An Overview," in Boskin, *Crisis in Social Security*, p. 33.

48. The wage ceiling for Social Security recipients under age sixty-five in 1981 was $4,080.

49. Louis Esposito, Lucy B. Mallan, and David Podoff, "Distribution of Increased Benefits Under Alternative Earnings Tests," *Social Security Bulletin* (September 1980), 43:5–7.

50. *Ibid.*, p. 7.

51. U.S. President's Commission on Pension Policy (PCPP), *Coming of Age: Toward A National Retirement Income Policy* (Washington, D.C.: GPO, February 26, 1981), p. 26.

52. Tish Sommers, "Commentary on Report of H.E.W. Task Force on the Treatment of Women under Social Security," February 1978. Mimeo.

53. U.S. Department of Health and Human Services (HHS), Social Security Administration, Office of Research and Statistics, "Program and Demographic Characteristics of Supplementary Security Income Beneficiaries," December 1979, p. 22.

54. Ball, *Social Security: Today and Tomorrow*, p. 352.

55. Federal Council on the Aging, *National Policy Concerns for Older Women* (Washington, D.C.: GPO, 1975), pp. 18–19.

56. HHS, "Program and Demographic Characteristics of Supplementary Security Income Beneficiaries," p. 22.

57. U.S. Senate, Special Committee on Aging (SSCA), *Developments in Aging: 1979*, part 1, 96th Cong., 2d sess., February 28, 1980, pp. 37–38.

58. For an insightful analysis of some problems with this type of approach see Hugh Mosley, review of *Fiscal Crisis of the State*, by James O'Connor, in *The Review of Radical Political Economics* (Spring 1979), 11(1):52–61.

59. O'Connor, *Fiscal Crisis*, p. 16.

60. Ball, *Social Security: Today and Tomorrow*, p. 408.

61. O'Connor, p. 16.

62. O'Connor, p. 14.

63. *Ibid.*

64. Daniel J. Beller, "Coverage Patterns of Full-Time Employees Under Private Retirement Plans," *Social Security Bulletin* 44(7):3. Out of the total private sector workforce, including part-time employees, only about 42 percent were covered under a private pension plan—32 percent of females as compared to 51 percent of males.

65. Beller, p. 10.

66. Alfred M. Skolnik, "Private Pension Plans, 1950–1974," *Social Security Bulletin* (June 1976), p. 3.

67. U.S. Bureau of the Census, Current Population Survey, "Consumer Income," March 1979, Special Tabulations.

68. William C. Greenough and Francis P. King, *Pension Plans and Public Policy* (New York: Columbia University Press, 1976), p. 165.

69. Greenough and King, p. 157.

70. "While Labor Looks Over ERISA Retroactively," *Pensions and Investments*, October 9, 1978, p. 3.

71. Gayle Thompson Rogers, "Vesting of Private Pension Benefits in 1979 and Change from 1972," *Social Security Bulletin*, 44(7):15.

72. SSA, Office of Research and Statistics.

73. HCA, *Retirement: The Broken Promise*, 116.

74. Gayle B. Thompson, "Pension Coverage and Benefits, 1972: Findings from the Retirement History Study," *Social Security Bulletin* (February 1978), pp. 3–17.

75. Ball, *Social Security: Today and Tomorrow*, p. 403.

76. Ball, p. 409.

77. Pension Rights Center, "A Report on Retirement Income," Washington, D.C., Fall 1979, p. 16.

78. James H. Schulz, *The Economics of Aging* (2d ed.; Belmont, Calif.: Wadsworth, 1980), p. 133.

79. HCA, *Retirement: The Broken Promise*, p. 131.

80. Ball, p. 415.

81. *Pensions and Investments*, April 9, 1979, p. 32.

82. Gayle P. Thompson, "Impact of Inflation on Private Pensions of Retirees 1970–1974: Findings from the Retirement History Study," *Social Security Bulletin* (November 1978).

83. PCPP, *Coming of Age*, p. 28; and "A Private Pension Forecasting Model," Final Report prepared by ICF, Inc., for the U.S. Department of Labor, October 1979, cited in House HCA, *Retirement: The Broken Promise*, p. 113.

84. Elizabeth L. Meier and Helen K. Bremberg, *ERISA: Progress and Problems* (Washington, D.C.: National Institute of Industrial Gerontology, National Council on the Aging, 1977), p. 18.

85. Marty Landsberg, Jerry Lembcke, and Bob Marotto, Jr., "Public Employees: Digging Graves for the System?" in Union of Radical Political Economists, eds., *U.S. Capitalism in Crisis* (New York: URPE, January 1978), p. 298.

86. U.S. House, Committee on Education and Labor (HCEL), *Pension Task Force Report on Public Employee Retirement Systems*, 95th Cong., 2d sess., March 15, 1978, p. 51.

87. Greenough and King, p. 124.

88. SSCA, *Developments in Aging: 1979*, part 1, pp. 6–7.

89. HCEL, *Report on Public Employee Retirement Systems*, p. 117.

90. Greenough and King, p. 129.

91. HCEL, *Report on Public Employee Retirement Systems*, p. 116.

92. *Ibid.*, p. 121.

93. *Ibid.*, p. 116.

94. PCPP, "Overview of Retirement Systems."

95. HEW, *Social Security and the Changing Roles of Men and Women*, p. 179.

96. Susan Grad and Karen Foster, "Income of the Population Aged 55 and Older," *Social Security Bulletin* (July 1979), 42(7):18, 25.

97. HEW, *Social Security and the Changing Roles of Men and Women*, p. 176.

98. HCEL, *Report on Public Employee Retirement Systems*, pp. 87–88.

99. However, a substantial number of state and local systems have built into them intrastate portability provisions.

100. HCEL, *Report on Public Employee Retirement Systems*, p. 90.

101. Approximately 85 percent of state and local workers, and all employees covered by the federal civil service retirement system, are required to contribute to their pension plans. The most common rate for state and local systems is between 5 and 7 percent of wages, on top of Social Security contributions. The rates for programs covering nonenrolled state and local employees tend to be slightly higher. Federal workers must pay 7 percent of their salaries into their retirement system, although the national government funds about 75 percent of program costs. The military retirement system, on the other hand, is noncontributory; employees pay only their regular Social Security taxes.

102. Department of Health and Human Services, Social Security Administration, Office of the Actuary; and Department of Defense, Manpower Reserve Affairs, and Logistics (Compensation).

103. Thirty-six states have community property laws.

104. HCEL, *Report on Public Employee Retirement Systems*, p. 126.

105. Pension Rights Center, "Retirement Income," p. 3.

106. Kolko, *Wealth and Power in America*, p. 47.

107. Grad and Foster, "Income of the Population," p. 21; and HEW, *Social Security and the Changing Roles of Men and Women*, p. 176.

108. Howard M. Wachtel, "Looking at Poverty from a Radical Perspective," in James H. Weaver, ed., *Modern Political Economy* (Boston: Allyn and Bacon, 1973), p. 209.

109. Grad and Foster, p. 18.

110. Joseph Friedman and Jane Sjogren, "The Assets of the Elderly as They Retire," ABT Associates, Cambridge, Massachusetts, March 1980, table 2.1, cited in U.S. President's Commission on Pension Policy, "Income of the Retired: Levels and Sources," Working Papers, October 1980, p. 64.

111. HEW, *Social Security and the Changing Roles of Men and Women*, pp. 176–177.

112. George S. Talley and Richard Burkhauser, "Federal Economic Pol-

icy Toward the Elderly," in Bernice L. Neugarten and Robert G. Havighurst, eds., *Social Policy, Social Ethics and the Aging Society* (Washington, D.C.: National Science Foundation, Rann Research Applications Directorate, 1976), p. 47.

113. Ball, *Social Security: Today and Tomorrow*, p. 90.

114. SSCA, *Developments in Aging: 1979*, part 1, p. 17.

115. PCPP, *Coming of Age*, p. 22.

116. Of the "official" poverty population, 59 percent are widows, 6 percent are divorced (or separated) women, and 7 percent are women who have never married.

117. HEW, *Social Security and the Changing Roles of Men and Women*, pp. 24, 167, 168; Grad and Foster, pp. 16–32; and Bureau of the Census, "Money Income and Poverty Status of Families and Persons in the U.S.: 1977," *Current Population Reports*, Series P-60, no. 116, July 1978.

4. Investment Capital and Pension Power

1. This chapter will explore only private, state, and local retirement systems since Social Security and the federal retirement systems primarily utilize pay-as-you-go funding methods and invest their modest accumulation of assets almost exclusively in U.S. Treasury securities.

2. Some major cities remaining as pay-as-you-go systems as of 1978 were: Washington, D.C., Boston, Pittsburgh, Indianapolis, and Denver. See Damon Stetson, "New York City Employees Lag in a Study on Total Compensation," *New York Times*, January 1, 1978, p. 23.

3. Under ERISA, only up to 10 percent of a pension plan's total assets can be invested in the securities of the sponsoring corporation.

4. William C. Greenough and Francis P. King, *Pension Plans and Public Policy* (New York: Columbia University Press, 1976), p. 137.

5. Roger F. Murray, *Economic Aspects of Pensions: A Summary Report* no. 85 (New York: Columbia University Press, National Bureau of Economic Research, 1968), p. 125.

6. Gabriel Kolko, *Wealth and Power in America: An Analysis of Social Class and Income Distribution* (New York: Praeger, 1962), p. 54.

7. Geoffrey N. Calvert, "Contrasting Economic Impact of OASDI and Private Pension Plans," in Richard Irwin, ed., *Social Security and Private Pension Plans: Competitive or Complementary* (Homewood, Ill.: Irwin-Dorsey, 1976), p. 68.

8. The "prudent man" rule is found in ERISA's section 404. It reads: "a fiduciary shall discharge his duties with the care, skill, prudence and diligence under the circumstances then prevailing that a prudent man acting in a like capacity and familiar with such matters would use in the conduct of an enterprise of a like character and with like aims."

9. Cited in A. H. Raskin, "Labor and Investment of Pension Funds," *New York Times*, November 9, 1977, p. 65.

10. U.S. House, Committee on Education and Labor (HCEL), *Pension Task Force Report on Public Employee Retirement Systems*, 95th Cong., 2d sess., March 15, 1978, pp. 206–207.

11. John Harrington, "New Pension Funds Investments: An Evaluation of Potential Allies and Opposition," in Lee Webb and William Schweke, eds., *Public Employee Pension Funds: New Strategies for Investment* (Washington, D.C.: Conference on Alternative State and Local Policies, July 1979), p. 123.

12. *Pensions and Investments*, November 6, 1978, p. 31.

13. See for example, U.S. Senate, Committee on Governmental Affairs, Subcommittee on Reports, Accounting, and Management, *Interlocking Directorates Among the Major U.S. Corporations*, 95th Cong., 2d sess., January 1978.

14. U.S. Senate, Committee on Governmental Affairs (SCGA), Subcommittee on Reports, Accounting, and Management, *Voting Rights in Major Corporations*, 95th Cong., 1st sess., January 1978.

15. *Ibid.*

16. U.S. House, Committee on Banking and Currency, Subcommittee on Domestic Finance, *Commercial Banks and Their Trust Activities: Emerging Influence on the American Economy*, vol. 1, 90th Cong., 2d sess., July 8, 1968, pp. 831–832.

17. David M. Kotz, "Finance Capital and Corporate Control," in Richard C. Edwards, Michael Reich, and Thomas E. Weisskopf, eds., *The Capitalist System* (2d ed.; Englewood Cliffs, N.J.: Prentice-Hall, 1978), p. 156.

18. SCGA, *Voting Rights*, p. 260.

19. *Pensions and Investments*, March 31, 1980, pp. 1 and 15.

20. *Pensions and Investments*, April 23, 1979, p. 1; and *Pensions and Investments*, April 24, 1978.

21. *Pensions and Investments*, March 31, 1980, p. 1.

22. *Ibid.*, see full issue, especially pp. 1 and 18.

23. Kotz, "Finance Capital and Corporate Control," p. 155.

24. For further details see SCGA, *Voting Rights*, pp. 263–292.

25. Richard Parker and Tamsin Taylor, "Strategic Investment," in Webb and Schweke, *Public Employee Pension Funds*, p. 9.

26. *Pensions and Investments*, October 9, 1978, p. 10.

27. Parker and Taylor, p. 9.

28. *Pensions and Investments*, January 1, 1979, p. 6.

29. David Leinsdorf and Donald Etra, *Citibank* (New York: Grossman, 1973), pp. 84–85 and 239; and U.S. House, H.R. Doc. no. 64, *Institutional Investor Study Report of the Securities and Exchange Commission*, 92d Cong., 1st sess., 1971, cited in Leinsdorf and Etra, p. 239.

30. Greenough and King, *Pension Plans and Public Policy*, pp. 145–146;

It has been suggested by several sources that ERISA's prudent man rule has encouraged more conservative investment practices. For instance, despite new rulings by the Labor Department which attempted to clarify what is meant by "prudent investments" there appears to be even less willingness by institutional investors to invest in venture capital funds or small businesses.

31. Quoted in Raskin, "Labor and Investment," p. 65.

32. Senator Lee Metcalf, "A Stronger Voice for Union Members in Pension Fund Investments," 95th Cong., 1st sess., January 4, 1978, *Congressional Record*, 123, 198, pp. SI 9951–9952.

33. Corporate Data Exchange, *Pension Investment: A Social Audit* (New York: Corporate Data Exchange, 1979), pp. 8 and 15.

34. Jeremy Rifkin and Randy Barber, *The North Will Rise Again: Pensions, Politics and Power in the 1980s* (Boston, Mass.: Beacon, 1978).

35. Quoted in *Pensions and Investments*, March 26, 1979, p. 2.

36. *Labor and Investments* (January 1981), 1(1):2.

37. HCEL, *Public Employee Retirement Systems*, p. 165. Other analysts have projected the unfunded liabilities to be over $300 billion.

38. Tamsin Taylor, Lee Webb, and Richard Parker, "Public Employee Pension Funds: Their Potential for Neighborhood Development," in Webb and Schweke, eds., *Public Employee Pension Funds*, p. 32.

39. HCEL, *Public Employee Retirement Systems*, p. 157.

40. *Ibid.*, pp. 22 and 36–37.

41. Les Stern, "State, Local Funds Would Fail ERISA Test," *Pensions and Investments*, September 10, 1979, p. 15.

42. House CEL, *Public Employee Retirement Systems*, p. 148.

43. *Pensions and Investments*, November 6, 1978, p. 35.

44. HCEL, *Public Employee Retirement Systems*, p. 102.

45. "Overview: Issues and Problems," in Webb and Schweke, p. 1.

46. *Labor and Investments* (January 1981), 1(1):5.

47. *Pensions and Investment Age*, January 19, 1981, p. 1.

48. *Ibid.*

49. See Webb and Schweke, eds., *Public Employee Pension Funds*.

50. Parker and Taylor, "Strategic Investment," p. 11.

51. Ray Rogers, "Confront Power with Power," in Webb and Schweke, p. 89.

52. Corporate Data Exchange, *Pension Investments*, pp. 15–16.

53. *Pensions and Investments*, November 16, 1978, p. 15.

54. Charles Dearing, *Industrial Pensions* (Washington, D.C.: Brookings Institution, 1954), p. 50.

55. Greenough and King, *Pension Plans and Public Policy*, pp. 44–46.

56. Raskin, "Labor and Investment," p. 65.

57. H. Robert Bartell, Jr., "Growth in Multiemployer and Union Pension Funds, 1959–1964," in Robert Bartell, Jr. and Elizabeth T. Simpson, eds.,

Pension Funds of Multiemployer Industrial Groups, Unions, and Non-profit Organizations, Occasional Paper 105 (New York: Columbia University Press, National Bureau of Economic Research, 1968), pp. 1–19.

58. The growing interest of union officials in pension fund investment policies is evidenced by the recently launched AFL-CIO publication *Labor and Investments*, the first issue appearing in January 1981.

59. Senator Metcalf, "A Stronger Voice," pp. S1 9951–9952.

60. *Labor and Investments* (January 1981), 1(1):1, 4.

61. In 1980, the union terminated Manufacturers Hanover Trust as its money manager.

62. *Pensions and Investments*, July 17, 1978, p. 44.

63. *Pensions and Investments*, June 5, 1978, p. 35.

64. *Pensions and Investments*, November 20, 1978, p. 52.

65. Quoted in *Labor and Investments* (January 1981), 1(1):3.

66. *Ibid.*

67. *Pensions and Investments*, December 22, 1980, p. 1.

68. *Pensions and Investments*, October 13, 1980, p. 52.

69. *Ibid.*, p. 2.

70. *Pensions and Investment Age*, February 16, 1981, p. 2.

71. *Pensions and Investments*, October 13, 1980, p. 2.

72. *Pensions and Investments*, November 24, 1980, p. 19.

73. Nathan Gardels, cited in *BNA Pension Reporter*, November 16, 1981, no. 368, p. A-7.

74. *Labor and Investments* (January 1981), 1(1):8.

75. Louis Harris and Associates, *1979 Study of American Attitudes Toward Pensions and Retirement*, New York, February 1979.

76. Quoted in *Pensions and Investments*, March 26, 1979, p. 2.

77. Runaway firms are those companies moving from northern and midwestern to southern parts of the United States, or to other countries, for the purpose of avoiding union labor or taxes.

78. Rogers, "Confront Power with Power," p. 95.

5. The Graying of the Medical-Industrial Complex

1. E. Richard Brown, *Rockefeller Medicine Men: Medicine and Capitalism in America* (Berkeley: University of California Press, 1979).

2. Brown, p. 5. The following discussion draws heavily from Brown's work.

3. Theodore R. Marmor, *The Politics of Medicare* (Chicago: Aldine, 1970), pp. 6, 9, 26.

4. Karen Davis, *National Health Insurance* (Washington, D.C.: Brookings Institution, 1975), p. 20.

5. Marmor, p. 6.

6. Barbara Ehrenreich and John Ehrenreich, *The American Health Empire: Power, Profits and Politics* (New York: Vintage, 1970), p. 103.

7. Ray Munts, *Bargaining for Health: Labor Unions, Health Insurance and Medical Care* (Madison: University of Wisconsin Press, 1967), pp. 1–6.

8. Robert J. Myers, *Medicare* (Homewood, Ill.: Richard Irwin, published for the McCahan Foundation, 1970), pp. 2–8.

9. Brown, *Rockefeller Medicine Men*, p. 122.

10. Robert Stevens and Rosemary Stevens, *Welfare Medicine in America: A Case Study of Medicaid* (New York: Free Press, 1974), pp. 43–44.

11. Brown, p. 229. For further discussion see section in this chapter on Health Care Under Capitalism: Some Limitations of the Medical Model for the Aged.

12. Paul P. Ginsburg, "Resource Allocation in the Hospital Industry: The Role of Capital Financing," *Social Security Bulletin* (October 1972), 35:21; and Stevens and Stevens, p. 43.

13. Marmor, *Politics of Medicare*, p. 18.

14. Stevens and Stevens, *Welfare Medicine*, p. 27.

15. The medically indigent older population included those people who were not receiving public assistance but whose incomes were insufficient to meet their medical bills. However, medically needy elegibility requirements were set at low and different levels by each participating state.

16. For a full discussion of the Kerr-Mills legislation see Stevens and Stevens, pp. 26–36.

17. U.S. Senate, Special Committee on Aging (SSCA), *Developments in Aging: 1980*, part 1, 97th Cong., 1st sess., May 13, 1981, p. xx; and Department of Health and Human Services, Health Care Financing Administration (HCFA), Office of National Health Statistics.

18. SSCA, *Developments: 1980*, pp. xx–xxi; and HCFA, Office of National Health Statistics.

19. U.S. Department of Health and Human Services, Social Security Administration, "Public Income-Maintenance Programs: Hospital and Medical Care Payments, 1940–80," Table M-2, *Social Security Bulletin* (January 1981), 44(1):34.

20. HCFA, Office of National Health Statistics.

21. U.S. Executive Office of the President, Office of Management and Budget (OMB), *Special Analysis: Budget of the United States Government, Fiscal Year 1982*, Special Analysis A (Washington, D.C.: GPO, 1981), p. 15.

22. Myers, *Medicare*, p. 129.

23. Beginning in January 1982, reimbursement under Medicare will be limited to 108 percent of the cost charged by comparable hospitals in a geographic area.

24. Brown, *Rockefeller Medicine Men*, p. 203.

25. SSCA, *Developments: 1980*, p. 44.

26. Brown, p. 203.

27. John Iglehart, "Health Report/Explosive Rise in Medical Costs Puts Government in Quandry," *National Journal* (September 20, 1975), 7:1322; and American Hospital Association, "Hospital Statistics, 1980," Chicago, Illinois, 1980.

28. U.S. Executive Office of the President, Office of Management and Budget (OMB), *Budget of the United States Government, Fiscal Year 1982* (Washington, D.C.: GPO, 1981), p. 232.

29. Cited in Inglehart, p. 1322.

30. Robert Charles Clark, "Does the Nonprofit Form Fit the Hospital Industry?" *Harvard Law Review* (May 1980), 93(7):1452.

31. Marmor, *Politics of Medicare*, p. 86.

32. American Medical Association, Center for Health Services Research and Development, "Profile of Medical Practice, 1981," Periodic Survey of Physicians, Monroe, Wisconsin, 1981.

33. SSCA, *Developments: 1980*, p. 45.

34. U.S. Senate, *Medicare-Medicaid Administration and Reimbursement Reform, Hearings before the Subcommittee on Health of the Committee on Finance on S. 3205*, 94th Cong., 2d sess., July 1976, esp. p. 175.

35. Ehrenreich and Ehrenreich, *American Health Empire*, pp. 94–123.

36. U.S. Department of Health, Education, and Welfare, Social Security Administration, Office of Research and Statistics, "Prescription Drug Data Survey, 1974," 1977.

37. Cited in Frances Tenenbaum, *Over 55 Is Not Illegal* (Boston: Houghton Mifflin, 1979), p. 154.

38. Bruce Vladick, *Unloving Care: The Nursing Home Tragedy* (New York: Basic Books, 1980), p. 131.

39. See Vladick, pp. 36–47, and p. 108.

40. SSCA, *Developments: 1980*, p. 83.

41. Of the 26,000 nursing homes in the United States, 21 percent participate in the Medicare program and 71 percent in the Medicaid program. SSCA, *Developments: 1980*, pp. 45, 77.

42. *Ibid.*, p. 45; and SSCA, *Developments: 1979*, pp. 54, 88, 92.

43. U.S. Senate, Report of the Subcommittee on Long-Term Care, *Nursing Home Care in the United States*, 94th Cong., 2d sess., March 1976, p. 24.

44. Elizabeth A. Taylor, "Policy Implementation of Long-Term Care for the Elderly," June 1979. Mimeo.

45. SSCA, *Developments: 1980*, p. 59.

46. For detailed and comprehensive accounts of economic and patient abuses by the nursing home industry see Mary A. Mendelson, *Tender Loving Greed* (New York: Random House, 1975); and Vladick, *Unloving Care*.

47. U.S. General Accounting Office, "State Audits to Identify Medicaid Over-Payment to Nursing Homes," January 24, 1977.

48. U.S. Senate, Special Committee on Aging, *Kickbacks Among Medicaid Providers*, Report 95-320, 95th Cong., 1st sess., June 30, 1977.

49. J. Terrence Brunner, executive director, Better Government Association, Chicago, Ill., quoted in U.S. Senate, *The Federal-State Effort in Long-Term Care for Older Americans: Nursing Homes and 'Alternatives,' Hearings before the Special Committee on Aging*, 95th Cong., 2d sess., August 30, 1978, p. 9.

50. American Federation of Labor-Congress of Industrial Organizations (AFL-CIO) Executive Council, "America's Nursing Homes: Profit in Misery," February 25, 1977, cited in U.S. Senate, Special Committee on Aging (SSCA), *Developments in Aging: 1977*, part 1, 95th Cong., 2d sess., April 27, 1978, p. 87.

51. Although the 1977 legislation stipulated that the states would receive 90 percent of such expenses until 1980, this was extended for an additional three years. Beginning in 1984 the states will receive 75 percent of the costs.

52. Senate Subcommittee on Long-Term Care, *Nursing Homes in the U.S.*, p. 269.

53. *Ibid.*, p. xi.

54. Vladick, *Unloving Care*, p. 18.

55. U.S. Department of Health and Human Services, "Report of Under Secretary's Task Force on Long-Term Care, staff draft, January 9, 1981, cited in SSCA, *Developments: 1980*, p. 89.

56. SSCA, *Developments: 1980*, p. 57. For a description of these changes in Medicare see note 67.

57. L. Gottesman and N. Bourestrom, "Why Nursing Homes Do What They Do," *Gerontologist* (1974), 14:501–506.

58. Barbara Bolling Manard, Ralph E. Woehle, and James M. Heilman, *Better Homes for the Old* (Lexington, Mass.: Heath-Lexington Books, 1977).

59. SSCA, *Developments: 1980*, p. 67.

60. Manard, Woehle, and Heilman, *Better Homes for the Old*, pp. 46, 92.

61. Jordan I. Kosberg, "Differences in Proprietary Institutions Caring for Affluent and Nonaffluent Elderly," *Gerontologist* (1973), 13:299–304.

62. Karen Davis and Cathy Schoen, *Health and the War on Poverty* (Washington, D.C.: Brookings Institution, 1978), pp. 73–75; and Manard, Woehle, and Heilman, *Better Homes for the Old*, p. 38.

63. Beginning in January 1982, reimbursements to nursing homes for publicly supported residents will be limited to 75 percent of cost, a decrease from the 80 percent allowed under prior legislation.

64. See, for example, Carol A. Dalany and Kathleen A. Davies, *Nursing Home Ombudsman Project Final Report: The Pennsylvania Experience*

(Harrisburg: Pennsylvania Advocates for Better Care, January 1979), pp. 15, 20, 23.

65. This deductible, which rose from $60 to $75 in 1982, was the first such increase since 1973.

66. Marian Gornick, "Ten Years of Medicare: Impact on the Covered Population," *Social Security Bulletin* (July 1976), 39:3–17; and SSCA, *Developments: 1980*, pp. 46–47.

67. Effective July 1981, Medicare recipients no longer had to be hospitalized for a period of at least three days before becoming eligible for home health benefits. The 1980 legislation also eliminated the prior limit of 100 home health visits, and removed the cost-sharing provisions for this service.

68. SSCA, *Developments: 1979*, p. 55.

69. Davis and Schoen, *Health and the War on Poverty*, p. 99.

70. Gornick, pp. 3–17.

71. SSCA, *Developments: 1979*, p. 54.

72. SSCA, *Developments: 1980*, pp. xxii, 45.

73. SSCA, *Developments: 1977*, p. 57.

74. *Senior Citizen News*, (January 1980), 5(221):2.

75. Majorie Smith Mueller, Robert M. Gibson, and Charles R. Fisher, "Age Differences in Health Care Spending, Fiscal Year 1976," *Social Security Bulletin* (August 1977), 40:7.

76. Brown, *Rockefeller Medicine Men*, pp. 212–213.

77. U.S. Department of Health, Education, and Welfare (HEW), *Health United States, 1976–1977* (1977), p. 16.

78. A one percent offset is offered for each of the following: having or establishing a hospital rate review program; enacting fraud or abuse controls; and reducing growth in annual program costs to under 9 percent. In addition, a one percent offset is provided automatically to states that have an unemployment rate exceeding 150 percent of the national average.

79. Davis and Schoen, *Health and the War on Poverty*, pp. 107–109.

80. Davis, *National Health Insurance*, pp. 44, 52–53.

81. Howard B. Waitzkin and Barbara Waterman, *The Exploitation of Illness in Capitalist Society* (Indianapolis, Ind.: Bobbs-Merrill, 1974), p. 87.

82. Waitzkin and Waterman, p. 73.

83. Abraham Ribicoff, *The American Medical Machine* (New York: Saturday Review Press, 1972), p. 43.

84. Rick J. Carlson, *The End of Medicine* (New York: Wiley, 1975), p. 41; and Brown, *Rockefeller Medicine Men*, p. 215.

85. Despite increasing specialization, medical schools have few training programs or even advanced courses in geriatrics.

86. Itzhak Jacoby, "Physician Manpower: GMENAC and Afterwards," *Public Health Reports*, (July-August 1981), 96(4):299.

87. Carlson, p. 41.

88. Jacoby, pp. 299–300.

89. Louis Harris and Associates, *The Myth and Reality of Aging in America* (Washington, D.C.: National Council on the Aging, July 1976), p. 29.

90. HEW, *Health U.S., 1976–1977*, pp. 14, 16.

91. Ribicoff, *The American Medical Machine*, p. 18.

92. Davis, *National Health Insurance*, pp. 155–156.

93. Jacoby, "Physician Manpower," p. 302.

94. See for example, John Ehrenreich, Introduction, in Ehrenreich, ed., *The Cultural Crisis of Modern Medicine* (New York: Monthly Review Press, 1978), and Brown, *Rockefeller Medicine Men*, p. 214.

95. Judith M. Feder, *Medicare: The Politics of Federal Hospital Insurance* (Lexington, Mass.: Heath-Lexington Books, 1977), pp. 9–25.

96. Sylvia Tesh, "Disease Causality and Politics," *Journal of Health Politics, Policy and Law* (Fall 1981), 6(3):369–388.

97. Respiratory diseases and injuries account for 72 percent of the acute health problems among the elderly.

98. Multiple chronic conditions are particularly unsuited to modern medical practice which subdivides illness and parcels out treatment to various specialists. Treatment for one disease may even result in adverse effects on other health problems.

99. SSCA, *Developments: 1980*, p. xxiii.

100. HEW, *Health U.S., 1976–1977*, p. 8.

101. Carlson, *End of Medicine*, p. 103.

102. Marc Renaud, "On the Structural Constraints to State Intervention in Health," in Ehrenreich, *Cultural Crisis*, pp. 101–123.

103. See for example Brown, *Rockefeller Medicine Men*, p. 229.

104. Tesh, "Disease Causality and Politics," p. 381.

105. U.S. Department of Health and Human Services, National Institute of Health (NIH), "National Cancer Program, 1980 Director's report and annual plan, FY 1982–1986," March 1981, p. i-2.

106. In 1981 the federal government spent $1.1 billion on cancer research, up from $.6 billion in 1974. NIH, "National Cancer Program," p. iii-31.

107. Samuel S. Epstein, *The Politics of Cancer* (San Francisco: Sierra Club Books, 1978), pp. 328–329.

108. *Ibid.*, pp. 328–329; and NIH, "National Cancer Program," p. v.

109. NIH, "National Cancer Program, p. i-2.

110. *Ibid.*, p. i-2.

111. U.S. Department of Health, Education, and Welfare, *Work in America* (Cambridge, Mass.: MIT Press, 1973), pp. 77–79.

112. Carlson, *End of Medicine*, p. 110.

113. Tesh, "Disease Causality and Politics," p. 372.

114. Louis Harris and Associates, *Myth and Reality of Aging*, pp. 29, 130.

115. HEW, *Health U.S., 1976–1977*, p. 11.

116. U.S. Senate, Committee on Labor and Public Welfare, Subcommittee on Aging, and the Special Committee on Aging, *Post-White House Conference on Aging Reports*, 93d Cong., 1st sess., 1973, p. 181.

117. Davis and Schoen, *Health and the War on Poverty*, p. 19.

118. HEW, *Health U.S., 1976–1977*, p. 226.

119. Davis and Schoen, p. 38.

120. U.S. Congressional Budget Office, Catastrophic Health Insurance (1977), p. 26.

121. Walter W. Kolodrubetz, "Group Health Insurance Coverage of Full-Time Employees, 1972," *Social Security Bulletin* (April 1974), 37:17–35.

122. Davis, *National Health Insurance*, p. 12.

123. *Ibid.*, pp. 35–37.

124. OMB, *Budget of the U.S., Fiscal Year 1982*, p. 232.

125. OMB, *Special Analyses: Budget of the U.S., Fiscal Year 1982*, Special Analysis G, p. 229.

126. OMB, *Budget of the U.S., Fiscal Year 1982*, p. 232.

127. E. Harvey Estes, Jr., "Health Experience in the Elderly," in Jon Hendricks and C. Davis Hendricks, eds., *Dimensions of Aging* (Cambridge, Mass.: Winthrop, 1979), p. 97.

6. The Housing Crisis: Private Power and Public Resources

1. Substandard housing is judged on the basis of whether the unit has adequate heating, plumbing, and sewage-disposal systems; how well the unit is designed and maintained; and on the type of electrical system and kitchen facilities available. See U.S. Department of Housing and Urban Development, *Annual Housing Survey Reports*, 1976.

2. U.S. Department of Housing and Urban Development (HUD), Office of Policy Development and Research, *How Well Are We Housed?: The Elderly*, by Anthony Yezer (Washington, D.C.: GPO, May 1979), pp. 8–9.

3. Five percent of older households live on farms. U.S. Senate, Special Committee on Aging (SSCA), *Developments in Aging: 1980*, part 1, 97th Cong., 1st sess., May 13, 1981, p. xxxvii.

4. HUD, *How Well Are We Housed?* p. 11.

5. U.S. Department of Housing and Urban Development, *Older Americans Facts About Income and Housing*, cited in National Council on Aging, *Fact Book on Aging: A Profile of America's Older Population* (Washington, D.C.: Council on Aging, 1979), p. 179.

6. Adjusted income is the household's cash income divided by the square root of the number of persons in the household. HUD, *How Well Are We Housed?* p. 14.

7. *Ibid.*, pp. 16–17.

8. Henry O. Pratt, *The Gray Lobby* (Chicago: University of Chicago Press, 1976), p. 79.

9. U.S. Senate, Special Committee on Aging (SSCA), *Developments in Aging: 1979*, part 1, 96th Cong., 2d sess., 1980, p. xxiv.

10. *Ibid.*, p. xxvi.

11. *Ibid.*

12. National Council on Aging, *Fact Book on Aging*, p. 182.

13. Department of Housing and Urban Development (HUD), "1979 Statistical Yearbook," (Washington, D.C.: GPO, 1979), p. 274.

14. U.S. Senate, Special Committee on Aging (SSCA), *Developments in Aging: 1977*, part 1, 95th Cong., 2d sess., April 27, 1978, p. iii.

15. National Council on Aging, *Fact Book on Aging*, p. 192.

16. See Gilbert W. Fairholm and Barbara Fairholm, "Policy Implications of Property Tax Relief for the Elderly," *Gerontologist* (October 1979), 19(5):432–437.

17. Circuit-breakers are tax relief programs for specified groups in society—usually for the elderly. There are different standards of eligibility and types of benefits among the localities in the United States. In general, an eligible household receives a rebate, or credit, against state income tax liabilities, when the property tax liability exceeds a specified percentage of the family's income. In some areas, households are expected to pay a set percentage of the property tax, a percentage that remains constant as taxes increase. See Federal Council on the Aging, *The Impact of the Tax Structure on the Elderly* (Washington, D.C.: GPO, December 29, 1975), pp. 95–96, 106.

18. Cited in SSCA, part 1, *Developments: 1979*, p. 99.

19. *Congressional Quarterly Weekly Report* (October 6, 1979), 37(40):2206.

20. U.S. Department of Labor, Bureau of Labor Statistics.

21. U.S. Department of Energy (DE), Economic Regulatory Administration, Fuel Oil Marketing Advisory Committee, "Low-Income Energy Assistance Programs," Washington, D.C., July 1980, cited in SSCA, part 1, *Developments: 1980*, pp. 96–97.

22. Energy Policy Project of the Ford Foundation, *A Time to Choose: America's Energy Future* (Cambridge, Mass.: Ballinger, 1974), pp. 128–129.

23. DE, "Low-Income Energy Assistance," cited in SSCA, part 1, *Developments: 1980*, p. 96.

24. SSCA, part 1, *Developments: 1979*, p. xliv.

25. In 1981, only $87.5 million was available for energy crisis intervention—an amount which is part of the total $1.85 billion authorized in that year.

26. Up to 15 percent of each state's allotment can be utilized for weatherization projects, and an additional 10 percent is allowed to be transferred into other block grant programs.

27. *Senior Citizen News* (April 1980), 5(224):S-4.

28. The following analysis is based on two articles by Michael E. Stone. Unless otherwise noted the data is drawn from these sources. See Michael E. Stone, "Gimme Shelter!" in Economics Education Project of the Union of Radical Political Economists (URPE), ed., *U.S. Capitalism in Crisis* (New York: URPE, January 1978), pp. 182–193; and Stone, "Federal Housing Policy: A Political-Economic Analysis," in Jon Pynoos, Robert Schafer, and Chester W. Hartman, eds., *Housing Urban America* (Chicago: Aldine, 1973), pp. 423–433.

29. Harold Wolman, *Politics of Federal Housing* (New York: Dodd, Mead, 1971), p. 27.

30. *Ibid.*, and National Council on Aging, *Fact Book on Aging*, p. 38.

31. HUD, "1979 Statistical Yearbook," p. 261.

32. Jonathan E. Zimmer, *From Rental to Cooperative: Improving Low and Moderate Income Housing* (Beverly Hills, Calif.: Sage, 1977), vol. 4, series 03-038, p. 7.

33. HUD, *How Well Are We Housed?* p. 7.

34. According to official estimates, "total housing starts in 1980 were about 1.3 million units, down from 1.7 million in 1979 and 2 million in both 1977 and 1978." U.S. Executive Office of the President, Office of Management and Budget, *Budget of the United States Government, Fiscal Year 1982* (Washington, D.C.: GPO, 1981), p. 169.

35. *Congressional Quarterly* (July 15, 1978), 36(28):1801–1804. The 1977 figures do not total 100 percent due to rounding.

36. Stone, "Federal Housing Policy," p. 423.

37. Councilwoman Ruth Messinger, quoted in *Village Voice* (January 21, 1980), 3(35):1, 19. The J-51 program offers tax incentives to landlords and developers who renovate or convert housing units. The program allows a twelve-year exemption from property taxes on the increased assessed value of the housing units, as well as up to twenty years of tax abatements. Since 1975, when the law was rewritten and hotels and commercial lofts became eligible for conversion benefits, most of the tax exemptions have supported conversions.

38. SSCA, part 1, *Developments: 1979*, p. 152.

39. Stephen E. Barton, "The Urban Housing Problem: Marxist Theory and Community Organizing," *The Review of Radical Political Economics* (Winter 1977), 9(4):16–30.

40. *Ibid.*

41. For a succinct analysis of the growing fiscal crisis in cities, see Kenneth Fox, "Cities and City Governments," in URPE, *U.S. Capitalism in Crisis*, pp. 174–181.

42. John M. Quigley, "Policies for Low and Moderate Income Housing," *Policy Studies Journal* (1979), 8(2):301.

43. For a good discussion of the National Association of Home Builders

and their lobbying efforts, see William Lilley III, "The Homebuilders Lobby," in Pynoos, Schafer, and Hartman, eds., *Housing Urban America*, pp. 30–48.

44. *Congressional Quarterly* (July 15, 1978), 36(28):1801–1804.

45. Frances M. Carp, "Housing and Living Environments of Older People," in Robert Binstock and Ethel Shanas, eds., *Handbook of Aging and the Social Sciences* (New York: Van Nostrand Reinhold, 1976), p. 247.

46. National Council on Aging, *Fact Book on Aging*, pp. 184–185.

47. These limited funds were allocated to both public housing authorities and section 202 housing developers. SSCA, part 1, *Developments: 1980*, p. 155.

48. See for example, U.S. Department of Housing and Urban Development, *Housing in the Seventies*, Report of the National Housing Policy Review, 1974.

49. Lawrence M. Friedman, "Public Housing and the Poor," in Pynoos, Schafer, and Hartman, eds., *Housing Urban America*, pp. 448–459.

50. Eugene J. Meehan, *The Quality of Federal Policymaking: Programmed Failure in Public Housing* (Columbia: University of Missouri Press, 1979), p. 36.

51. Pynoos, Schafer, and Hartman, Introduction, pp. 16–17.

52. SSCA, part 1, *Developments: 1980*, p. 153; and Leonard Freedman, *Public Housing: The Politics of Poverty* (New York: Holt, Rinehart, and Winston, 1969), p. 179.

53. Marilyn Moon, *The Measure of Economic Welfare: Its Application to the Poor* (New York: Academic Press, 1977).

54. Robert Butler, *Why Survive? Being Old in America* (New York: Harper and Row, 1975), p. 108.

55. Meehan, p. 37.

56. Meehan, p. 197.

57. *Ibid.*

58. Meehan, p. 196.

59. SSCA, part 1, *Developments: 1980*, p. 154.

60. Wolman, *Politics of Federal Housing*, p. 36.

61. SSCA, part 1, *Developments: 1977*, p. 109.

62. Cited in Butler, *Why Survive?* p. 128.

63. U.S. Department of Housing and Urban Development (HUD), "Annual Housing Survey: 1978," part A, *General Housing Characteristics*, November 1980, p. xv; and HUD, "1979 Statistical Yearbook," p. 204.

64. HUD, "1979 Statistical Yearbook," p. 37.

65. Jon Hendricks and C. Davis Hendricks, *Aging in Mass Society* (Cambridge, Mass.: Winthrop, 1977), p. 278.

66. Butler, *Why Survive?* p. 128.

67. National Housing Policy Review, *Housing in the Seventies*, p. 122.

68. Mahlon R. Straszheim, "The Section 8 Rental Assistance Program: Costs and Policy Options," *Policy Studies Journal* (1979), 8(2):311–312.

69. HUD, "1979 Statistical Yearbook," table 72.

70. SSCA, part 1, *Developments: 1980*, p. 153; and U.S. Senate, Special Committee on Aging, *Omnibus Budget Reconciliation Act of 1981, Selected Provisions Affecting the Elderly*, Information Paper, 97th Cong., 1st sess., September 1981, p. 19.

71. SSCA, part 1, *Developments: 1979*, pp. 143–145.

72. Lilley, "Homebuilders Lobby," p. 38; Section 235, also enacted as part of the 1968 Housing and Urban Development Act, subsidized mortgage interest rates for suppliers of low-income single-family dwellings.

73. Butler, *Why Survive?* p. 130.

74. Cited in Zimmer, *From Rental to Coop*, p. 9.

75. SSCA, part 1, *Developments: 1979*, p. xxvii.

76. SSCA, part 1, *Developments: 1980*, p. 154.

77. *Ibid.*, p. 154.

78. Barton, "Urban Housing Problems," pp. 16–23.

7. Human Services

1. See Frances Fox Piven and Richard A. Cloward, *Regulating the Poor: The Functions of Public Welfare* (New York: Pantheon Books, 1971), esp. pp. 248–330.

2. Henry J. Pratt, *The Gray Lobby* (Chicago: University of Chicago Press, 1976), pp. 113–117.

3. Pratt, pp. 118–128.

4. John C. Donovan, *The Politics of Poverty* (2d ed.; Indianapolis, Ind.: Bobbs-Merrill, 1973), p. 178.

5. Robert N. Butler, *Why Survive? Being Old in America* (New York: Harper and Row, 1975), p. 330.

6. See U.S. Department of Health, Education, and Welfare, Office of Human Development, Administration on Aging, *Older Americans Act of 1965, As Amended and Related Acts*, Bicentennial Compilation, March 1976, pp. 2–3.

7. Carroll L. Estes, *The Aging Enterprise* (San Francisco: Jossey-Bass, 1979), p. 54.

8. Under OAA regulations, a state meeting certain criteria does not have to subdivide its jurisdiction into separate planning and service areas or establish local area agencies on aging. As of 1981, there were thirteen such single-state agencies on aging.

9. Approximately 60 percent of the local area agencies on aging function as units of government and 40 percent operate as private, nonprofit organ-

izations. U.S. Department of Health and Human Services, Federal Council on Aging (FCA), "Toward More Effective Implementation of the Older Americans Act," a staff report, April 1981, p. 51.

10. This figure excludes the old title IX (currently title V) Community Service Employment Program which is run by the Department of Labor. In 1981 these activities totaled $277 million. Appropriations for OAA in 1982 were $715 million.

11. Prior to 1973, grants under title III were used primarily to develop community services.

12. Theodore Marmor and Elizabeth Kutza, "Coordinated Government Services: Aging Agencies and the Coordination Dream," paper presented at the 37th annual meeting of the Midwest Political Science Association, Chicago, Illinois, April 19–21, 1979, pp. 3, 9.

13. Sheldon S. Tobin, Steven M. Davidson, and Ann Sack, *Effective Social Services for Older Americans* (Detroit: Institute of Gerontology, University of Michigan–Wayne State University, 1976), p. 48.

14. Leonard E. Gottesman, Barbara Ishizaki, and Stacey MacBride, "Service Management: Concepts and Models," *Gerontologist* (August 1979), 19(4):384.

15. Jurgen Schmandt, Victor Bach, and Beryl A. Radin, "Information and Referral Services for Elderly Welfare Recipients," *Gerontologist* (February 1979), 19(1):24.

16. Raymond M. Steinberg, *A Longitudinal Analysis of 97 Area Agencies on Aging* (Los Angeles: University of Southern California, Andrus Gerontology Center, May 1976), p. 42.

17. Marmor and Kutza, p. 25.

18. Dan Fritz, "The Administration on Aging as an Advocate: Progress, Problems and Prospects," *Gerontologist* (April 1979), 19(2):141–157.

19. Estes, *Aging Enterprise*, p. 119.

20. Federal outlays were $2.7 billion in 1977 and 1978, $2.9 billion in 1979, $2.7 billion in 1980, and $2.9 billion in 1981. All of the increases from the initial $2.5 billion level was designated for use as 100 percent federally funded child care services.

21. Federal allotment formulas are based on the ratio of the state's population to the population in the United States. For most programs, states were reimbursed for 75 percent of their title XX expenditures. Only 11 states spent their own funds beyond the required match. U.S. Department of Health and Human Services (HHS), Office of the Secretary, "Annual Report to the Congress on Title XX of the Social Security Act, Fiscal Year 1980," March 1981.

22. HHS, "Annual Report on Title XX," p. 4.

23. The total for 1981 was $4.3 billion.

24. HHS, "Annual Report on Title XX."

25. The Community Services Administration (CSA) which funded antipoverty programs totaling $526 million in 1981, was abolished effective January 1982. It was replaced by a community services block grant which will be administered by the Department of Health and Human Services. Funding was reduced to $389 million for 1982. The program had served about 1.5 million older persons in addition to other needy groups.

26. Fritz, "The Administration on Aging as an Advocate," p. 148.

27. See Estes, *The Aging Enterprise*, pp. 44, 198–220.

28. Forrest Malakoff and Michael McQuaide, "The Role and Composition of Advisory Councils to Area Agencies on Aging: The Pennsylvania Example," Philadelphia, November 29, 1979. Mimeo.

29. Estes, p. 71.

30. Douglas F. Dowd, *The Twisted Dream: Capitalist Development in the U.S. Since 1776* (Cambridge, Mass.: Winthrop, 1974), p. 165.

31. In response to a congressional mandate that federally funded transportation projects be made accessible to the elderly and handicapped, the transportation department developed a "transbus" at a cost of $27 million. However, attempts to make these buses available to older people have been thwarted by powerful monopoly interests. Since General Motors, one of the few bus manufacturers in the United States, has been unwilling to alter its current production method to meet specifications mandated by the transportation department, the expected $480 million purchase of the transbus by the national government was put off indefinitely.

32. U.S. Senate, Special Committee on Aging (SSCA), *Developments in Aging: 1977*, part 1, 95th Cong., 2d sess., April 27, 1978, p. 120.

33. Motor Vehicle Manufacturers Association, *Motor Vehicles Facts and Figures, 1976*, cited in National Council on Aging, *Fact Book on Aging: A Profile of America's Older Population* (Washington, D.C.: National Council on Aging, 1979), p. 212.

34. Louis Harris and Associates, *The Myth and Reality of Aging in America* (Washington, D.C.: National Council on Aging, July 1976), pp. 114, 143.

35. Schmandt, Bach, and Radin, p. 23.

36. Lehigh Valley Community Council, "A Generic I&R System for the Lehigh Valley," Bethlehem, Pa., October 1979, p. 3. Mimeo.

37. Schmandt, Bach, and Radin, "Information and Referral Services," pp. 23, 25.

38. See for example, Linda Noelker and Zeo Harel, "Aged Excluded from Home Health Care: An Interorganizational Solution," *Gerontologist* (February 1978), 18(1):37–41.

39. Barbara Skolnick, "Home Health Care Now," *Network* (July/August 1979), p. 5.

40. Pennsylvania Department of Public Welfare, Office of the Aging,

Serving Older Persons in Pennsylvania, A Summary Report and Proposals for the State Plan on Services for Older Persons, April 4, 1977, p. 17.

41. Funding under the Older Americans Act provides up to 85 percent of the costs.

42. E. Kahoma, B. Felton, and T. Fairchild, "Community Services and Facilities Planning," in M. Powell Lawton, Robert J. Newcomer, and Thomas O. Byerts, eds., *Community Planning for an Aging Society* (Stroudsburg, Pa.: Dowden, Hutchinson, and Ross, 1976), p. 230.

43. Estes, *Aging Enterprise*, pp. 17–18.

44. FCA, "Toward More Effective Implementation of the Older Americans Act," p. 51.

45. See Ian Rawson et al., "Nutrition of Rural Elderly in Southwestern Pennsylvania," *Gerontologist* (February 1978), 18(1):24–36.

46. Dieter Hessel, ed., *Maggie Kuhn on Aging* (Philadelphia: Westminster Press, 1977).

47. Robert L. Schneider, "Barriers to Effective Outreach in Title VII Nutrition Programs," *Gerontologist* (April 1979), 19(2):164.

48. Robert M. Ball, *Social Security: Today and Tomorrow* (New York: Columbia University Press, 1978), p. 365.

49. The number of participants grew from 6.5 million in 1970, to 19 million in 1975, and to 22.6 million in 1981.

50. Persons aged sixty and over have income eligibility standards that are higher than those for other age groups. Eligibility for younger households now is set at 130 percent of the nonfarm poverty guidelines prescribed by the Office of Management and Budget.

51. The benefit reduction rate, currently set at 30 percent, specifies the portion of income that a family is expected to spend on food. For every dollar that is above 30 percent of an eligible household's income, the amount of food stamps it would have been entitled to is reduced by one-third.

52. The 1982 spending cap was set at $11.3 billion.

53. U.S. General Accounting Office, *Improvements Needed in Contracting for On-the-Job-Training under the Manpower Development and Training Act of 1962*, 1970, cited in Larry Sawyers and Howard M. Wachel, "The Distributional Impact of Federal Government Subsidies in the United States," *Kapitalistate* (Spring 1975), 3:61.

54. U.S. Executive Office of the President, Office of Management and Budget, *Budget of the United States Government, Fiscal Year 1982* (Washington, D.C.: GPO, 1981), p. 220.

55. U.S. House, Select Committee on Aging, *Funding of Federal Programs For Older Americans*, 94th Cong., 2d sess., September 1976, p. 16.

56. *Ibid.*, p. 16.

57. Remarks by Representative William S. Cohen and Senator H. John Heinz, *ibid.*, p. 47.

58. *Ibid.*, p. 18.

59. U.S. Senate, Special Committee on Aging (SSCA), *Developments in Aging: 1979*, part 1, 96th Cong., 2d sess., 1980, pp. 212–213.

60. SSCA, p. 214.

61. Maggie Kuhn, "Open Letter," *Gerontologist* (October 1978), 18(5):422–424.

62. Rufus S. Lynch, "Utilization and Dissemination of Research on Aging," paper presented at the 37th annual meeting of the Midwest Political Science Association, Chicago, Illinois, April 19–21, 1979, p. 1. For additional problems of dissemination see R. Steinberg and Neal Cutler, "Policy Research, Dissemination, and Utilization," (Los Angeles: University of Southern California, Ethel Andrus Gerontology Center, 1976).

63. Raymond T. Coward, "Planning Community Services for the Rural Elderly: Implications from Research," *Gerontologist* (June 1979), 19(3):275.

8. Epilogue: Perspectives on Reform

1. Robert B. Hudson, "The 'Graying' of the Federal Budget and Its Consequences for Old-Age Policy," part 1, *Gerontologist* (October 1978), 15(8):428.

2. David Plotke, "Facing the 1980s," *Socialist Review* (January-February 1980), 10(1):21.

3. Robert M. Ball, *Social Security: Today and Tomorrow* (New York: Columbia University Press, 1978), p. 90.

4. The credit currently is set at 1 percent of the worker's PIA for each year that he or she forgoes Social Security, up to a maximum of 15 percent.

5. Juanita M. Kreps, "Economic Growth and Income Through the Life Cycle," in Mildred M. Seltzer, Sherry L. Corbett, and Robert C. Atchley, eds., *Social Problems of the Aging: Readings* (Belmont, Calif.: Wadsworth, 1978), p. 186.

6. U.S. Senate, Special Committee on Aging, *Emerging Options for Work and Retirement*, prepared by James Storey, 96th Cong., 2d sess., June 1980, p. 9.

7. A new CPI formula is being developed for use shortly. It will exclude the rise in home mortgage interest rates, thus lowering the overall official inflation rate in the United States.

8. David Hackett Fischer, *Growing Old in America* (expanded ed.; New York: Oxford University Press, 1978), p. 163.

9. James H. Schulz, *The Economics of Aging* (2d ed.; Belmont, Calif.: Wadsworth, 1980), p. 126.

10. Alan Wolfe, "Jimmy Carter—Going Places with Stagflation," *Socialist Review*, nos. 50–51 (March–June 1980), 10(2–3):136.

11. Howard B. Waitzkin and Barbara Waterman, *Exploitation of Illness in Capitalist Society* (Indianapolis, Ind.: Bobbs-Merrill, 1974), pp. 15–16.

12. Carroll L. Estes, *The Aging Enterprise* (San Francisco: Jossey-Bass, 1979), p. 17.

13. André Gorz, "Reforms and the Struggle for Socialism," in Richard C. Edwards, Michael Reich, and Thomas E. Weisskopf, eds., *The Capitalist System* (2d ed.; Englewood Cliffs, N.J.: Prentice-Hall, 1978), pp. 529–530.

14. Gosta Esping-Anderson, Roger Friedland, and Erik Olin Wright, "Modes of Class Struggle and the Capitalist State," *Kapitalistate* (Summer 1976), 4–5:199.

15. Gorz, p. 530.

16. Dudley Burton and M. Brian Murphy, "Planning, Austerity, and the Democratic Prospect," *Kapitalistate*, (1980) no. 8, pp. 78–80.

17. Gorz, pp. 530–531.

18. U.S. Senate, Special Committee on Aging, *Developments in Aging: 1979*, part 1, 96th Cong., 2d sess., 1980, p. 13.

19. Michael Kieschnick, "Issues of Social Costs, the Multiplier, and Pension Fund Investments," in Lee Webb and William Schweke, eds., *Public Employee Pension Funds: New Strategies for Investment* (Washington, D.C.: Conference on Alternative State and Local Policies, July 1979), p. 58.

Index

Revenue sharing, 194; and state and local retirement systems, 115–16
Rhode Island, public employee retirement plans, 124
Rifkin, Jeremy, 113, 121
Rodgers, Harrell R., 58
Rogers, Ray, 122, 127
Rubinow, Isaac M., 41
Ryan, John, 38
Ryan, William, 233n39

Sack, Ann, 192
Sanders, Daniel, 49
Saville, Lloyd, 50
Schmandt, Jurgen, 200
Schoen, Cathy, 151, 159
Schulz, James, 63, 84
Scudder, Stevens and Clark, 110, 114
Seattle First National Bank, 122
Section 8 housing program, see Subsidized housing programs
Section 202 housing program, see Subsidized housing programs
Section 236 housing program, see Subsidized housing programs
Seidman, Burt, 106
Senior centers, see Older Americans Act
Senior Community Service Employment Program, 193, 208–9, 210, 213, 258n10; see also Employment services
Share the Wealth Movement, 45–46
Sheppard, Harold, 17
Sjogren, Jane, 96
Sligh, Charles R., Jr., 12
Small Business Administration, 139–40
Social investing, see Pension trust funds
Social policies affecting the aged; growth of, 1–6, 55; impact on society, 214–17, 225–26; perspectives on, see Free market conservatives, Liberal accomodationists, Radical reformers; prior to 1935, 38–40; see also Federal budget; Federal income

taxes; Federal tax expenditures; and under individual programs
Social Security, 65–75; actuarial reductions of, 67–68, 69; alternative perspectives on, 13–14, 18, 22–23, 218–21, 224–25; and cost-of-living adjustments, 50, 71, 72, 219–20; coverage under, 45, 50, 65; and high-income workers, 68, 71, 73–74; increasing costs of, 6–8, 9; and minimum benefit, 66, 67, 70, 90, 240n40; and payroll tax, 47, 70–73, 115, 220–21, 224–25; PIA formula, 66–67, 239n26; ratio of taxpayers to beneficiaries, 4; and retirement test, 73–74, 241n48; and wage replacement, 66–67, 68; see also Blacks; Social Security Act of 1935; Women
Social Security Act of 1935: expansion of, 5, 49–50, 132; history of, 42–48, 52, 53–54, 129, 236n65; see also Social Security
Social services: need for and problems with, 187–88, 197–204, 212–13; under title XX of Social Security Act, 193, 194–95, 258nn20–21; see also Housing of aged; Older Americans Act
Sommers, Tish, 75
State and local retirement systems, 88–94; assets of, 101, 102 (table), 118; benefit levels, 90; and cost-of-living adjustments, 94; coverage under, 89; effect of depression on, 43; establishment of, 41–42; expansion of, 236nn49, 59; funding of, 101, 114–17, 243n101; integration with Social Security, 91; investments of, 101, 103, 116; and portability, 92–93, 243n99; roles of, 117; vesting under, 92; and wage replacement, 89–90, 91; see also State sector
State sector, 23, 77, 84–94, 114–17, 215–16; see also Competitive sector; Monopoly sector
Steinberg, Raymond, 193